PROPERTY
TAX
REFORM

D1207862

PROPERTY TAX REFORM

DICK NETZER • JOHN SHANNON
HENRY AARON • MASON GAFFNEY • DAVID C. LONG
GEORGE E. PETERSON • BRUCE W. HAMILTON
WILLIAM H. OAKLAND • RICHARD R. ALMY

EDITED BY GEORGE E. PETERSON

THE JOHN C. LINCOLN INSTITUTE

AND

THE URBAN INSTITUTE

FOREWORD

The property tax is nothing if not durable. It has been decried for generations as one of the worst of taxes, yet it remains the pillar of local government finance. All the while economists and politicians were forecasting that the property tax well was about to run dry, its revenue producing power multiplied many times over until the tax, nationwide, now yields almost forty-five billion dollars annually. Despite state constitutional limitations and requirements for voter support that are far more stringent than those for almost any other tax, instances of "taxpayer rebellion" are outweighed year after year by examples of substantial citizen support for higher property tax rates.

These anomalies are among the reasons that the property tax in recent years has been getting more serious examination, but they are not the only reasons. The school finance question brought the spotlight sharply on the disparities that result from separate property taxation by very small jurisdictions. Several suits by poor residents alleging assessment discrimination have focused public interest on the importance of assessment administration. The tenaciousness of severe housing problems for poor and moderate-income Americans in the face of large national programs has drawn attention to indications that the property tax may seriously affect the conditions, supply, and price of housing. The continuous battle of city officials to meet growing demands for urban services with restricted budgets has been another reason for taking a closer look at all local taxes. Additionally, the property tax has been linked in various degrees to the problems and possible remedies for urban sprawl and other forms of land waste, distortions of the job market, and the exclusion of low-income households from suburbia.

All of these matters evoke a wide range of responses, not only from politicians and citizens, but also from tax administrators and economists. Some of the controversies go to the very heart of social philosophy, revolving around the kind of cities, institutions, and society that people want. It is our belief that such questions, however complex and perplexing, are not intractable, but can be resolved through continued analyses and thorough airing of the facts and interpretations that are developed. This book, like the conference for which the authors originally prepared their chapters, airs such vital matters. The authors who prepared the separate chapters are exceptionally well qualified to give informed judgments on issues that are high on the national agenda of property tax reform. Their differences stem from both value differences and limitations in our understanding of the systems of which the property tax is a part.

This volume, then, should be considered not as the definitive map of the territory so much as a description of the current frontiers and jumping-off places for new exploration. The Urban Institute is pleased to join with The John C. Lincoln Institute in the presentation of these timely and important contributions to the understanding of property tax reform.

WILLIAM GORHAM, *President*
The Urban Institute

Washington, D.C.

PREFACE

The late John C. Lincoln was a prolific inventor, chiefly in the field of electric arc welding. He was also a man of wide-ranging intellectual interests and of deep social conscience. During the 1920s and 1930s he became much interested in Henry George's ideas of social and economic justice, especially as regards the use of land in the public interest, and he left a Foundation to encourage continued attention to this subject.

The Foundation has carried on his interest through a program for the training of tax economists at the Claremont Graduate School, Claremont, California, and through various programs carried out by the Henry George School of New York, and the John C. Lincoln Institute, allied with the University of Hartford in Hartford, Connecticut. The John C. Lincoln Institute has worked closely with the International Association of Assessing Officers to improve property tax administration, has sponsored a wide range of programs to focus attention on Henry George's ideas of social and economic justice, and has maintained very lively programs in East Asia where the parallel ideas of Henry George and Sun Yat-sen have led several governments to undertake major programs of land tenure reform.

In America the cry for property tax reform is never stilled. From time to time attention is directed to the income tax with its annual moments of anguish, or to the sales tax; but of late years the property tax has been the most consistently and unpleasantly visible of all taxes. Hence, the taxpayers have been demanding with ever-increasing fervor that "something be done about it."

To add to the tumult, the school litigation of the 1950s and 1960s concerning equal education opportunity has raised penetrating questions whether the small local units of government are appropriate to levy and administer so massive a tax as is now required to pay the costs of public schools in the face of manifest geographical imbalance of fiscal capability.

Because the high interest in these topics coincides with the basic purpose of the Foundation, the John C. Lincoln Institute was most pleased to cooperate with The Urban Institute in conducting a seminar on current property tax developments and issues, and in publishing this volume.

A. M. WOODRUFF
Director, John C. Lincoln Institute
President, University of Hartford

Hartford, Connecticut

CONTENTS

TABLES

FIGURES

ACKNOWLEDGEMENTS

The chapters in this volume are revised and updated versions of papers originally presented in May 1973 at a conference on property tax reform held in Hartford, Connecticut under the joint sponsorship of The John C. Lincoln Institute and The Urban Institute.

Special thanks for handling the organization of the conference are due to Carleton F. Sharpe, Administrative Officer, and Melton L. Spivak, Research Assistant, both of the Lincoln Institute.

In revising their papers the authors benefitted greatly from the vigorous discussions that marked the conference proceedings. For this reason, and because their participation contributed so importantly to the success of the conference, I would like to acknowledge the others who were in attendance: Jay Adams, Edgar E. Belleville, James Brown, Robert Franklin, Harvey Galper, J. Ted Gwartney, James Hoben, Harold M. Hochman, James Hull, Richard Martin, Edward McDonough, James Ruth, Theodore R. Smith, Thomas K. Standish, John J. Sullivan, John Walsh, and Gregory H. Wassall.

G.E.P.

PROPERTY TAX REFORM

1

THE ISSUES
OF PROPERTY TAX REFORM

by George E. Peterson

No part of the American tax system evokes more controversy than the property tax. In all, property taxes now raise some $45 billion per year for local and state governments. About half of that amount comes from taxes that, in one form or another, are levied on commercial and industrial property. Approximately 36 percent is paid directly by private households, in the form of taxes on owner-occupied homes. Another 12 percent is charged to residential rental properties.

Intermittently over the last few years, popular irritation with the property tax has reached such peaks that commentators have thought they discerned the beginnings of a genuine property tax revolt. Opposition to the property tax, as expressed by the electorate in public opinion polls or local tax referenda, would seem to indicate that there is political mileage in the issues of property tax reform and property tax relief. During the early months of the 1972 presidential campaign, both major candidates promised to come up with campaign planks on the property tax issue. Although these promises never materialized into specific proposals, in part because of the complexity of finding a way for the federal government to intervene effectively in what always has been a local matter, Senators Muskie and Percy subsequently introduced a bill (S 1255) that staked out a role for the federal government in encouraging property tax relief and administrative reform.

At the state level, the "property tax revolt" has enjoyed a rather checkered history. In California, more than $1.1 billion recently was slashed from the state's property tax bills by substituting new sales taxes for a portion of the property tax. In Minnesota, several months of legislative debate led to the reversal of a previous history of spiraling property tax payments. The decision to shift part of the cost of public schooling to other tax sources and to grant tax reductions for low-income households actually decreased that state's property tax bill by more than 11 percent in 1972. However, in states where pro-

GEORGE E. PETERSON, Senior Research Staff, The Urban Institute.

1

posals to replace the property tax have been put directly to the voters in referendum, the voters have elected to retain the "known evil"—property taxation—rather than to accept the risk of "unknown evils" in the form of new taxes.

What seems to be emerging across the country is a movement to distribute property tax relief in more specific fashion without requiring massive replacement of the property tax. Property tax relief measures now have been adopted in one form or another by all 50 states, as described in detail by John Shannon in Chapter 3. This movement may well represent the most significant change in the country's tax structure since World War II. As Shannon remarks, states' satisfaction with the first phase of property tax relief probably presages its application on a much larger scale, with property tax rebates being extended not just to the elderly, as is the case at present in most areas, but to other low-income homeowners and renters, and even to middle-income families as well.

Besides these tax *relief* measures, whose sole purpose is to alleviate the property tax burden, property tax *reform* stands at the center of several fundamental political issues. Almost every state in the union has debated the advisability of reducing the role that local property taxes play in financing public schools. The decision by the Supreme Court that it is constitutionally permissible to pay for public schooling through local property taxes doubtless has taken some of the edge off the school finance reform movement; but courts in California, Michigan, and New Jersey have found that present school funding arrangements may violate the *state* constitutions, even if they are consistent with the federal Constitution. Modification of the property tax seems necessary to comply with court rulings in these states. In many of the country's big cities, fear that high property tax rates discourage industry from locating within the cities, and fear that stiff property taxes may also discourage owners from making needed improvements to the residential housing stock, has led to widespread adoption of property tax abatement plans. These exempt designated forms of new investment from all or part of their property tax liability in order to offset the investment disincentives the property tax is thought to provide.

In short, there is much agitation to do *something* about the property tax. If the truth be told, this desire to change the property tax has far outrun economists' capacity to analyze the effects of the various "reforms" that have been proposed, and even their ability to identify what is wrong with the property tax as currently administered.

It is the purpose of this book to take stock of property tax reform proposals, as well as the criticisms that have led to the conclusion that the property tax requires reform. The succeeding four chapters are intended to give the reader a feeling for the principal reform issues. Dick Netzer and John Shannon present the analysis that underlies the current direction of property tax reform. Probably more than anyone else, these two authors are responsible for the current trend in property tax legislation—Netzer through his writings and congressional testimony, and Shannon through the work of the Advisory Commission on Intergovernmental Relations. In Chapter 2 Netzer presents a comprehensive critique of the local property tax and its shortcomings. In Chapter 3 Shannon describes the current course of property tax reform and property tax relief, and argues its suitability. Following this affirmative case for the present direction of change, Henry Aaron and Mason Gaffney offer contrary views. Aaron argues that property tax relief legislation, as currently drafted, distributes government assistance in an irrational manner, since the magnitude of government aid is made to vary directly with the value of the property which a household occupies. The families who benefit most are those that are poor in terms of current income but wealthy in terms of the assets they control. Gaffney contends that far from reducing reliance on the property tax, governmental authorities ought to make still greater use of it, since it is the only means these authorities have of taxing *wealth* rather than productive economic activity. Gaffney offers his own agenda for how the property tax (and its administration) ought to be reformed in order to make it function more efficiently as a wealth tax.

In the second half of the book, the case for property tax reform is examined by investigating in detail the adverse effects that the current system of property taxation is alleged to have. David Long carefully analyzes the school finance reform movement and the inequities that the courts have found in the use of local property taxes to pay for public schooling. He contrasts the cases now being brought before state courts with the ruling handed down by the Supreme Court in *Rodriguez*. In Chapter 7 I have scrutinized the common contention that property tax burdens play an important role in the deterioration of the low-income housing stock in urban areas. I argue that the manner of administering the property tax makes its influence on housing investment and abandonment quite different from what it usually is thought to be. Bruce Hamilton analyzes the incentive to fiscal zoning that is created by the use of property taxes, and investigates the degree of income segregation and other effects that have resulted from fiscally motivated zoning restrictions. He concludes that fiscal zoning does contribute to income stratification and probably has reduced the overall supply of low-income housing as well. William Oakland looks at the most basic function of the property tax—its role in paying for government operations. Oakland uses a case study of Baltimore City and its suburbs to appraise the fiscal plight of the cities. Finally, Richard Almy examines current assessment practices and considers how the adoption of certain constructive assessment practices would make the property tax more effective and more palatable.

Needless to say, a partitioning of property tax issues into separate categories such as those indicated by the chapter headings is largely arbitrary. It may be more useful to review four major points of discussion that recur throughout the volume. In doing so, I have made no attempt to minimize the differences of opinion that are expressed by the authors. The truth of the matter is that no professional consensus exists as to the effects of the property tax as currently administered, nor as to the property tax reforms that ought to be carried out. Consequently, I have sought to identify the most important areas of disagreement and will leave it to the reader to weigh the arguments adduced on behalf of each position.

REGRESSIVITY

Certainly in political terms, and perhaps in economic terms as well, the principal charge lodged against the property tax—or rather the residential portion of the property tax—is that it is a regressive tax, which obliges poor families to' pay a larger portion of their incomes for taxes than wealthy families. Within the class of low-income households, certain types of families are thought to suffer especially severe hardships from the property tax—the most obvious group being the elderly, whose property tax bills seem to rise inexorably, despite the fact that they must live on relatively fixed incomes.

The argument that seeks to establish the property tax's regressivity is well expressed by Shannon. In Table 1 he illustrates the property tax burden, as a percentage of household income, for homeowners at different income levels. This comparison reveals a dramatic fall-off from the lowest income categories, where households with incomes below $3,000, pay 10 percent or more of their incomes for property taxes, up to the highest income categories, where households pay a mere 3 percent or less of their income for property taxes. Similar tabulations have been compiled by others for renter households. These seem to show that the inequality of the tax burden among renters is even more extreme than it is among homeowners.

Several difficulties present themselves in interpreting these figures, however. As Aaron points out, at the low end of the income scale the figures on the percentage of income that families spend for property taxes are highly misleading: when the several expenditures of low-income families are added up, one finds that their *total* expenditures, on average, are almost twice as great as their income. For example, low-income households according to this kind of data may spend 80 percent of their income on housing, 40 percent on food, 30 percent on clothing, and so on. Obviously, this is a situation that could not continue forever. And the explanation seems to be that among the households with low current-year incomes are many families who are suffering temporary setbacks—families where the household head has been sick or unemployed during part of the year, or families with business losses or crop failures. These families' average income over the long run—or as economists would say, their "permanent" income—considerably exceeds their actual income for this one year alone. Such families will have adjusted their housing consumption to their long-run income expectations. Thus it is altogether natural that their expenditures on housing, and consequently their expenditures on property taxes, should prove to be a high percentage of the current year's unusually low income level.

In addition, the standard calculations of the property tax burden for renters assume that the entire amount of the property tax is shifted forward to the tenant in the form of higher rents. As Aaron discusses, the theory of tax incidence is exceedingly complicated, and judgment as to the distribution of property tax burdens may change significantly with assumptions about the manner in which the markets involved function, but it is certain that it is a vast (and biased) oversimplification to assume that tenants bear all the burden of a property tax levied on the capital value of the structures in which they live.

There is considerable agreement among the authors that the property tax as administered today, with all the variations of property tax rates that actually occur among jurisdictions, and with all the flaws of assessment, is a regressive tax, although there is disagreement as to how regressive the current property tax system is. Whether a uniform-rate property tax, administered uniformly, also would be a regressive tax is a subject of keen dispute. Netzer and Shannon find the property tax so severely regressive, in terms of measured current income, that any reasonable definition of permanent or long-term income would have to preserve this regressivity. Others, like Aaron and myself, argue that once permanent income is properly defined, property taxes will be found to be approximately neutral with respect to income; that is, that property tax payments will account for approximately the same proportion of long-term family income at all income levels. Still others, among whom Gaffney is conspicuous, judge a uniform-rate property tax to be definitely *progressive*.

In addition to this dispute as to whether a uniform-rate property tax would be regressive, neutral, or progressive in terms of permanent income, there was some discussion at the conference where these papers were presented as to the proper concept of income, against which property tax payments ought to be compared, in calculating tax burdens. Shannon, arguing what has become the position of the Advisory Commission on Intergovernmental Relations, maintained that the proper way to measure a household's tax burden is by comparing its annual tax obligations with the annual stream of cash receipts, from which it must pay those taxes. This is a cash flow or current income criterion which, Shannon argued, accords most closely with popular judgment of ability to pay. Most of the other participants at the conference thought that permanent or long-run income is the appropriate criterion of ability to pay. Gaffney argued for moving away from income altogether, whether current or permanent, as the criterion of ability to pay and using wealth for this purpose. He argued, for instance, that households which derive their income from a return on invested assets do not have to work for this income, and therefore should be taxed more stiffly than families that earn their livelihood through labor.

The difference in proposed ability-to-pay standards is perhaps best illustrated by the case of a moderately wealthy retired family. As long as the household's current income from retirement benefits is low, Shannon would judge that the family has a low ability to pay. By the permanent income criterion, however, this same family probably would have an above-average ability to pay, since its current low income reflects its point in the life cycle rather than strained circumstance. By a wealth criterion, measured in terms of present net worth, the family would be still better off.

The methods one deems appropriate for analyzing the effects of the property tax, of course, are directly related to the reforms he is likely to advocate. If current income is taken as the proper measure of household ability to pay, then it makes perfectly good sense to support tax relief legislation that measures the "excess" tax burden in terms of the percentage of current income that a household spends in property taxes. Furthermore, if one is willing to adopt a view of incidence that says that tenants bear the full burden of the property tax, it makes sense, as several states have done, to calculate property tax relief for renters, on the assumption that *their* tax burden is equal to the full amount of taxes that the landlord pays on the rental units they occupy. Thus it is the ACIR analysis of the property tax, described by Shannon, that underlies most of the recent state legislation in the property tax field.

If, on the other hand, one is convinced that permanent income is the proper measure of household ability to pay, he will balk at tax relief schemes that take account of current income only and increase the size of the tax rebate in direct proportion to the assets (and hence permanent income) that a family controls. Similarly, if one is convinced that a uniform-rate property tax would be approximately neutral in terms of permanent income, he will not be alarmed at the prospect of using statewide property taxation to pay for public school expenditures, especially if, as seems increasingly to be the case, the alternative is to adopt stiffer sales taxes on other commodities. In short, the agenda for property tax reform that one adopts follows implicitly from the standards he uses to judge the property tax, and the manner in which he carries out the positive analysis as to its effects.

THE LOCAL NATURE OF THE TAX

Virtually the only proposition that commands universal assent among the authors represented in this volume is that too much use currently is made of the *local* property tax, or indeed local taxes of any kind. Netzer puts this argument succinctly in Chapter 2.

Perhaps the most flagrant example of excessive reliance on local financing occurs with respect to public schooling. In the original *Serrano* case, where the California Supreme Court ruled that reliance on local property wealth introduced unacceptable disparities in some local districts' ability to pay for public schooling, the objection was essentially a regressivity argument. Plaintiffs held that because wealthy school districts are able to raise a given amount of revenue per pupil at a lower property tax rate than are poor districts, they enjoy an unfair advantage in the provision of schooling. Plaintiffs maintained that equity requires that all school districts either be provided equal educational services, or be allowed to buy their own services at the same tax *rate* as other districts. The actual situation was alleged to force poor school districts to pay higher tax rates than wealthy districts, and thus to discriminate against the poor.

Now several observers have pointed out that this original *Serrano* argument trades somewhat on an ambiguity in the term "wealth." The claim that wealthy school districts can raise funds at a lower property tax rate than poor districts is obviously true if what one means by "wealthy" is that the school districts in question enjoy a higher value of taxable property per pupil. However, school districts that are wealthy in this sense need not also be wealthy in the sense that the families living there have above-average incomes. In many states, poor families are concentrated in the large cities which, because of the large amount of industrial and commercial property located within their boundaries, have higher per pupil taxable wealth than the rest of the state. These districts are wealthy in terms of property values, but poor in terms of household income. Consequently, a mere shifting of the responsibility for raising school taxes to the state level, or an equalizing of property tax bases among school districts, would not necessarily alleviate the tax burden of the poor. In some cases, it would greatly exacerbate the tax burden of low-income households.

As David Long makes clear in Chapter 6, a second generation of school finance cases now seems to be emerging. In these, the courts may be forced to take a broader view of the objections to using local property taxes to pay for public schooling. The key question may prove to be not whether poor households on balance are better off or worse off, but whether any *educational purpose* is served by making school expenditures dependent upon the amount of local taxable wealth. If not, the financing of schools through local property taxes may violate several state constitutions, even though those who suffer from the tax-base discrimination are not always the poor.

As long as public services like schools are paid for at the local level, it will be in the interests of affluent suburban communities to do what they can to preserve the competitive edge conferred upon them by their high tax bases. The most direct method of tax base preservation is to exclude from the community those who cannot pay their own way fiscally; that is to say, families which would live in homes that generate insufficient property tax revenue to cover the cost of the public services they demand. In most areas, the favorite exclusionary device is zoning restrictions. In Chapter 8 Bruce Hamilton looks at the property tax's incentive to fiscal exclusion and its effects. He shows that in states where there is a high degree of reliance on locally raised revenue to pay for public schools, there seems to be a discernibly higher degree of income segregation among communities than elsewhere. In areas where a high proportion of school costs are paid out of state revenues the same incentive to protect the local tax base, of course, does not exist. Hamilton then examines what this attitude of fiscal mercantilism means for the supply of low-income housing throughout the metropolitan area as a whole and finds some evidence that fiscally motivated zoning has restricted the total amount of land available for low-income housing.

Yet another consequence of reliance on *local* property taxation is to place poor communities—those low in per capita wealth—in an even greater fiscal bind than they otherwise would face. William Oakland looks at the demands for public services and the ability to pay for them in Baltimore City and contrasts these with the situation in Baltimore County and the other surrounding suburban jurisdictions. Baltimore is one of the nation's metropolitan areas where flight to the suburbs has robbed the central city even of its traditional edge in industrial and commercial activity. Per capita taxable commercial and industrial wealth in Baltimore City now lags behind the suburbs. And like most cities, Baltimore's tax base is growing at only a small fraction of the suburban rate of growth. The dilemma this poses for the city is the following: either the city must tax itself at a stiff rate and provide the services its citizens demand, but in the process risk driving many of the remaining firms, industries, and affluent households out of the city to the suburbs, where property tax rates already are some 50 percent lower; or else the city can opt to retain its property tax base, but frustrate its citizens' demands for public services by refusing to levy the taxes the majority of households want. Oakland examines the causes and consequences of this dilemma in considerable detail. If property tax rates were uniform across jurisdictions, the tax structure would not create this situation where prosperous communities thrive because of their relative advantage over their impecunious neighbors.

LAND USE EFFECTS

The American property tax is a tax on both the value of land and the value of structures. For purposes of analysis, however, it often is useful to distinguish these two components of the property tax, and speak of a land tax and a structure tax. As economists long have pointed out, because there is a fixed amount of land in supply, a land tax cannot cause owners to reduce the amount of land they offer to the market. However great the tax burden on land, it always is in a landowner's interest to utilize his parcel in the way that maximizes his income before property tax payments. For this reason, a tax on land values should not disturb market outcomes at all.

A tax on structures, however, has a quite different effect. Over the long run, at least, there is an elastic supply of reproducible real capital. If the government decides to slap a tax on the value of physical improvements, some investors will decide that they can earn a better return by investing their capital in other ways, and sooner or later the diminished attractiveness of investment in structures will result in a decreased volume of capital improvements. A tax on structures, therefore, *will* alter the outcome of economic markets, and in particular will cause less investment in physical improvements than there would be without a tax.

As Netzer notes, one market where the above argument often has been applied is the housing market. Because the American property tax extends to structures (in fact there is evidence that in most areas structures are assessed for tax purposes at a higher proportion of true market value than land), the property tax commonly is thought to discourage investment in housing. For well-off families this property tax disincentive may be offset by the favorable treatment granted homeowners in the federal income tax structure, but for low-income markets, and especially for low-income renter markets where there is no income tax offset, the presence of the property tax is argued to lead to a much lower volume of housing capital than would exist in the absence of a tax. This underinvestment in low-income housing is expressed not only in a reluctance to undertake new construction, but (more importantly for the low-income market) in decisions not to upgrade or improve existing properties, and in more rapid housing abandonment than otherwise would occur.

In Chapter 7 I examine the empirical validity of this argument. Because of the way assessments are administered in the cities, the disincentive effect of the property tax may have been exaggerated. Most improvements to the housing stock seem to escape assessment, and in blighted areas almost all improvements to existing stock fail to result in reassessment. Since the *incremental* tax levied on the value of improvements is small, the disincentive to investment also should be small. Most landlords in low-income neighborhoods agree that the property tax is a minor obstacle, or none at all, to their housing investment decisions.

At the other end of the scale, excessive property taxes often are thought to lead to premature abandonment of still useful housing. Failure to reduce assessments in line with a neighborhood's declining property values could in fact accelerate abandonment, if a city were strict in its collection of taxes. In practice, however, most cities are so slow to force tax payments that overassessment of poor neighborhoods creates tax delinquency rather than abandonment. The true effect of property taxation in low-income areas, I think, takes a different form. Extremely high tax rates drain small owners of cash flow which they normally use to make annual repairs and maintenance. In this way, high tax rates lead to a gradual, but cumulatively significant, disinvestment in the housing stock.

Housing for the poor is not the only land use issue. Both Netzer and Gaffney advocate placing much greater reliance on land taxes as opposed to taxes on the combined value of land and structures.

As noted before, land taxes do not distort the structure of profit incentives. As a result, they carry some presumption of encouraging economic efficiency. Netzer and Gaffney also see land taxes as a means of generating more intensive development of land in metropolitan areas, since the presence of a land tax would make it more costly for owners or speculators to hold their land out of production while awaiting price appreciation. Gaffney puts forward the argument that the greater concentration of economic activity encouraged by land taxation would lower the cost of providing citizens with public services.

Others at the conference were reluctant to use the tax system to encourage more intensive land use. Shannon points out that the favorable tax treatment most states grant to farmland and undeveloped parcels may well reflect taxpayer preferences as to land use, although he acknowledges that there probably are more efficient means of preserving open space than by subsidizing inactivity through the tax system. Others noted that in most cities zoning rules prevent greatly increased land use, whatever the profit incentives may be.

THE ASSESSMENT SYSTEM

Among public officials and academics alike, perhaps the most neglected aspect of the property tax system is the assessment process. Assessment methods crucially affect each of the property tax issues discussed in this introductory chapter. Especially in the nation's older cities, assessment bias is a prime contributor to property tax regressivity. There exists substantial evidence that in many cities low- and moderate-income properties are assessed at a much higher proportion of market value than are upper-income properties. This, of course, is equivalent to levying the property tax at a higher rate on low-income households. Similarly, the local nature of the tax system compounds the difficulty of assessment. There are more than 14,000 assessment jurisdictions in the United States, many of which are so small as to make professional assessment impossible. Even in metropolitan areas, assessment practice often suffers from jurisdictional fragmentation. The underassessment of high-income neighborhoods may be largely inadvertent, but at least on occasion it is a deliberate attempt to keep from pushing out the wealthier families that the city needs by shielding them from the full force of the central city tax rate.

In the last chapter Almy argues that the relative isolation of the assessor's office from other local public authorities is injurious to both parties. Assessment policy affects the distribution of tax burdens among local residents; it may serve to attract or repel new commercial investment; and it can encourage or discourage improvement to the housing stock. For this reason, it is disingenuous for assessors to hide behind the façade that their job is policy-neutral, consisting only of the determination of the market value of parcels. Almy argues that we would do better to give explicit recognition to the policy importance of assessment. Moreover, he shows that many of the products of the assessment system potentially are of great value to the local economy. The information that assessors do or should generate include market value trends, land use patterns, cadastral maps, and inventories of the housing stock and the conditions of that stock. All of this information can be utilized in both public and private economic planning. Almy provides an agenda for assessment reform, consisting in part of measures designed to improve the accuracy of market value appraisals and in part of recommendations as to how to integrate assessors more fully into local economic planning and policies.

2

IS THERE TOO MUCH RELIANCE ON THE LOCAL PROPERTY TAX?

by Dick Netzer

To answer the question posed in the chapter heading, I must begin with another question: compared to what? or rather, comparing what with what?

I doubt that any reader would disagree with the proposition that there is too much reliance on "the local property tax," if we define it strictly to mean the property tax as used in the United States today with every one of its attributes, including all the disparities and inequities in tax bases, tax rates, assessment quality, and the like. All of us agree that there is too much reliance on *this* tax, whether we call for moderate reform of the property tax, drastic reform of it, or large-scale replacement of it.

I prefer to approach the question more narrowly: to consider the appropriate role of a local property tax that is at least somewhat reformed, but remains fundamentally an ad valorem tax largely on land and buildings levied by conventional local government units possessing some degree of fiscal autonomy and therefore free to levy the tax at non-uniform rates.

Even so, the question needs to be separated into a number of distinct ones if it is to be answered coherently. One form of the question is this: Should a larger share of public sector expenditure be financed from non-local revenue sources, without regard to the form that the local share takes? Since the local property tax accounts for over half of the locally financed share of public expenditure, any reduction in the aggregate role of local finance in the public sector is likely to mean less reliance on the *local* property tax. If one answers that the local role is too large, he is thus implicitly answering that there is indeed too much reliance on the local property tax, even though he may not have made any comparison of the merits of the property tax with the merits of alternative local finance instruments.

DICK NETZER is Professor of Economics and Dean, Graduate School of Public Administration, New York University.

13

The second form of the question deals with this latter issue explicitly: Is the property tax better or worse than the local finance alternatives? In view of the many proposals for statewide property taxation for the schools, this probably should be generalized to compare the property tax, whether imposed by local units or statewide, with alternative forms of state-plus-local finance. But this comparison is more complicated than it seems. Are we assuming a *tabula rasa* and designing an ideal system of local (or state-local) finance? If so, we can ignore windfall gains and losses associated with major changes in fiscal institutions, the destabilizing second-order economic effects of such changes, and all the other advantages of inertia that lead us in the real world to make incremental rather than radical changes. Are we assuming an optimal geographic configuration of local governments, for spatial structure does count a good deal in the comparative evaluation of the property tax? Are we assuming that the administration of the property tax can achieve a high degree of uniformity, largely free from the all too apparent defects of the present-day fiscal institution?

In this chapter, I propose to pay some attention to the relative merits of an idealized property tax, assuming away the dislocations associated with radical institutional change. Rapid conversion of the existing property tax into an ideal one would be one of the most radical and destabilizing changes in fiscal institutions imaginable. However, the most useful discussion for policy purposes compares the property tax, under conservative assumptions with regard to the likelihood or feasibility of major changes in its geographic scope and quality of administration, to the likely alternatives.

Before going any further, it is worthwhile stopping to place the notion of non-radical change in reliance on the property tax in some historical context. Currently, based on 1970-71 Census data, the property tax finances roughly 40 percent of local government expenditure and 24 percent of the expenditure of the consolidated state-local sector. It accounts for 60 percent of *own-source* revenue of local governments and 29 percent of own-source revenue for the entire state-local sector. For local governments, these percentages have changed little over the past twenty years (that is, from 1950 to 1970-71); but for the combined state-local sector they have declined appreciably, from 30 percent to 24 percent in the case of expenditure and from 33 percent to 29 percent in the case of own-source revenue.

The new conventional wisdom is that state-local expenditure is unlikely to rise as rapidly relative to GNP in the next twenty years as it did in the past twenty years. Suppose that the increase in state-local expenditure as a percentage of GNP between 1970-71 and 1990-

91 is half as great as in the twenty years up to 1970-71, in absolute percentage points. Suppose also that the property tax does not increase at all as a percentage of GNP. Under these assumptions, the property tax will be financing only 30 percent of local government expenditure in 1990-91 (compared to 40 percent in 1970-71) and 19 percent of combined state-local expenditure (compared to 24 percent in 1970-71).

If we further assume that intergovernmental fiscal transfers remain a constant share of expenditure of the receiving levels of government, at the 1970-71 percentages, then the property tax by the year 1990-91 will account for 45 percent of local government own-source revenue (compared to 54 percent in 1970-71) and 23 percent of state-local own-source revenue (compared to 29 percent in 1970-71).

Thus, if nonradical change simply means not utilizing the property tax to satisfy rising demands for state-local expenditure, relative to GNP, a fair-sized reduction in reliance on the local property tax can be achieved. The question is, should it be done?

THE LOCAL FINANCE ROLE

One of the strongest traditions in the literature of American public finance is criticism of the inappropriately large role of local governments in financing civilian public expenditure in this country. This criticism grew much louder and more effective in the 1930s and reached *ad nauseam* levels in the 1960s. As a frequent contributor to such discussions over the past decade, I would have hoped that repetition of the basic argument would now be unnecessary. However, since considerable revisionist writing on fiscal federalism has emerged in the last few years, such repetition seems unavoidable.

The gist of the argument goes like this: In a contemporary, advanced, industrial society characterized by a high degree of mobility of labor and capital, heavy reliance on geographically small local governments to finance civilian public expenditure is inconsistent with widely held views on fiscal equity and inefficient from the standpoint of resource allocation.[1] The equity side of the argument is fairly obvious. It is neither feasible nor appropriate in an open, complexly-interrelated economy for local governments to attempt to achieve different degrees of income redistribution through the public sector. (The argument applies almost as strongly to state governments as well.) And to relegate to local governments important responsibilities for financing overtly income-redistributive services is to insure that there will be *less* income redistribution than would be the case

---

1. Local governments financed roughly 28 percent of the $250 billion in civilian public expenditure in 1970-71.

with nationwide financing. This is so because of the spatial concentrations of wealth and poverty which reduce the capacity of *local* governments to pay for redistributive services and because in communities with a sizable spread in incomes the possibility that the losers from local fiscal redistribution can migrate to places where less fiscal redistribution is carried out acts as a severe restraint on the process.

Thus, the financing of 10 percent of the overtly income-redistributing public expenditure (health, welfare, public housing, etc.) by local governments—and another 15 percent by the states—seems most inappropriate. The public school finance system also contains a significant income-redistribution element, or at least includes redistribution as one goal. If it did not, the appropriate role for government would be confined to the administration of compulsory school attendance laws, with little or no tax financing of schools per se. Moreover, the essence of the *Serrano*-type arguments is income redistribution.[2]

The efficiency side of the argument is based on geographic spillovers of benefits and costs, combined in some instances with economy of scale considerations. Some public sector activities such as fire protection generate benefits with very limited spatial extension; others generate benefits that are largely internal to the immediate consumer of the service, an example of which in my own view is higher education. Where income redistribution is not a major consideration, such activities can appropriately be locally financed. A Tiebout-type solution or the theory of clubs may then offer the right normative models.[3] But other activities, including many assigned to small-area local governments and financed largely by them, do involve geographic externalities. Environmental protection activities are the most obvious ones. In such cases, an efficient solution requires either performance of the functions by a governmental unit with considerable spatial extension— a state government or an interstate or intrastate regional body—or

---

2. In Serrano v. Priest the California Supreme Court in 1971 found it unconstitutional to finance local school districts in such a way as to make "the quality of a child's education a function of the wealth of his parents and neighbors."

3. In the Tiebout model consumers choose a jurisdiction in which to reside by comparing the public service mix the jurisdiction provides and the taxes it levies. If there are a large number of small jurisdictions, each with its own public service bundle and tax rate, the choice available to the consumer may resemble the choice he would have if public goods were provided on the private market.

In the club model, groups of consumers voluntarily combine to share the costs of providing themselves facilities which many persons can use simultaneously.

Both models attempt to show that market-like solutions exist for the provision of public goods. A market solution is efficient, however, only if all the benefits of consumption redound to the purchaser; if other persons stand to gain from his consumption (if there are "externalities") market solutions generally will lead to nonoptimal consumption. See Charles M. Tiebout, "A Pure Theory of Local Expenditure," Journal of Political Economy, Vol. 64 (October 1956), pp. 416-424.

subventions and controls from the higher levels of government to induce optimal expenditure patterns.

The revisionism alluded to previously mainly concerns school finance. The conventional wisdom may be exemplified by the position of the Advisory Commission on Intergovernmental Relations which for several years has urged statewide financing of the public schools. Significant federal aid along the lines of Title I of the Elementary and Secondary Education Act of 1965 (providing for federal aid to districts with large numbers of children from low-income families) would not be inconsistent with this stance since ACIR also has recommended federalization of the income maintenance system. On an individual state level, increasing numbers of governors and study commissions, notably in New Jersey and New York, have urged statewide financing of schools.

The revisionist argument [4] celebrates the virtues of the local property tax per se; more on that later. But it appears to have two other main strands, which are closely related to each other. One is some skepticism about the dimensions of the "public goods" aspect of the benefits from schooling: if the great bulk of the benefits are internal to the child and his family, then the fact that our population is highly mobile will not necessarily produce an inefficient allocation of resources to education. Parents should be willing to pay, in the form of taxes levied by the local district providing the schooling, for such benefits as the school expenditure brings. Geographic spillovers or externalities, calling for finance on a wider geographic basis, can exist only in respect to benefits that are *not* internalized by the immediate consumers of a publicly provided service. Such benefits, in education, consist of the generalized advantage of a reasonably well-educated populace *as voters* in a democratic society; but one can easily doubt whether any incremental expenditure, above and beyond that called for by the private benefits that schooling yields, is necessary to adduce these public benefits. The broader social benefits may be an incidental byproduct of the private benefits.

If this is so, then there is only an equity argument for nonlocal government intervention into school finance: the need to equalize for wide disparities in local income and wealth. The revisionists argue, quite correctly, that simply shifting to statewide uniform financing of schools, paid for, say, by a statewide property tax, may not be satisfactory from a redistributive standpoint. The highest per pupil expendi-

---

4. I take as reasonable examples Robert D. Reischauer and Robert W. Hartman, *Reforming School Finance, Washington, D.C., Brookings, 1973,* and George E. Peterson and Arthur P. Solomon, "Property Taxes and Populist Reform", The Public Interest, No. 30, Winter, 1973.

tures on schools presently are made by the big cities and the rich suburban districts. However, school tax rates in the suburbs are much higher than in the cities. In many cases, therefore, a shift to statewide finance with uniform expenditures and uniform tax rates would tend to shift tax burdens regressively on balance and in the aggregate. This is not always the case, however. For example, Governor Cahill's proposal in New Jersey would have increased school expenditure fairly sharply in poor central cities, frozen it in rich suburbs, and financed the lot from a newly instituted state personal income tax with a fair degree of graduation (essentially, the New York State personal income tax structure divided by two). But there is validity in the general argument that a proper concern for equity requires that care be taken in formulating the details of nonlocal financing.[5]

My own view is that the income distribution element in school finance combined with the merit-good benefit spillover call for nonlocal financing of the schools to an extent far in excess of the current 50 percent national average. It probably should be more like 80 percent. Such a change in school finance, combined with a shift to state or regional levels of the financing of other services which have important geographic externalities, could result in a reduction of the local finance share of civilian public expenditure by as much as 40 percent. In these circumstances, given only the present, modest utilization of user charges by local governments, reliance on the local property tax would be substantially reduced, even if local governments were to utilize no nonproperty taxes at all.

THE PROPERTY TAX AS THE MAIN INSTRUMENT OF LOCAL FINANCE

The major criticisms of the property tax *as it exists today,* relative to alternative fiscal instruments, are the following:

ONE. It is regressive in incidence as presently levied and administered.

TWO. It has unfavorable resource allocation effects. It tends to discourage investment in the production and consumption of goods and services that require large amounts of reproducible capital subject to the property tax, in particular, types of housing that are not afforded fiscal advantages by other features of the nation's tax system.

---

5. The so-called power equalization plans advocated by some school finance reformers would have this effect. Under such plans, each taxing district would be able to raise the same amount of tax revenue (per-pupil or per-capita) from a mill of locally imposed property tax rates. In localities with little taxable property, much of the revenue would actually come from state funds. However, the power equalization formula retains local decisionmaking as to the rate at which a locality will tax itself. The effect in this case is the same as if all localities had equal tax bases.

THREE. The tax rate disparities produce spatial distortions as well. One is the deterrent effect on location in older central cities and poorer suburban communities. Another is more indirect: the inevitable tendency toward fiscal zoning that occurs when small local units with the authority to control land use raise most of their money from a revenue source that is highly sensitive to land-use decisions.

FOUR. The administration of the tax is anything but uniform, which creates or aggravates the difficulties just described and gives rise to additional horizontal inequities as well.

I doubt whether anyone seriously questions the validity of these charges in respect to the property tax as it now stands. The real bone of contention is the extent to which the defects inhere in the tax. Assuming that the defects are correctable rather than inherent, a further point of controversy focuses on how feasible the needed reforms are.

It is easy to conceive of a property tax that is neither regressive in incidence nor significantly distorting in its resource allocation effects. Such a tax would be a uniform percentage of the value of *all* capital, uniform with respect to both types of capital and location of capital. If the supply of savings is price inelastic, as it is conventionally held to be, this uniform tax would have only one significant first-order economic effect: it would lower the rate of return on capital generally. The second-order effects on production and consumption would depend upon how great the differences in preference patterns are between capitalists and noncapitalists, but it would not be unreasonable to ignore such effects.

However, the property tax we have is very far from this ideal and, indeed, it must always be so. *First,* it is hard to imagine a real-world property tax that actually covers all forms of capital, much less one that covers them uniformly. Yet any major exemptions convert the property tax, at least in part, into an excise tax and produce the excess burden on nonexempt capital that is associated with any type of excise taxation. One major exemption is based on ownership: capital owned by public agencies and many nonprofit organizations is not taxed. Another major exemption is granted to capital not held in the form of real estate. It may be alleged that the century-old trend toward removing most personal property from the tax base has been in error, but the administrative difficulties in discovering and valuing personalty afford arguments that must be persuasive to anyone concerned with the practicalities of implementing tax policy, not merely with theoretical purity.

Second, if the tax is to remain a major element in *local* finance, it is hard to see how it could be applied across jurisdictions at a uniform rate. Equalization of local tax bases may go very far; but differences in local tax rates will remain as long as local authorities are permitted to reflect differences in preferences for public goods, geographic and demographic characteristics, and everything else that makes decentralized decision making efficient in the public sector, as in the private sector. Clearly, if the property tax is viewed by each taxpayer as the equivalent of the price for a package of public services, with alternative packages and prices readily available at substitute locations, that is, if the conditions for a Tiebout solution exist, then the tax will not be distorting.[6] But as the extensive literature on this shows, those conditions are even more restrictive than Tiebout himself allowed and market-like choices for public service consumption simply do not exist, except in the rarest of cases. In any event, were the property tax to be used as the local tax in a Tiebout solution, it would have to be confined to household property. This selective use of the tax would violate the first uniformity condition: uniform application of the tax to all forms of capital.[7]

Thus, the real-world property tax is both rampantly nonuniform and anything but an element of a Tiebout optimality solution. Since so much capital is not taxed at all, the tax rate on a very large fraction of the capital that is taxed is well above the average effective rate calculated with the value of all capital as the denominator. Therefore, excise tax effects are at least as important as capital tax effects. Since the effective rate of property tax is by now far from trivial in most urban areas, the excise tax distortions cannot be trivial.

The distortion are both sectoral and spatial. The sectoral effects increase the land intensity of site uses, since buildings generally bear high tax rates relative to land. They deter investment in types of structures such as office buildings that generally attract especially high tax rates. And they have negative impacts on all activities that are relatively real-property-intensive. Among the most important of such activities is housing. I have argued elsewhere that, except in those cases where the residential property tax-public service nexus is very close indeed,

---

6. See Tiebout, loc. cit. In the Tiebout model, local jurisdictions, within a metropolitan area compete for residents by offering alternative combinations of public services and local tax rates. The Tiebout model involves a number of simplifying assumptions which seldom hold in the real world of local finance. Thus, the pattern of tax rates and public service levels and the residential migration patterns the model would predict are hard to discover in American metropolitan areas, although a fair number of doctoral dissertations and journal articles have been written in recent years about the empirical validity of the Tiebout model. However, if the necessary assumptions did hold, the model would be a "solution" in that, by enabling individual preferences for public goods to be revealed, it permits outcomes that approach Pareto efficiency.

7. In the Tiebout model, all taxes must fall directly on households.

the residential property tax must discourage housing consumption in favor of nonhousing consumption, since the excise tax effect of this tax on housing expenditure is far greater than the corresponding consumption taxes applied to nearly all forms of nonhousing consumer expenditure.[8]

The spatial effects are like those of other local taxes where the rate differentials are large ones. There are aggravated effects for central cities because the tax-public service nexus tends to be wholly invisible to central city taxpayers and because central cities generally have more rental housing than suburbs, so that fewer central city households can offset residential property taxes with income tax deductions.

This also bears on the ancient claim that the real-world property tax is objectionable on vertical equity grounds, a claim now undergoing heavy revisionist attack.[9] It is possible to grant virtually all the points of the revisionists and still maintain that the residential component of the property tax is very regressive indeed, provided one recognizes the pattern of tax rate differentials in metropolitan areas, the associated geographic distribution of renters and owners at various income levels and the way in which assessments are actually done.

Were the property tax to be imposed on a metropolitan areawide basis (or at least much more so than it is now, e.g., by substantially increasing the relative role of county governments in local finance), the regressivity would be substantially lessened and the spatial distortions virtually eliminated. There is little in our experience over the past twenty-five years to suggest that this is a very likely prospect, however. Considering the property tax as it typically exists with many variations from one jurisdiction to the next, the relative merits of nonproperty taxes, local or state, are considerably enhanced. Moreover, abolition of the role of small local units would discard whatever Tiebout-type efficiency advantages exist in the present system of public sector organization.

Broadening the geographic areas over which the tax is imposed would not reduce its deterrent effects on housing consumption; indeed, this could increase them, by breaking the tax-public services

8. See the following: Economics of the Property Tax, Washington, D.C., Brookings, 1966, pp. 74-85; "Housing Taxation and Housing Policy," in Adela Adam Nevitt, Ed., The Economic Problems of Housing, New York, St. Martin's Press, 1967, pp. 123-136, especially p. 133; and "Federal, State and Local Finance in a Metropolitan Context," in Perloff and Wingo, Eds., Issues in Urban Economics, Baltimore, Johns Hopkins Press, 1968, p. 446.

9. See, for example, Peter Mieszkowski, "The Property Tax: An Excise Tax or a Profits Tax?" Journal of Public Economics, Vol. 1, April 1972, pp. 72-96, and George E. Peterson, "The Regressivity of the Residential Property Tax," Working Paper S1207-10, Washington, D.C., The Urban Institute, October 1972.

nexus that now does exist in dormitory suburbs. Of course, it would be possible to revise the federal income tax provisions so that federal tax offsets would make housing consumption decisions as attractive to tenants and low-income homeowners as they now are to high-income homeowners. This would involve converting deductions into credits and extending the credits to renters as well as to owner-occupants. Like most people concerned with the quality of the federal income tax, this strikes me as a decidedly second-best alternative, one that accentuates horizontal inequities. Rather than extend income tax preferences that are a function of preferences for housing vis-à-vis other goods, I would prefer to see less discriminatory taxation of housing consumption on the state-local level.

It is also possible to overcome the bias against housing by an ever-increasing array of state and local abatement and exemption schemes. These frequently have high administrative and compliance costs and, all too often, create serious distortions of their own between those consumers living in housing eligible for rebate and those living in ineligible housing.

Unquestionably, the quality of property tax administration can be improved. Indeed, the Census of Governments evidence indicates that it has improved significantly in recent years. But I remain skeptical about whether the feasible improvements can go far enough. There is a very real inherent problem in estimating the market value of diverse types of capital assets that are sold infrequently, illustrated by the fact that the largest cities, with large professional assessment organizations, tend to have substantial within- and between-class non-uniformity. Some of this could be eliminated readily enough, for example, by not permitting assessors to use different types of evidence of value for different properties, or by foregoing the use of clearly erroneous rules-of-thumb, like uniform gross rent multipliers for all types of rented residential properties. But some of the nonuniformity simply reflects the fact that the market value of some types of infrequently traded assets is not only unknown, but unknowable. Moreover, in some of the larger cities, the nonuniformity among classes is a deliberate policy choice in which some political and economic costs and benefits are traded off against others. We may believe that the trade-off calculations are in error, but it is not a simple "good government" issue.

CONCLUSION: TURN TO USER CHARGES AND
LAND VALUE TAXATION

In my estimation, the likely and feasible reforms in the local property tax will be relatively marginal in their ability to overcome the defects of the existing institution. Therefore, I conclude that there is indeed too much reliance on the tax, and would continue to be even if the overall role of locally-raised finance were significantly reduced.

My own agenda for property tax reform, for this reason, is to reduce reliance on the conventional tax, in favor of the two local finance alternatives that seem distinctly superior on efficiency and equity grounds. The first is heavier reliance on properly designed user charges, particularly congestion and pollution charges. The second is reliance on land value taxation. Since my bent is for incremental reform, I would accomplish the latter in stages, starting with elimination of the existing drastic under-taxation of land relative to improvements. Twenty years hence, my ideal system of local finance would comprise user charges and land value taxation, period.

3

THE PROPERTY TAX: REFORM OR RELIEF?

by John Shannon

Before it is possible to answer the central question—whether the country ought to seek property tax reform or property tax relief—it is necessary to confront four subsidiary issues:

ONE. Why is the property tax the most hated of all major taxes?

TWO. Will assessment reform—bringing local assessment levels into alignment with state valuation law—make the property tax more popular?

THREE. Why has the "circuit-breaker" become the legislative instrument of choice for extending property tax relief?

FOUR. Will the "circuit-breaker" movement work for or against fundamental assessment reform?

THE UNPOPULARITY ISSUE

Three recent public opinion surveys dramatically highlight the fact that the property tax is considered to be the most onerous tax. When specifically asked in a 1972 poll sponsored by the Advisory Commission on Intergovernmental Relations [ACIR], "which do you think is the worst tax, the least fair?", 45 percent of the nationwide respondents selected the property tax.[1] Regardless of age, income, area of residence, type of employment, race, and other socioeconomic factors, each subclassification voted the property tax as least fair—generally by margins of two-to-one.

When asked in a 1971 National League of Cities poll to choose among five tax instruments if additional local tax revenue were needed, citizens in each of ten cities placed the property tax at or near the bottom of the list—while uniformly placing the sales tax at the

JOHN SHANNON is Assistant Director, Advisory Commission on Intergovernmental Relations. Mr. Shannon gratefully acknowledges the contributions of John Gambill, Research Assistant, ACIR, especially for his help in gathering data and preparation of tables.

1. ACIR, Public Opinion and Taxes, Washington, D.C., May 1972.

top.[2] When asked in 1973 by pollster Lou Harris, "From your personal standpoint, which of these taxes do you feel are too high, which about right?", 68 percent of those interviewed replied that the property tax was too high—a larger percentage than given for any other tax.[3]

The Causes of Unpopularity

Why is the property tax the most unpopular of all major taxes? This question takes on added significance because over the last twenty years the property tax load borne by the average family has grown more slowly than have the burdens of most of the other major taxes.

While no tax is popular, the property tax possesses certain irritating characteristics that are quite unique.

• No other major tax in our public finance system bears down so harshly on low-income households, or is so capriciously related to the flow of cash into the household.[4] (See Table 1.)

• When compared to the preferential treatment accorded outlays for shelter under both the income and sales taxes, the property tax stands out clearly as an anti-housing levy. Moreover, as the tax increases steadily, it is viewed by a growing number of families as a threat to homeownership.

• Unlike income and sales taxes, the property tax imposes a levy on unrealized capital gains. Undoubtedly, many property owners do not share the view held by most economists that this constitutes an acceptable method for measuring ability to pay taxes. Homeowners, especially, are apt to dismiss the increase in the value of their home as mere "paper profit" that they do not intend to convert into "spendable income."

• The administration of the property tax is far more difficult than is the case with either the income or sales tax. At best, the property tax assessment is based on an informed estimate of the market value of the property. The subjective judgment of market value seems all the more arbitrary during times of inflation and in jurisdictions experiencing rapid changes in property values.

• The dramatic increase in taxes (and the resultant taxpayer shock) that often follows in the wake of an infrequent mass reappraisal

2. Nations Cities, *August 1971, p. 15.*

3. Washington Post, *April 14, 1973, p. A 13.*

4. *In preparing its forthcoming report,* Financing Schools and Property Tax Relief— A State Responsibility, *the ACIR staff examined the recently published theoretical works purporting to demolish the view that the property tax is highly regressive. After weighing the conflicting claims, the staff concluded that the property tax, especially the residential component, bears down harshly on low-income households. This is especially clear in the case of homeowners, who combine the role of capital owner and tenant, since they pay the tax under any theory.*

Table 1.
REAL ESTATE TAXES AS A PERCENTAGE OF FAMILY INCOME, OWNER-OCCUPIED SINGLE-FAMILY HOMES, BY INCOME CLASS AND BY REGION, 1970

Family income[a]	United States Total	North-east Region	North-central Region	South Region	West Region	Number and distribution of homeowners	
						No. (000)	% dist.[b]
Less than $2,000	16.6	30.8	18.0	8.2	22.9	1,718.8	5.5
$ 2,000 - 2,999	9.7	15.7	9.8	5.2	12.5	1,288.7	9.7
3,000 - 3,999	7.7	13.1	7.7	4.3	8.7	1,397.8	14.1
4,000 - 4,999	6.4	9.8	6.7	3.4	8.0	1,342.8	18.5
5,000 - 5,999	5.5	9.3	5.7	2.9	6.5	1,365.1	22.8
6,000 - 6,999	4.7	7.1	4.9	2.5	5.9	1,530.1	27.8
7,000 - 9,999	4.2	6.2	4.2	2.2	5.0	5,377.4	45.0
10,000 - 14,999	3.7	5.3	3.6	2.0	4.0	8,910.3	73.6
15,000 - 24,999	3.3	4.6	3.1	2.0	3.4	6,365.6	94.0
25,000 or more	2.9	3.9	2.7	1.7	2.9	1,876.9	100.0
All incomes	4.9[c]	6.9[c]	5.1[c]	2.9[c]	5.4[c]	31,144.7	

a. Census definition of income (income from all sources). Income reported was received in 1970.
b. Cumulated from lowest class.
c. Arithmetic mean—median for U.S. is 3.4.

Source: U.S. Bureau of the Census, *Residential Finance Survey, 1970* (conducted in 1971), special tabulations prepared for the Advisory Commission on Intergovernmental Relations. Real estate tax data were compiled for properties acquired prior to 1970 and represent taxes paid during 1970.

has no parallel in the adminstration of the income or sales tax. As inflation pushes property values up, the assessment hikes become more pronounced and the taxpayer shocks become more severe.

• The property tax is more painful to pay than the "pay as you go" income and sales taxes. This is especially true for those property taxpayers who are not in a position to pay the tax on a monthly installment basis.

• The property tax has the worst public image. For more than fifty years, this tax has been cited by both political leaders and tax scholars as the most wretchedly administered tax.

The factors cited above have combined to make the property tax the most disliked of all of our major revenue instruments. They also explain why the "felt burden" of this tax is greater than that suggested by the comparative tax burden analysis set forth in Table 2.

Certain Virtues—and Fiscal Realism

Despite its obvious defects and poor public image, the property tax has significant political and fiscal virtues. First, it is the one major

revenue sources directly available to local government and therefore
serves as the sheet armor against the forces of centralization. Second,
it is the one tax in general use that can recapture for the community
the property values the community has created. Third, its high visibility
forces local officials to maintain high standards of public account-
ability.

Table 2.
ESTIMATED DIRECT TAX BURDEN FOR A HYPOTHETICAL FAMILY
WITH TWO CHILDREN, EARNING $5,000 IN 1953 AND
$12,000 IN 1972[a]

Type of tax	1972		1953		Percentage increase in tax related to income 1953-1972
	Tax as % of family income	Percentage distribution	Tax as % of family income	Percentage distribution	
Total	20.2%	100.0%	11.8%	100.0%	71.2%
Federal personal income tax	9.7	48.0	7.6	64.4	27.6
Social security tax (OASDHI)	3.9	19.3	1.1	9.3	254.5
Major State and local taxes:	6.6	32.7	3.1	26.3	112.9
Property	3.4	16.8	2.2	18.6	54.5
Personal income	1.8	8.9	0.3	2.5	500.0
General sales	1.4	6.9	0.6	5.1	133.3

a. Assumes all income is earned by one spouse and is from wages and salaries.

Source: ACIR staff computations.

Beyond these three considerations there is the inescapable element
of fiscal realism—the nation's local governments will not quickly come
up with an acceptable substitute for this powerful $45 billion revenue
producer. Prudent public policy, therefore, would dictate the adoption
of measures designed to reduce the irritant content of this levy.

EQUALIZED TAX RATES AND ASSESSMENT REFORM

Before it is possible to determine whether assessment reform will
make the property tax more acceptable to taxpayers we must be quite
clear as to what is meant by assessment reform. In our mind, this term
does not necessarily connote the appointment of well-trained asses-

sors, nor the use of comprehensive tax maps and high-powered computers, nor any of the other instrumental tests that reformers usually apply in order to determine the character of an assessment operation.

In the final analysis, *fundamental assessment reform* boils down to one test. Does the remedial action substantially resolve the perennial conflict between state valuation law and local assessment practice? The property tax laws of most states require that *all* classes of property be assessed at the same percentage of current market value and "full value" still remains the most common valuation standard.

These two mandates—full value assessment and the uniformity requirement—appeared in most state constitutions before the turn of the century. Much of their support for this type of legislation came from business interests who feared that state legislative bodies might fall under the control of populist leaders and develop progressive property tax systems designed to "stick" big business.

Despite these precautions, state valuation law has more often been honored in the breach than in the observance. In fact, most state tax administrators are unable to hold county assessment levels at *any* uniform percentage of current market value, let alone at full value. Thus, the actual assessment system is usually characterized by the pervasive and time-honored practice of fractional assessment with each local assessor selecting his own fractional standard. Local assessors have also deviated from the uniformity mandate by formulating their own extra-legal system of classification under which certain preferred classes of property are often assessed at a lower percentage of current market value than are other classes of property.

Farmers and homeowners are more frequently the beneficiaries— not the victims—of extra-legal assessment practices. Although instances can be (and have been) found of relative underassessment of high-value industrial plants, especially in "company towns," it is more likely, *especially in the large cities,* that income-producing properties are assessed at a higher percentage of market value than are single-family homes. Moreover, farmland is generally assessed at a lower percentage of market value than residential property.

Data for Large Cities on Assessment Ratios

An unpublished tabulation of 1966 assessment ratio data for large cities, gathered for the *1967 Census of Governments* taxable property values survey, reveals a generally progressive situation: as values rise so do assessment ratios.[5] This was true in 85 percent of the 117 cities for which valid data are available.

---

5. *The Census data are for "ordinary real estate," i.e., excluding real estate that is presumed to have a market value of over $250,000.*

In only three of the 24 cities with 1970 populations of 500,000 or more (excluding three large Texas cities for which valid data were not available) were the ratios of lower-value properties (primarily homes) generally above those of higher-value properties (primarily income-producing properties). See Table 3. The three cities where this situation existed are Baltimore, Philadelphia and San Diego.

In New York City, the properties in the lower half of the assessed value scale were assessed at 63 percent of the properties in the upper half. This kind of situation apparently still exists there, as is noted in a recent *New York Times* article:

> Generally, the homes are assessed at a much lower ratio to their market value—the price the house could be sold for—than income-producing properties. "This undervaluation," according to a report by the State Commission on Investigation, (is) "apparently a traditional and deliberate decision on the part of various city administrations to deter middle-income families from leaving the city for the suburbs."[6]

An intensive study of assessment ratios in Boston, based on 1962 sales prices and assessments, found that without question commercial property was assessed at a much higher ratio than residential property.[7] In central Boston, single-family homes were assessed at 44 percent of market value, while commercial property carried a ratio of 78 percent. Indeed, looking at the ratios for the city as a whole, there was a smooth progression of ratios: from 34 percent for single-family homes to 41 percent for two-family residences, 52 percent for three-to-five family residences, 58 percent for six-or-more families, and 78 percent for commercial properties.[8]

A recent report on assessment practices in Cook County notes that the assessment ratio for commercial and industrial properties is about double that for single-family homes.[9] In fact, the recently adopted Illinois Constitution legalizes differential assessment by providing that the larger counties (those with over 300,000 population) can assess one class of property at a level or assessment ratio up to two-and-one-half times the level of another class.

---

6. *Robert E. Tomasson, "840,000 Parcels Recorded by Hand,"* New York Times, *February 22, 1973, p. 35.*

7. *Oliver Oldman and Henry Aaron, "Assessment-Sales Ratios Under the Boston Property Tax,"* National Tax Journal, *Vol. XVIII, No. 1, March 1965.*

8. *Ratios varied considerably as between sections of the city as well.*

9. *Real Estate Research Corporation,* Report on 1971 Activities and Plans for Future Improvements, *prepared for Cook County Assessor P. J. Cullerton, Chicago, May 1972, pp. 23 and 24.*

Table 3.
**RELATIVE ASSESSMENT RATIOS IN 1966 FOR LOW- AND
HIGH-VALUE PROPERTIES IN CITIES WITH POPULATIONS
OF 500,000 AND OVER**[a]

City	Ratio of assessed value to sales price (percent)		Lower half as percent of upper half [Col 1 ÷ Col 2] (3)
	Lower half of assessed value classes (1)	Upper half of assessed value classes (2)	
Baltimore	69.4	64.5	108
Boston	31.6	43.5	72
Chicago	31.5	49.7	63
Cleveland	34.8	40.6	86
Columbus	37.6	39.0	96
Dallas	NA	NA	NA
Denver	28.0	29.8	94
Detroit	35.8	47.9	75
Honolulu	56.0	63.9	88
Houston	NA	NA	NA
Indianapolis	31.1	32.6	95
Jacksonville	78.7	105.2	75
Kansas City	23.1	32.8	70
Los Angeles	17.7	21.1	84
Memphis	41.6	47.7	87
Milwaukee	49.7	54.0	92
New Orleans	16.4	24.0	68
New York	37.5	59.4	63
Philadelphia	60.0	57.1	105
Phoenix	17.6	20.4	86
Pittsburgh	36.0	46.7	77
St. Louis	32.2	45.2	71
San Antonio	NA	NA	NA
San Diego	22.6	18.3	124
San Francisco	9.3	14.5	65
Seattle	14.8	18.0	82
Washington, D.C.	43.0	43.3	99

Notes: Data apply only to "Ordinary Real Estate"; i.e., real estate with a presumed market value of less than $250,000.

NA—Data not available.

a. Population category as of 1970.

Source: ACIR staff calculations based on unpublished assessment ratio data from the *1967 Census of Governments*.

Statewide Evidence in Kentucky

When Kentucky was forced by court action in 1965 to quadruple its assessed values from about a 25 percent level to the constitutionally required fair cash value, the result was as follows (in millions of dollars:[10]

Class of real estate	Assessed valuation (millions of dollars)		Percent increase
	Jan. 1965	Jan. 1966	
Residental	$1,639	$ 5,617	342.7%
Farms—Acreage	788	3,777	479.3
Commercial—Industrial	685	2,243	327.4
Oil, Mineral Rights, etc.	75	174	232.0
Total	$3,187	$11,811	370.6%

Before the reassessment, residential and farm properties apparently were assessed at a lower level on the average than commercial and industrial property—and considerably lower than oil and mineral rights.

Political Implications of Fundamental Reform

The political implications of assessment reform are rather grim because for many state tax officials the decision to raise all local assessments to the state legal valuation standard places them in double jeopardy. First, local ratemakers may take advantage of this situation by failing to cut back their tax rates commensurate with the state hike in local assessments. If this happens, then state officials will usually be blamed by irate property owners for the resultant increase in their taxes. Even if state officials are successful in mandating a rollback of local tax rates, they still face the second nemesis—the prevalent and time-honored practice of giving farmers and homeowners a "little assessment break." Thus, if state officials demand compliance with the uniformity provision there is the unpopular shift in tax burden from the utilities and other business firms to homeowners and farmers. To paraphrase Hamlet, "Under such circumstances, great reform plans often become sicklied over with a pale cast of doubt and lose their name of action."

In view of this basic misdirection of political responsibility for higher property tax loads, it is not difficult to appreciate the natural reluctance of both governors and senior state tax officials to raise the assessments of all classes of property to the state valuation standard.

10. J. E. Luckett, "The Administrator's Response to Full Value Assessment," in 1966 Proceedings: National Tax Association, Columbus, 1967, p. 190.

As seen from the perspective of the professional assessor, calls for reform are no simple matter:

"If it is suggested that the officials are lacking in courage, there is
the obvious rejoinder that it takes *extraordinary courage* to do something that is predestined to have an undesirable development for
which you are not responsible but for which you know that you will
be blamed."[11]

As a result, virtually all of the basic assessment reform action that
has taken place in recent years has come about because the judges
mandated state remedial action. Two states—Kentucky and Washington—that in the past decade were handed court mandates to equalize
their assessments attempted to soften the blow by rolling back property
tax limits. In addition to the rollback, the Kentucky legislature adjusted
the rate on utilities—which had always been appraised at market value
by the State Department of Revenue—*to assure that utility property
would produce at least as much revenue for 1966 and 1967 as it did
for 1965.*[12]

In the case of Washington, the utility assessments were sharply
reduced over a three-year period prior to embarking on a general
reassessment of all properties. This was done to avoid a sudden shift
in taxes from state assessed utilities to locally assessed property. Washington's reappraisal experience also verified the fact that as a class
farmers had been assessed at a lower level than had other classes of
property owners.

Three other States—Alabama, Arizona, and Tennessee—took
another approach, also in response to court mandates. They established (de jure) classification systems which, in effect, legalized the
prior de facto situation of preferential treatment for farmers and homeowners. These three states—as well as the other states that have
enacted property tax classifications earlier—set higher ratios for industrial and commercial properties than for owner-occupied dwellings
and farm properties. (See Table 4.) Arizona adopted its classification
system in 1967 while both Alabama and Tennessee enacted their
plans in 1972.

Should Obeying the Law Require Heroic Action?

While the evidence strongly suggests the existence of a de facto
assessment arrangement that generally tends to favor farmers and
homeowners at the expense of income-producing properties, this de

---

11. *California State Board of Equalization,* Annual Report 1950-1951, *Sacramento,
1951, p. 6.*

12. *The Kentucky constitution authorizes the legislature to establish different rates
on different classes of property—a form of property tax classification.*

Table 4.
PROPERTY CLASSIFICATIONS AND ASSESSMENT LEVELS IN ALABAMA, ARIZONA, AND TENNESSEE

Class of property	Assessment ratio		
	Alabama	Arizona	Tennessee
Railroad property	30% [a]	60% [b]	55% [a]
Utility property	30	40	55
Commercial and industrial[c]	25	25	40
Residential and farm	15	18	25 [d]

a. Included with utility property classification.
b. Also producing mines and standing timber.
c. Includes multi-family residential property (apartment houses).
d. Farm property established as a separate class, but with the same ratio as residential property.

facto situation certainly cannot be endorsed. If the public wants to favor farmers and homeowners, the terms of this preferential treatment should be hammered out in the open—in legislative debate—not behind the closed doors of the local assessor's offices.

In view of the fact that most state political leaders view basic assessment reform as a "no win" situation, progress is bound to be slow. Perhaps the best political strategy for assessment reformers is riveted insistence that the state tax departments make annual local assessment ratio studies and give the widest publicity to the results of these studies: It is hard for state tax leaders to be against a "full disclosure" policy, and while taxpayers do not want their assessments increased, they certainly can be expected to be receptive to a state policy that would enable them to judge the fairness of their own assessments.[13]

In the absence of a full disclosure policy, the so-called "public" assessment roll allows the assessor simultaneously to pursue policies of favoritism and bury mistakes.

By quantifying and publicizing local assessment practices, a full disclosure policy provides the judges with the evidence they need to resolve the conflict between state assessment law and local assessment practices.

As a frustrated property tax reformer, I must concede that there is something basically wrong with a tax that requires the heroic action of elected officials or tenured public servants to bring law and practice into reasonable alignment.

13. For an outline of necessary institutional reforms, see the appendix to this chapter which summarizes the ACIR property tax reform agenda.

TAX RELIEF—THE CIRCUIT-BREAKER

If state legislators have any failing, it is their eagerness to respond to requests for property tax relief. For example, the state "circuit-breaker" movement is now moving so rapidly that it is extremely difficult for the ACIR staff to keep up with the latest developments.

Current Status of Tax Relief Efforts

In May 1973, the Michigan Legislature approved Governor Milliken's massive $250 million circuit-breaker plan designed to help every household in Michigan—the nonelderly as well as the elderly, renters as well as homeowners. For those under the age of 65, relief comes in the form of a substantial rebate on that part of the residential tax that exceeds 3.5 percent of household income. For the elderly low-income households, the Milliken plan provides even greater aid.

This major breakthrough in Michigan came hard on the heels of the news that Vermont had also adopted a universal circuit-breaker, albeit with a somewhat different formula. The significance of these two state actions is that they represent "Phase II" of the circuit-breaker movement, characterized by virtually universal protection for all low- and moderate-income families and with an estimated per capita cost of approximately $25 in both cases. The typical "Phase I" state circuit-breaker, in sharp contrast, was restricted to low-income elderly households with per capita cost ranging from $1 to $5.

To convey the momentum and coverage of the state tax relief movement, Table 5 sets forth the chronology of state property tax relief action. (Table 7 outlines the salient program features for each state.) States are obviously moving rapidly on the property tax relief question, but in most cases, they still have a long way to go before they reach the Michigan and Vermont standards of protection from extraordinary tax burden in relation to household income. For example the current state effort can be summarized as follows:

- All 50 states now either finance, mandate, or authorize property tax relief for *elderly homeowners.*
- Fifteen states now finance property tax relief for low-income *elderly renters.*
- Ten states now finance property tax relief for *nonelderly homeowners.*
- Three states now finance property tax relief for low-income *renters under the age of 65.*

Because most of the state remedial property tax action has taken place since 1970,[14] the tax burden situation for the elderly low-income

---

14. *For a more detailed description of state property tax relief programs, see Table 7.*

Table 5.
SUMMARY OF STATE PROPERTY TAX RELIEF PROGRAMS FOR THE ELDERLY AND DATES OF ENACTMENT (AS OF MAY 15, 1973)[a]

```
-----------------LEGEND-----------------
A—Date of Adoption
L—Date of Most Recent Liberalization
```

State-Financed Circuit-Breaker* [21 States]	Other State-Financed Programs [10 States]	State-Mandated— Locally-Financed [13 States]	State-Authorized— Locally-Financed [6 States]
ADOPTED PRIOR TO 1971			
Wisconsin (A-1964, L-1971)	Mississippi[b]	Louisiana[b]	R.I. (A-1960, L-1973)
California (A-1967, L-1972)	New Jersey (A-1953, L-1972)	Oklahoma[b]	N.Y. (A-1966, L-1972)
Minnesota (A-1967, L-1973)	Iowa (A-1967, L-1971)	Mass. (A-1963, L-1971)	Utah (A-1967, L-1973)
Vermont (A-1969, L-1973)		Georgia (A-1964, L-1972)	N.H. (A-1969)
Kansas (A-1970, L-1973)		Delaware (A-1965, L-1967)	
		Maryland (A-1967, L-1969)	
		Hawaii (A-1969, L-1972)	
		Idaho (A-1969, L-1973)	
		Montana (A-1969, L-1971)	
ADOPTED IN 1971			
Colorado (L-1972)	Florida	Kentucky	Virginia (L-1973)
Maine	South Carolina (L-1973)	North Carolina	
Ohio (L-1972)	Alabama[d]	Washington (L-1972)	
Oregon			
Pennsylvania			
ADOPTED IN 1972			
Illinois	Alaska (L-1973)	South Dakota	Texas
New Mexico (L-1973)	Nebraska		
West Virginia	Tennessee		
ADOPTED IN 1973			
Arizona	Wyoming		
Arkansas			
Connecticut			
Indiana			
Michigan[e]			
Missouri			
Nevada			
North Dakota[e]			
Vermont[e]			

* "Circuit-breaker"—tax relief phases out as household income rises.
a. In addition the elderly are also helped by a general tax credit financed by the state in Wisconsin, Indiana, Minnesota, and California.
b. Elderly receive tax relief under general homestead tax relief provisions. The state reimburses local governments in Louisiana and Mississippi.
c. North Dakota provides a locally-financed partial homestead exemption for elderly homeowners and a state-financed circuit-breaker for elderly renters.
d. Alabama gives relief from state taxes only.
e. Broad circuit-breaker (all ages, homeowners and renters, potentially all incomes), adopted 1973.
Source: ACIR Staff.

homeowner today is not as oppressive as that depicted by the data in Table 1. That evidence of property tax regressivity was derived from 1970 census data.

Nothing Succeeds Like Success

As clearly evidenced by the dramatic growth of state-financed circuit-breakers—increasing from four in 1970 to twenty-one by May 15, 1973—this method is rapidly becoming the instrument of choice for granting property tax relief.

Underpinning this dramatic growth is legislative recognition of the fact that the residential property tax can place truly extraordinary burdens on low-income families, both elderly and nonelderly. To put it bluntly, legislators are not buying the new economic doctrine that the property tax is a truly progressive levy if properly administered. Nor are state legislators buying the correlative policy implication to be derived from this new school of thought—that property tax relief for low-income families should receive, at best, a rather low legislative priority.

It is becoming increasingly clear that state legislators will not pursue the ad valorem logic to its ultimate conclusion—they will not allow the ad valorem tax collector to force a homeowner into a position where he must either liquidate his capital or turn to his relatives for help in order to meet his residential property tax payment.

With increasing frequency, state legislators are subjecting the residential property tax to the cash flow test. If the property tax takes an excessively large bite out of the households' cash income *(from all sources)*, then part of the tax is deemed to be excessive and rebatable by the state. To put it another way, state legislators will not permit the residential property tax to become the inheritance tax for elderly low-income homeowners.

The circuit-breaker method owes part of its popularity to its ability to maximize the residential tax relief "bang" for the state rebate "buck"—the amount of state aid decreases as family income rises.

The partial homestead exemption approach—once typical—does not diminish as family income rises, and therefore is a less efficient device for shielding family income from extraordinary property tax loads.

It should also be noted that the typical homestead assessment exemption places great pressure on local assessors to use a small fraction of market value for tax purposes. For example, a $3,000 homestead exemption becomes a $15,000 exemption if the assessed value is put at 20 percent of market value.

In sharp contrast, the assessor is under no such functional valuation pressure when the circuit-breaker is selected as the instrument of property tax relief. In fact, the circuit-breaker does not interfere with either the assessment or the tax levying process. It is only after the liability has been created and the tax bill received that the remedial action takes place.

It must also be emphasized that by pulling the regressive stinger from the tax, the circuit-breaker approach will tend to make this levy a more equitable and *productive* revenue instrument for local government. In recommending that states take this remedial action, the Advisory Commission has emphasized its concern for increasing the productivity of this tax.

Tax Relief for Farms

State legislators apparently are as cognizant of the potentially large property tax bite that can be taken out of farm income as they are of the large residential property tax bite—particularly because of those pleas for farm property tax relief that come from farmers located on the urbanizing fringe. In 1970, 17 states authorized preferential farm assessment; by July of 1973 the number had increased to 31. See Table 6.

State legislators exhibit a general reluctance to force farmers to liquidate their rapidly appreciating land holdings in order to pay a real estate tax. Some would argue that the states are preparing (by means of preferential farm land assessment) a banquet for urban land speculators in order to provide some property tax relief crumbs for dirt farmers. Just over half of the thirty states currently authorizing preferential farm land assessment recapture a part of the tax foregone at the time of sale. Only five states now impose some type of restrictive land use in return for preferential farm land assessment.

Will Circuit-Breaker Success Undercut Local Fiscal Autonomy?

As long as circuit-breaker coverage was restricted to low-income elderly homeowners, the fiscal implication of state-financed circuit-breakers was negligible. Now, however, with the development of Phase II circuit-breakers that extend property tax relief to virtually all low- and middle-income households, a new and very serious inter-governmental fiscal dimension has been added. For example, if virtually all the households in a low- or middle-income community are receiving state-financed property tax relief, voter resistance to property tax increases evaporates. This could become the equivalent of backing a local truck up to an open state treasury door.

In order to achieve broad state-financed circuit-breaker coverage while retaining local fiscal responsibility, it is necessary for the state to limit property tax relief in some way. Michigan restricts the amount of state-financed relief to 60 percent of the amount of tax in excess of 3.5 percent of household income and further stipulates that in no case will the state rebate exceed $500. Vermont attempts to handle this problem by cutting back on the state-financed rebate in the same proportion that the locality's tax exceeds 103 percent of the previous year's levy.

Table 6.
STATES WITH DIFFERENTIAL FARMLAND ASSESSMENT PROVISIONS (AS OF JANUARY 1973)

Preferential Assessment[1] (10 States)	Deferred Taxation[2] (16 States)	Contents and Agreements[3] (5 States)	Not Yet Determined[4] (3 States)
Arkansas	Alaska	California	Massachusetts
Colorado	Connecticut[7]	Hawaii	New Hampshire
Delaware	Illinois[8]	Pennsylvania	Pennsylvania[15]
Florida	Kentucky	Vermont[14]	
Indiana	Maine	Washington	
Iowa	Maryland		
New Mexico	Minnesota		
North Carolina[5]	Montana[9]		
South Dakota[6]	New Hampshire[10]		
Wyoming	New Jersey		
	New York[11]		
	Oregon[12]		
	Rhode Island		
	Texas		
	Utah		
	Virginia[13]		

Notes

1. *Preferential assessment:* Land to be assessed at value in agricultural use, with no penalty if it is later converted to another use.

2. *Deferred taxation:* Additional taxes collected if use of land changes.

3. *Contracts and agreements:* Local government and landowner agree on restrictions on land use in return for lower property taxes. Typically there are penalties for not complying with the agreement.

4. Constitutional amendments were approved recently. The actual method of differential assessment had not yet been formulated by the legislature.

5. Effective January 1974.

6. South Dakota limits preferential assessment for agricultural property to independent school districts.

7. Connecticut does not collect a deferred tax upon a change in land use but imposes a special real estate transfer tax on the total sales price at rates ranging from 1 to 10 percent, depending on the length of time the land was held subsequent to its classification as farmland (up to ten years). The tax applies also if the use is changed by the original owner during the ten-year period.

8. Applies only to counties with more than 200,000 population.

9. April 1973.

10. New Hampshire's law is temporary, pending the report of the Open Space Land Study Commission.

11. New York's deferred tax law is based chiefly on the establishment of agricultural districts, though land not in agricultural districts may be eligible for agricultural use assessment if the landowner enters into an agreement with the local government.

12. Oregon collected deferred taxes on farmland which is not zoned for farm use. Land which is zoned for farm use gets preferential assessment.

13. Virginia's law enables local governments to enact a deferred tax ordinance.

14. Vermont has provided for contracts between farmers and local government to fix the tax rate for land. Vermont also enables local governments to purchase rights and interests in farmland, with the farmer being taxed according to the value of the rights and interests left him.

15. May 1973.

Source: U.S. Department of Agriculture, Rural Development Service. For further details, see Thomas F. Hady, "Differential Assessment of Farmland on the Rural Urban Fringe," *American Journal of Agricultural Economics*, Vol. 52, No. 1, February 1970, p. 25. See also, John Kolesar and Jaye Scholl, *Misplaced Hopes, Misspent Millions: A Report on Farmland Assessments in New Jersey*; Princeton, The Center for Analysis of Public Services, 1972.

It is too early to determine whether these fiscal constraints are too easy or too harsh on local authorities. But, once a state decides to extend circuit-breaker relief to a substantial fraction of homeowners and renters, it is clear that the state must in self-protection exercise a far greater degree of fiscal surveillance over its localities than was the case in the pre-circuit-breaker era.

THE FEDERAL PRESENCE

Will state circuit-breaker success encourage unnecessary federal involvement in the property tax field? The key term here, of course, is *unnecessary* federal involvement. If one shares the view of the majority of the Advisory Commission that questions of property tax relief and assessment reform should be resolved by state authorities, then there is some reason to be concerned about the growing popularity of the circuit-breaker idea.

For example, the Administration now favors a 100 percent federally financed and administered circuit-breaker to protect all elderly homeowners and renters below the $25,000 income level. This proposal conjures up the vision of federal policymakers both climbing aboard the state circuit-breaker bandwagon and then pushing the states off—hardly an exercise in intergovernmental fiscal comity.

Also, Senator Muskie and several of his fellow senators have devised a proposal (S. 1255) which would provide support for a state circuit-breaker but then later withdraw that support if the state failed to meet certain federally prescribed assessment reform guidelines. It is quite understandable that frustrated property tax reformers would seize upon the popular property tax relief issue in general and the circuit-breaker technique in particular as the "lever" for forcing states to reform their local property tax assessment systems.

The use of this "federal stick" approach, however, reinforces the case of those who are opposed to any federal involvement in the property tax field. They argue that once the federal government moves into the circuit-breaker field, there is the irresistible temptation to go further and to impose coercive guidelines on state and local policymakers. In this case, low- and moderate-income families become the "hostages" held by the federal government for effecting state assessment reforms.

THE CIRCUIT-BREAKER AND ASSESSMENT REFORM

In my judgment the circuit-breaker movement represents an added impetus to assessment reform. Obviously, if Senator Muskie's bill (S. 1255) becomes a law of the land, federal incentive grants can be expected to reinforce other factors that are promoting assessment reform. But, even if S. 1255 fails to win congressional support, state circuit-breakers will work *for* rather than *against* assessment reform. This optimistic judgment rests on the premise that the circuit-breaker introduces a badly needed element of fiscal realism into the residential property tax. To put it bluntly, the assessor will no longer be under the same pressure to deviate from state valuation law and grant property tax relief to low-income families by means of preferential assessment practices. The assessor can turn back the demand for this type of "break" by pointing to the state financed circuit-breaker program as the appropriate means for effecting property tax relief.

It should also be noted that the presence of heavy duty circuit-breaker protection should make state tax authorities far less willing to tolerate preferential residential assessment practices. The circuit-breaker, in effect, becomes the new form of property tax classification, thus obviating the need for the time-honored but extra-legal method of granting preferential assessment treatment.

CONCLUSION: RELIEF MAY PAVE THE WAY TO REFORM

If the recent past permits us to obtain a "feel" for the near future, it is fairly safe to predict that the policymakers will continue to exhibit more interest in tax relief than in fundamental assessment reform.

Indeed, property tax relief and its instrumentality, the circuit-breaker, have already become so popular that federal policymakers are now beginning to compete with state authorities for a piece of the property tax relief action.

While prognosis for assessment reform is not nearly so bright, the introduction of the family income test into the residential property tax field is bound to make this levy more acceptable to low- and moderate-income families. This fact, in turn, coupled with a vigorous full disclosure policy, should permit state and local assessment officials to bring their assessment levels more in line with state valuation law.

Table 7.
DETAILED FEATURES OF PRINCIPAL STATE PROPERTY TAX RELIEF PROGRAMS FOR HOMEOWNERS AND RENTERS (AS OF JULY 1, 1973)

State	Financed by	Date of Adoption (Latest Liberalization)	Description of Beneficiaries (estimated number of claimants)	Income Ceiling (Asset Test)	Tax Relief Formula (or general remarks)	Form of Relief (estimated per capita cost)
Alabama	State (exemption applies to state taxes only)	1971	Homeowners 65 and over (N.A.)	None	The $2,000 general exemption of assessed value is increased to $5,000 for homeowners 65 and over for state ad valorem taxes only.	Reduction in tax bill (N.A.)
Alaska	State	1972 (1973)	Homeowners 65 and over (1,000)	None	Total exemption.	No tax liability ($1.54)
Arizona	State (circuit-breaker)	1973	Homeowners and renters 65 and over	$3,500 single $5,000 married (value of property not to exceed $5,000)	A percentage of tax is given back as a credit, percentage declines as income rises. Only taxes on first $2,000 of assessed value are considered. (25% of rent = tax equivalent, not to exceed $225)	State income tax credit or rebate
Arkansas	State (circuit-breaker)	1973	Homeowners 65 and over (90,000)	$5,500	Relief ranges from maximum of $400 for income below $1,500 to $175 for income to $5,500 on graduated scale.	State income tax credit or rebate ($1.39)
California	State (circuit-breaker)	1967 (1972)	Homeowners 62 and over (292,999)	$10,000 net $20,000 gross	Relief ranges from 96% of tax payment on first $7,500 of value if net household income is less than $1,400 to 4% of tax payment if net household income is $10,000 (in addition to homestead exemption of $1,750).	State rebate only ($2.93)
	State	1972	All renters (N.A.)	None	Relief ranges from $25 if adjusted gross income is less than $5,000 to $45 on income of $8,000 and over.	State income tax credit or rebate (N.A.)

Table 7. (continued)

State	Financed by	Date of Adoption (Latest Liberalization)	Description of Beneficiaries (estimated number of claimants)	Income Ceiling	Tax Relief Formula (or general remarks)	Form of Relief (estimated per capita cost)
Colorado	State (circuit-breaker)	1971 (1972)	Homeowners and renters age 65 and over (11,000)	$2,400 single $3,700 married (Net worth less than $20,000)	Relief limited to 50% of the tax payment and cannot exceed $250. The credit or refund is reduced by 10% of income over $500 for individuals and 10% of income over $1,800 for husband and wife. (10% or rent-tax equivalent.)	State income tax credit or rebate ($.32)
Connecticut	State (circuit-breaker) [replaces 1965 state-financed program.]	1973	Homeowners and renters 65 and over	$7,500	Taxes exceeding 5% of income. Maximum refund ranges up to $500 for incomes below $3,000. (20% of rent = tax equivalent)	Reduction in tax bill
Delaware	Localities (mandated)	1965 (1967)	Homeowners 65 and over (N.A.)	$3,000	Exemption of $5,000 assessed value from state or county property taxes.	Reduction in tax bill (N.A.)
	Localities (optional)	1969 (1970)	Homeowners 65 and over (N.A.)	$3,000	Exemption of $5,000 assessed value from municipal property tax.	Reduction in tax bill (N.A.)
Florida	State	1971	Homeowners 65 and over (362,000)	None	The general homestead exemption of $5,000 for all homeowners is increased to $10,000 for homeowners 65 and over for taxes levied by district school boards for current operating purposes.	Reduction in tax bill ($1.47)
Georgia	Localities (mandated)	1964 (1972)	Homeowners 65 and over (100,000)	$4,000	Exemption of $4,000 assessed value from state and county property taxes.	Reduction in tax bill ($1.48)
	Localities (mandated)	1972	Homeowners 62 and over (N.A.)	$6,000	Exemption of ad valorem taxes for school districts.	Reduction in tax bill (N.A.)

Table 7. (continued)

State	Financed by	Date of Adoption (Latest Liberalization)	Description of Beneficiaries (estimated number of claimants)	Income Ceiling	Tax Relief Formula (or general remarks)	Form of Relief (estimated per capita cost)
Hawaii	Localities (mandated)	1969 (1972)	Homeowners 60 and over (180,000)	None	Exemption of $16,000 of assessed value for homeowners age 60 to 69. Exemption of $20,000 of assessed value for homeowners age 70 or more.	Reduction in tax bill ($4.40)
Idaho	Localities (mandated)	1969 (1973)	Homeowners 65 and over (N.A.)	$4,800 (value of property not to exceed $15,000)	Elderly homeowners are exempt from property tax up to $75.	Reduction in tax bill ($.72)
Illinois	State (circuit-breaker)	1972	Homeowners and renters age 65 and older or disabled (290,000)	$10,000 implicit	Relief based on amount by which property tax (or rent constituting property tax) exceeds 6 percent of household income for that year on the amount of such income between zero and $3,000 plus 7% on that amount in excess of $3,000. Relief limit is $500 less 5% of household income. (25% of rent = tax equivalent)	Direct rebate ($2.58)
	Localities (mandated)	1971	Homeowners 65 and over (N.A.)	None	Maximum reduction of $1,500 from assessed value.	Reduction in tax bill (N.A.)
Indiana	Localities (mandated)	1957 (1971)	Homeowners 65 & over (80,000)	$6,000 (realty value not in excess of $6,500)	Exemption of $1,000 assessed value.	Reduction in tax bill ($1.59)
	State (circuit-breaker)	1973	Homeowners and renters, 65 and over	$5,000	Relief ranges from 75% of property tax for incomes below $500 to 10% for incomes above $4,000. Limitation on amount of property tax liability considered for relief is $500. (20% of rent = tax equivalent, but 15% if furnished or utilities provided). [In addition, all homeowners, regardless of age or income, receive a general credit financed by the state.]	

Table 7. (continued)

State	Financed by	Date of Adoption (Latest Liberalization)	Description of Beneficiaries (estimated number of claimants)	Income Ceiling (Asset Test)	Tax Relief Formula (or general remarks)	Form of Relief (estimated per capita cost)
Iowa	State	1967 (1971)	Homeowners 65 and over or totally disabled (N.A.)	$4,000	Deduction from tax bill of $125 or amount of tax liability, whichever is less.	Reduction in tax bill ($2.71)
Kansas	State (circuit-breaker)	1970 (1973)	Homeowners 60 and over (N.A.)	$8,192	Similar to Wisconsin but with different percentages. Limitation on amount of property tax liability considered for relief is $400.	State rebate ($2.88)
Kentucky	Localities (mandated)	1971	Homeowners 65 and over (125,000)	None	Exemption of $6,500 assessed value, except for assessment of special benefits.	Reduction in tax bill ($3.12)
Louisiana	A general homestead exemption of $2,000 for all homeowners, mandated by state. No reimbursement to local government.					
Maine	State (circuit-breaker)	1971	Homeowners and renters age 65 and older for males, 62 and older for females (16,000)	$4,000 (in addition net assets must not exceed $30,000)	Relief equal to 7% of the difference between household income and $4,000. Limited to the total property tax levied. (20% of rent = tax equivalent) (at least 35% of household income must be attributable to claimant)	State rebate only ($1.60)
Maryland	Localities (mandated)	1967 (1969)	Homeowners 65 and over (61,000)	$5,000	Credit of 50% of assessed value or $4,000, whichever is less, multiplied by the local property tax rate.	Reduction in tax bill ($1.81)
	Localities (optional)	1968 (1972)	Homeowners 65 and over (females 62 and over in Cecil Co.)	Varies by county	Relief varies from an increase in the credit provided by the state mandated law to a lessening or modification of conditions of eligibility for such credit.	Reduction in tax bill (N.A.)
Massachusetts	Localities (mandated)	1963	Homeowners 70 and over (74,000)	$6,000 single $7,000 married (maximum estate: $40,000 single $45,000 married)	Exemption of $4,000 assessed value or the sum of $350, whichever would result in an abatement of the greater amount of taxes due.	Reduction in tax bill ($5.18)

Table 7. (continued)

State	Financed by	Date of Adoption (Latest Liberalization)	Description of Beneficiaries (estimated number of claimants)	Income Ceiling (Asset Test)	Tax Relief Formula (or general remarks)	Form of Relief (estimated per capita cost)
Michigan	State (circuit-breaker)	1973	All homeowners and renters	None	Excess taxes are taxes above 3.5% of income (various lower percentages for elderly with incomes below $6,000). Credit = 60% of excess taxes [100% for all elderly]. Maximum relief is $500. [17% of rent = property tax equivalent].	State income tax credit or rebate ($27.53)
Minnesota	State (circuit-breaker)	1967 (1973)	Homeowners and renters 65 and over (95,000)	$6,000	A percentage of tax is given back as a credit, percentage declines as income increases. Not more than $800 tax considered. (20% of rent = tax equivalent.) [In addition, all homeowners, regardless of age or income, receive a general credit financed by the state.]	State income tax credit or rebate ($2.38)
Mississippi	State finances a partial homestead exemption of $5,000 for all homeowners with a reimbursement to local governments.					
Missouri	State (circuit-breaker)	1973	Homeowners and renters 65 and over	$7,500	Taxes exceeding various percentages are rebated: percentages range from 3% for incomes below $3,000 to 4% for incomes above $4,500. Not more than $400 tax considered for relief. (18% of rent = tax equivalent)	State income tax credit or rebate
Montana	Localities (mandated)	1969 (1971)	Retired homeowners (N.A.)	$4,000 single $5,200 married	50% reduction	Reduction of tax bill ($1.39)
Nebraska	State	1972	Homeowners 65 and over (60,000)	$2,800 single $3,550 married $4,300 married and spouse over 65	Reduction of tax by 25% (max. $125) in 1973 and by 50% (max. $250) in 1974.	Reduction of tax bill ($4.41)

Table 7. (continued)

State	Financed by	Date of Adoption (Latest Liberalization)	Description of Beneficiaries (estimated number of claimants)	Income Ceiling (Asset Test)	Tax Relief Formula (or general remarks)	Form of Relief (estimated per capita cost)
Nevada	State (circuit-breaker)	1973	Homeowners and renters 62 and over (13,000)	$5,000	Property tax in excess of 7% is refunded. (15% of rent = property tax equivalent). Maximum relief is $350.	State rebate ($1.42)
New Hampshire	Localities (optional)	1969	Homeowners 70 and over (9,300)	$4,000 single	Equalized valuation reduced by $5,000 times the local assessment ratio.	Reduction of tax bill ($1.99)
New Jersey	State 50% Localities 50% (mandated)	1953 (1972)	Homeowners 65 and over (163,000)	$5,000 (excluding social security)	Reduction of tax bill by $160, but not more than amount of tax.	Reduction of tax bill (one-half reimbursed by state) ($3.50)
New Mexico	State (circuit-breaker)	1972 (1973)	All persons (70,000)	$6,000	Person receives credit based on all state-local taxes which he is presumed to have paid. Credit varies depending on income and number of personal exemptions, ranges up to $133.	State income tax credit or rebate ($1.88)
New York	Localities (optional)	1972	Renters in rent-controlled housing, 62 and over (N.A.)	$3,000 (can be raised to $5,000 by locality)	Not to exceed amount by which maximum rent exceeds one-third of combined household income.	Reduction of maximum rent (N.A.)
	Localities (optional)	1966 (1972)	Homeowners 65 and over (82,000)	$3,000 (can be raised to $6,000 by locality)	Assessed valuation reduced by 50%.	Reduction of tax bill ($1.14)
North Carolina	Localities (mandated)	1971	Homeowners 65 and over (retired) (19,000)	$3,500	Assessed valuation reduced by $5,000.	Reduction of tax bill ($.16)

Table 7. (continued)

State	Financed by	Date of Adoption (Latest Liberalization)	Description of Beneficiaries (estimated number of claimants)	Income Ceiling (Asset Test)	Tax Relief Formula (or general remarks)	Form of Relief (estimated per capita cost)
North Dakota	Localities (mandated)	1969 (1973)	Homeowners 65 and over (5,000)	$3,500	Assessed valuation reduced by $1,000.	Reduction in tax bill ($.47)
	State (circuit-breaker)	1973	Renters 65 and over	$3,500	Property tax in excess of 5% of income is refunded. (20% of rent = tax equivalent). Maximum relief is $350.	State rebate
Ohio	State (circuit-breaker)	1971 (1972)	Homeowners 65 and over (N.A.)	$8,000	Benefits range from reduction of 70% or $5,000 assessed value (whichever is less) for incomes below $2,000 to 40% or $2,000 for incomes above $6,000.	Reduction of tax bill ($2.78)
Oklahoma	Homestead exemption of $1,000 of assessed value for all homeowners is mandated by state. No reimbursement to local government.					
Oregon	State (circuit-breaker)	1971	All homeowners (100,000)	None	Relief based on amount by which property taxes exceed percentage of income ranging from 3% on income below $1,500 (max. relief $400) to 7% for income above $8,000 (max. $100).	Reduction of tax bill (reimbursed) or tax credit ($7.80)
Pennsylvania	State (circuit-breaker)	1971	Homeowners 65 and over; widows 50 and over; totally disabled (264,000)	$7,500	100% of tax for income less than $1,000; 10% of tax for income greater than $6,000. Maximum rebate $200.	State rebate ($2.30)
Rhode Island	Localities (optional)	1960 (1973)	Homeowners 65 and over (19,000)	$4,000 ($5,000 in one locality)	Various formulas; most reduce assessed valuation by $1,000. [Also a tax freeze.]	Reduction in tax bill ($1.02)
South Carolina	State	1971 (1973)	Homeowners 65 and over (78,000)	None	Assessed valuation reduced by $10,000. Not related to income.	Reduction in tax bill ($1.31)

Table 7. (continued)

State	Financed by	Date of Adoption (Latest Liberalization)	Description of Beneficiaries (estimated number of claimants)	Income Ceiling (Asset Test)	Tax Relief Formula (or general remarks)	Form of Relief (estimated per capita cost)
South Dakota	Localities (mandated)	1972	Homeowners 65 and over (N.A.)	$4,000 married $2,400 single	Assessed valuation reduced by $1,000.	Reduction in tax bill ($5.15)
Tennessee	State	1972	Homeowners 65 and over (81,000)	$4,800	Equivalent to reduction of assessment by $5,000.	State rebate to taxpayer ($.74)
Texas	Localities (optional)	1972	Homeowners 65 and over (N.A.)	None	Assessment reduced by $3,000.	Reduction in tax bill ($4.29)
Utah	Localities (optional)	1967 (1973)	Indigent homeowners (presumed to be 65 and over) (N.A.)	$2,500 single $3,000 married	Taxes may be reduced by $100 or 50%, whichever is less.	Reduction in tax bill ($.16)
Vermont	State (circuit-breaker)	1969 (1973)	All homeowners and renters (60,000)	None	Income — Tax excessive when exceeding following percent of income 0-$3,999 — 4% $4,000-$7,999 — 4.5% $8,000-$11,999 — 5.0% $12,000-$15,999 — 5.5% $16,000- — 6.0% Maximum relief is $500. (20% of rent = tax equivalent)	State rebate (or income tax credit for elderly) ($23.38)
Virginia	Localities (optional)	1971 (1973)	Homeowners 65 and over	$7,500 ($20,000 asset test)	At discretion of locality.	Reduction in tax bill
Washington	Localities (mandated)	1971	Homeowners 62 and over or disabled (72,000)	$6,000	Income — Percentage of excess levies abated $0 - $4,000 — 100% $4,000 - $6,000 — 50% (minimum relief of $50 for income below $4,000)	Reduction in tax bill ($1.81)

Table 7. (continued)

State	Financed by	Date of Adoption (Latest Liberalization)	Description of Beneficiaries (estimated number of claimants)	Income Ceiling (Asset Test)	Tax Relief Formula (or general remarks)	Form of Relief (estimated per capita cost)
West Virginia	State (circuit-breaker)	1972	Homeowners and renters 65 and over (N.A.)	$5,000	Relief based on ratio of property tax to household income. Taxes exceeding a given percent of income are remitted. These percents range from .5% to 4.5%. Not more than $125 tax considered for relief. (12% of rent = tax equivalent.)	Direct state payment ($.84)
Wisconsin	State (circuit-breaker)	1964 (1971)	Homeowners and renters 62 and over (79,000)	$5,000	Tax burden excessive when exceeding following percents of household income (cumulative rates). See table below. Not more than $500 tax considered for relief. (25% of rent = tax equivalent) [In addition, all homeowners, regardless of age or income, receive a general credit financed by the state.]	State income tax credit or rebate ($2.21)

Income		% of excessive burden relieved
$0 - $1,000	0%	75
$1,000 - $1,500	5%	60
$1,500 - $2,000	10%	60
$2,000 - $5,000	14%	60

State	Financed by	Date of Adoption	Description of Beneficiaries	Income Ceiling	Tax Relief Formula	Form of Relief
Wyoming	State	1973	Homeowners 65 and over (8,000)	$2,000 single $2,500 married	Exemption of $1,000 assessed value.	Reduction in tax bill ($1.16)
District of Columbia				Plan under active congressional consideration.		

Notes:

N.A.—Data not available.

Circuit-breaker—A state-financed program of property tax relief in which the amount of tax relief phases out as household income rises.

Per capita cost—Total cost divided by total state population.

Source: ACIR Staff compilation.

APPENDIX:
THE ACIR AGENDA FOR PROPERTY TAX REFORM

A decade ago the Advisory Commission on Intergovernmental Relations submitted a comprehensive list of prescriptions for strengthening the property tax.[15] Undergirding the 29 policy recommendations are the following basic principles:

1. The prevailing joint state-local system for administering the property tax can work with a reasonable degree of effectiveness only if the state tax department is given sufficient executive support, legal authority, and professional stature to insure local compliance with state law calling for uniformity of tax treatment.

2. Professionalization of the assessment function can be achieved only if the assessor is selected on the basis of demonstrated ability to appraise property.

3. The perennial conflict between state law calling for full value assessment and the local practice of fractional assessment can be resolved most expeditiously by permitting local assessment officials to assess at any uniform percentage of current market value above a specified minimum level provided this policy is reinforced with two important safeguards:

    a. A full disclosure policy, requiring the state tax department to make annual assessment ratio studies and to give property owners a full report on the fractional valuation policy adopted by county assessors.

    b. An appeal provision specifically to authorize the introduction of state assessment ratio data by the taxpayer as evidence in appeals to review agencies on the issue of whether his assessment is inequitable.

The commission recently examined the desirability of a federal categorical grant to encourage states to improve assessment administration. The commission did not vote to recommend such a grant, but did urge the President and Congress to take steps to coordinate and strengthen existing federal programs that have clear potential for stimulating improvement of state and local assessment practices. Examples of such activities are:

• The Department of Housing and Urban Development, under its research and demonstration program, can make grants to, or enter into contracts with, states and localities for innovative projects aimed at improving assessment administration.

• The FHA appraisal activities of the Department of Housing and Urban Development might be extended and coordinated with those of the local assessors.

• Other federal agencies—such as the Department of Transportation, the General Services Administration and the Department of Defense—are continuously involved in land acquisition and undoubtedly conduct appraisals in connection with these activities. Such appraisals should also be coordinated with local assessment work.

• The various mapping operations of the Department of Commerce and the Department of Interior might be available to the state property tax

15. ACIR, The Role of the State in Strengthening the Property Tax, A-17, Washington, D.C., June 1963.

agencies as they develop land use maps in connection with property tax assessment.

• Treasury regulations and practices regarding depreciation of buildings for income tax purposes should be examined to determine whether such practices do indeed—as has been alleged—encourage over-assessment of improvements vis-à-vis the land on which the improvements stand.

• The activities of the Civil Service Commission under the Intergovernmental Personnel Act might be expanded in the areas of assessor training and interchange of state and federal personnel concerned with property appraisal.

• The experience that has been gained by the Bureau of the Census in conducting sales-assessment ratio studies might be built upon to help states strengthen and standardize their own studies.[16]

In addition the Commission recommended that the states finance the cost of relieving extraordinary residential property tax burdens on low-income families.[17]

---

16. ACIR, Financing Schools and Property Tax Relief—A State Responsibility, *A-40, Washington, D.C., January 1973.*

17. ACIR, *Fiscal Balance in the American Federal System, A-31, October 1967, Washington, D.C., p. 22.*

4

WHAT DO CIRCUIT-BREAKER LAWS ACCOMPLISH?

by Henry Aaron

"Practical men, who believe themselves to be quite exempt from any intellectual influence, are usually the slave of some defunct economist. . . . [I]n the field of economic and political philosophy there are not many who are influenced by new theories after they are twenty-five or thirty years of age, so that the ideas which civil servants and even agitators apply to current events are not likely to be the newest."[1]

Nineteen states now—as of May, 1973—have circuit-breakers and the number seems to be increasing hourly. Rarely has an idea gained such widespread and immediate acceptance. Rarely has policy been so unequivocally supported by such dubious analysis.

No trend at the state level has matched the circuit-breaker movement since states individually, but unanimously, established foundation programs for the support of elementary and secondary education. It seems likely that left to their own devices, most states over the next few years will enact some form of circuit-breaker. But the federal government may well hasten the process by underwriting state circuit-breakers (e.g., S. 1255, the Muskie-Percy bill), or it may enact a federal circuit-breaker (e.g., the Administration's proposals of April 30, 1973).

This tidal movement toward property tax relief rests on the following clear, strongly held, and, in my opinion, indefensible analysis of the impact of property taxes:

HENRY AARON, Senior Fellow, Economic Studies Division, The Brookings Institution. The views presented are those of the author and not necessarily those of the officers, trustees, or other staff members of the Brookings Institution. All computer operations described in the paper were performed at the Brookings Social Science Computation Center and the programming was done by Andrew Pike, whose efforts are gratefully acknowledged.

1. John Maynard Keyes, The General Theory of Employment, Interest and Money, Harcourt Brace, 1936, pp. 383-84.

> The property tax is a kind of excise tax borne by
> —renters through higher rents,
> —homeowners through direct billing, and
> —consumers through higher prices on commodities and
>   services produced with taxed nonresidential property.

On these assumptions property tax burdens (assigned in the fore-going manner) are clearly regressive, ranging from 16.6 percent of family income for families with incomes below $2,000 per year (30.8 percent in the Northeast census region) to 2.9 percent for families with incomes of $25,000 or more per year.[2] These burdens are alleged to represent an unconscionable burden on low-income households, especially on the aged who have little prospect of higher income.

In this chapter, I a) sketch the characteristics of circuit-breakers already enacted; b) indicate how direct benefits under typical circuit-breakers are distributed, i.e. who gets the check; c) evaluate the analysis of property taxes on which the movement toward circuit-breakers rests; and d) indicate how states are likely to respond to inducements for the adoption of circuit-breakers, such as S. 1255, the Muskie-Percy bill.

CHARACTERISTICS OF EXISTING CIRCUIT-BREAKERS

Property tax relief comes in many forms—homestead exemptions of various kinds, deductibility under the federal income tax, percentage reductions in tax bills for certain classes of taxpayers, and circuit-breakers, which provide partial or complete relief for property tax payments that exceed a stipulated fraction of income.

The typical existing circuit-breaker (see Table 7) covers only the aged (variously defined), aids renters as well as homeowners, limits benefits to households with incomes below $5,000 to $6,000 but contains no asset test, and imposes a maximum on total relief of $500 or less.

This pattern conceals immense differences and may well be a misleading guide to the form future circuit-breakers will take. The annual cost per state inhabitant of existing circuit-breakers ranges from 32 cents in Colorado to $27.53 under a newly enacted plan in Michigan. The amount of tax households must pay before becoming eligible for relief varies significantly. For example, a household with income of $1,000 pays no property tax if its liability is less than $200 in Pennsylvania, but pays the first $60 of tax obligation in Illinois.

Two recently enacted circuit-breakers, those of Michigan and Vermont, are vastly more generous than any previously enacted. Both cover all homeowners and renters regardless of age, have no income or net asset limitations, and provide relief when property taxes exceed

---

2. *See Table 1 in preceding chapter.*

rather modest fractions of income—3.5 percent in Michigan, 4 to 6 percent in Vermont. Based an average effective property tax rates in those states—2.02 percent in Michigan and 2.53 percent in Vermont in 1971[3]—typical consumption patterns, and normal relations between incomes and home value or rent, half or more of all households will qualify for some aid.[4] Preliminary estimates of those states confirm this supposition.

WHO GET THE BIGGEST REBATES?

The distributional effect of circuit-breakers depends critically on their specific provisions and limitations. These include:

—Income limits. Is aid completely denied if income exceeds a certain threshold?

—Net worth limits. Is aid completely denied if net worth exceeds a certain threshold?

—Deductibles and coinsurance. Must taxpayers pay some amount of tax before aid is provided; and, after aid commences, does it cover all or only part of taxes over the relevant range?

—Eligibility. Does the plan cover only the aged or everyone; only homeowners or renters as well?

—Benefit formulas. How much aid is provided as a function of household income and property tax liability? In this connection, is a fixed or variable fraction of rent regarded as property taxes?

—Maximum benefits. Is there a ceiling on benefits apart from that contained in the benefit formula, and if so, at what level?

—Definitions. How are income and (where relevant). net worth defined?

Tables 8 and 9 illustrate distribution of total aid and the average aid per household under the most generous circuit-breaker authorized by S. 1255, the Muskie-Percy bill. Under this bill the federal government would reimburse states for up to half of the cost of circuit-breakers which exempt households from property tax liability in excess of the following fractions of income:

Income	Property tax in excess of
$ 3,000 or less	3 percent
$ 3,001 to $ 7,000	4 percent
$ 7,001 to $10,000	5 percent
$10,001 to $15,000	6 percent

3. *Advisory Commission on Intergovernmental Relations,* Financing Schools and Property Tax Relief—A State Responsibility, *Washington, D.C., January 1973, Table 7, p. 22.*

4. *This statement presumes that a) homeowners own homes valued at twice annual income and b) renters spend 25 percent of income on apartments valued at eight times gross rent.*

Maximum aid is $500 per household. The bill limits federal sup-
port to rebates for families with incomes under $15,000, contains no
limit on net worth, and defines income broadly, except for the exclusion of capital gains and imputed rent, and for the failure to add
back excess depreciation. The estimates in Tables 8 and 9 are based
on the Brookings MERGE file, a statistical combination of the Survey
of Economic Opportunity and the Brookings Tax File. Values for cells
with fewer than 10 sample cases are omitted.

Table 8.
AVERAGE ASSISTANCE PER HOUSEHOLD RECEIVING ANY AID FROM S. 1255 (PROPOSED) BY INCOME AND NET WORTH CLASS, 1972 (in dollars)

Income class[a]	All net worth classes	Net worth class			
		Less than $0	$0-10,000	$10,000-20,000	Over $20,000
Less than $0	216	b	123	298	281
$ 0- 3,000	133	122	113	145	210
$ 3,000- 5,000	122	92	93	111	196
$ 5,000-10,000	122	83	85	102	193
$10,000-15,000	191	b	b	123	203
Average	129	95	103	124	201

Source: Brookings MERGE file, updated to 1972 values.
a. Income is equal to Census money income plus realized capital gains.
b. Cell contains fewer than 10 sampling observations.

Table 9.
TOTAL GOVERNMENT COST OF ASSISTANCE UNDER S. 1255 (PROPOSED) BY INCOME AND NET WORTH CLASS, 1972 (in millions of dollars)

Income class[a]	All net worth classes	Net worth class			
		Less than $0	$0-10,000	$10,000-20,000	Over $20,000
Less than $0	26	b	b	b	14
$ 0- 3,000	990	103	458	186	244
$ 3,000- 5,000	466	47	147	90	183
$ 5,000-10,000	526	25	139	90	271
$10,000-15,000	55	b	b	5	47
All classes	2,064	175	754	377	758

Source: Brookings MERGE file, updated to 1972 values.
a. Equal to Census money income plus realized capital gains.
b. Contains fewer than 10 sampling observations.

These tables contain some rather striking features. First, on a per family basis, benefits increase with net worth. This pattern occurs within income brackets and for all beneficiaries. Second, the largest per household benefits accrue to households with negative incomes, although total estimated benefits for this group are small. The estimates seriously understate actual benefits for households with negative incomes, since the MERGE file lacks data on net worth for households with high gross incomes. Many such households have low or negative net incomes, typically because of business losses. These households would qualify for aid under virtually all circuit-breakers except those with a net worth test. To the extent that housing expenditures are correlated with normal income, a point discussed below, this pattern suggests that households with temporarily depressed incomes, and hence with high ratios of home value or rents to current income, will receive substantial aid. Households in the same current income bracket whose incomes are not depressed will have lower rates of home value or rent to current income and will qualify for less aid or none at all. A third feature, shown in Table 10, is that any nationally uniform circuit-breaker overwhelmingly favors states of the Northeast because these states have the highest property tax rates in the nation; households in southern states would receive little aid because southern states tend to have low property tax rates.

These distributions may fairly reflect the actual patterns of benefits in Oregon and, for the aged, in a few other states, but most existing plans have different provisions and are less generous than the simulated version.[5]

Despite the "unrepresentativeness" of the results in Tables 8 and 9, they do reveal the essential structure of circuit-breakers. That

5. *Vermont and Michigan are striking exceptions.*

Table 10.
DISTRIBUTION OF CIRCUIT-BREAKER BENEFITS UNDER S. 1255 (PROPOSED) BY CENSUS REGION

Census Region	Total benefits (millions of dollars)	Percent of total benefits	Average benefit (dollars)
Northeast	917	44	164
North Central	594	29	124
South	140	7	58
West	413	20	130
National	2,064	100	129

Source: Brookings MERGE file, updated to 1972 values.

structure selects households whose expenditure on a particular item —real property taxes—is large in relation to current measured income. Since property tax liabilities are closely correlated to holdings of real property which are, in turn, correlated with net worth, the largest direct benefits on the average must accrue to the wealthiest households within each bracket. Plans that are confined to the aged, such as the administration's proposal, would exhibit this pattern even more dramatically, since the aged within each income bracket have more net worth than do other age groups.

I have some doubt whether a political consensus on behalf of circuit-breakers could be assembled if the fact were stressed that they provide most direct aid to those within each income bracket who have most net worth.

PROPERTY TAX INCIDENCE REVISITED

The intellectual rationale for circuit-breakers rests on the alleged regressivity of the property tax. This position has been widely accepted by economists at least since the landmark study of tax incidence by Richard Musgrave and others in 1951.[6] The assumptions underlying this study have been adopted in numerous subsequent studies and have achieved official sanctification in publications of the Advisory Commission on Intergovernmental Relations. The principal assumptions are that:

—The incidence of the property tax falls on users of commodities produced by taxed real property, housing in the case of residential property, and other commodities in general in the case of nonresidential property.

—Property tax burdens are fairly measured as a fraction of current measured income.

Each new study based on these assumptions reconfirms Keynes fatalism regarding the lag between discoveries and their application. It is more than a decade since Harberger set analysis of tax incidence squarely within a general equilibrium framework,[7] although it is only four years since Peter Mieszkowski extended the Harberger model to property taxes.[8] The use of current measured income has persisted

6. *"Distribution of Tax Payments by Income Groups: A Case Study for 1948,"* National Tax Journal, March 1951, pp. 1-53.

7. *Arnold C. Harberger, "The Incidence of Corporation Income Tax,"* Journal of Political Economy, June 1962, pp. 215-40.

8. *"The Property Tax: An Excise Tax or a Profits Tax?"* Journal of Public Economics, Vol. 1, April 1972, pp. 73-76. This paper circulated among economists for some time before publication.

despite the demonstration by Milton Friedman,[9] Margaret Reid,[10] Richard Muth,[11] and countless others that many consumption decisions, especially those, such as housing, which entail long-term commitments, are better explained by normal income than by current measured income. If the incidence of the residential property tax follows housing outlays, the use of measured rather than normal income distorts estimates of effective rates.

Incidence Theory

According to general equilibrium tax theory, a proportional tax on the value of all capital will be borne by all capital. If one ignores changes in demand patterns caused by the imposition of such a tax or by the replacement of some other tax, relative before-tax prices of factors and prices of commodities will not change. Accordingly the net-of-tax yield of capital falls by the amount of the tax. If the burden of the property tax were distributed in proportion to the ownership of all capital, one would conclude that it is at least proportional and very likely progressive with respect to normal income.[12]

If capital in some regions is taxed at higher rates than in others, the average rate is a burden on capital and the deviations from this average act as regional excise taxes or subsidies on the use of capital in those regions whose tax rates are above or below average, respectively. It is not clear whether regional variations in property taxes in fact reduce or increase progressivity. Low-income families are concentrated both in central cities, where property taxes tend to exceed the national average, and in rural areas (particularly in the South), where property taxes typically are much below the national average.

If capital in some industries is taxed at higher rates than in others, the impact on incidence depends on elasticities of substitution, differences in factor proportions among industries, and elasticities of demand, and no general conclusion about incidence is possible, although under plausible values of these parameters the burden of a property tax may remain substantially on capital.[13]

9. A Theory of the Consumption Function, *Princeton, 1957.*

10. Housing and Income, *University of Chicago Press, 1962.*

11. *"The Demand for Nonfarm Housing,"* in Arnold C. Harberger, *Ed.,* The Demand for Durable Goods, *University of Chicago Press, 1960, pp. 29-96.*

12. *Distributions of wealth against current measured income are misleading for reasons set forth in the text below.*

13. *Harberger describes parameter values that will cause the burden of a corporation income tax to be borne by capital in general,* op. cit. *Mieszkowski presents another numerical illustration in which owners of capital and apartment dwellers share the burden of a property tax on apartments only; see his "Tax Incidence Theory: The Effects of Taxes on the Distribution of Income," Journal of Economic Literature, December 1969, p. 1110-1111.*

Some recent attempts have been made to relax the highly restrictive assumptions of the models employed by Harberger and Mieszkowski, specifically their assumption that factor supplies are unaffected by taxation. Feldstein[14] has reaffirmed the traditional conclusions of comparative static analysis that part of the burden of a tax on capital will be borne by labor if the elasticity of supply of capital with respect to its after-tax yield is positive.[15] However, his subsequent analysis of the steady-state incidence of a payroll tax within a dynamic model,[16] as well as Peter Diamond's earlier analysis of an interest income tax,[17] both suggest that the long-run effects of a uniform tax on capital are very different from those suggested by comparative static analysis.

Whatever form the theory of the incidence of a tax on capital value or property income eventually takes, it is quite clear that the theory will not assign tax burdens in proportion to the consumption of housing or other goods produced with taxed capital. The theory of tax incidence embodied in the numerous studies now influencing public policy, most notably the recent computations of the Advisory Commission on Intergovernmental Relations, can be described, perhaps unfairly, as an atavistic attachment to naive and obsolete theory in defiance of published theoretical advances that demolish the previous orthodoxy.

Tax Burdens and Measured Income

Let us now assume, contrary to recent theoretical work, that the burden of the property tax is borne by users of housing and other commodities produced by taxed property. Even under this assumption the estimates of the regressivity of property taxes are badly exaggerated, so much so that a well-administered property tax may be progressive.

Under a perfectly administered residential property tax, the

---

14. See Martin Feldstein, "Tax Incidence in a Growing Economy with Variable Factor Supply," Harvard Institute for Economic Research, Discussion Paper Number 263, December 1972.

15. Empirical work by Weber suggests that the elasticity of savings with respect to the interest rate may be negative; if true, this conclusion would imply that capital would bear more than the full burden of a property tax; i.e., labor would benefit. See Warren E. Weber, "The Effect of Interest Rates on Aggregate Consumption," American Economic Review, September 1970, pp. 591-600.

16. Feldstein, op. cit., pp. 25-37.

17. "Incidence of an Interest Income Tax," Journal of Economic Theory, September 1970, pp. 211-24. Diamond finds that, within a rigidly simplified growth model, a tax on interest income raises the gross yield of capital, lowers wages and may increase or decrease the net yield of capital. As Feldstein points out, the most interesting questions may concern short-run incidence, because the period of adjustment to a new steady growth path after a tax has changed may be measured in decades.

burdens would be borne in proportion to the ratio of house (or apartment) value to income. Property tax collections in relation to actual or imputed rent are shown in equation (1).

$$T = \frac{T}{V} \cdot \frac{V}{R} \cdot R = t \cdot g \cdot R \tag{1}$$

where T = residential property tax liability
     V = market value of residence
     R = actual or imputed gross rent of residence

$$t = \frac{T}{V}, g = \frac{V}{R}$$

Taking logs and differentiating with respect to normal income yields:

$$e_{TY} = e_{RY}(1+e_{GR}), \tag{2}$$

where e_{TY} is the elasticity of property tax collections with respect to normal income, e_{RY} is the elasticity of gross rent (actual or imputed) with respect to normal income, and e_{GR} is the elasticity of the value/rent ratio (i.e., gross rent multiplier) to gross rent.[18]

Clearly, if $e_{GR} = 0$, i.e. if the value/rent ratio is the same at all rent levels, then the elasticity of the residential property tax is the same as the normal income elasticity of demand for housing, e_{RY}. Unfortunately, economists do not seem to be converging in their estimates of e_{RY}.[19] DeLeeuw concluded a recent survey with the judgment that the cross-sectional income elasticity of demand for rental housing probably fell between 0.8 and 1.0 and that of owner-occupied housing possibly higher.[20] Peterson reports some evidence

---

18. *Equation (2) is a combination of equations (3) and (4) in George Peterson's "The Regressivity of the Residential Property Tax," Working Paper 1207-10, Washington, D.C., The Urban Institute, November 1972, p. 8. The remainder of this section is little more than a summary of Peterson's paper.*

19. *In part, this circumstance may be due to the fact that e_{RY} has various meanings. It may refer to the proportionate change in housing expenditure as normal income varies over time—for households, groups, or the nation—which is a time series phenomenon. Or it may refer to the proportionate differences in housing expenditures among groups with different normal incomes—a cross-sectional phenomenon. To the extent that housing is used to maintain social distinctions, one would expect the cross-sectional e_{RY} to exceed the time series e_{RY}. See Robert Hartman, Demand For the Stock of Nonfarm Housing, unpublished Ph.D. dissertation, Harvard University, 1964. In comparing the burdens of a forward shifted property tax among income classes, clearly the cross-sectional e_{RY} is the relevant elasticity.*

20. *Frank deLeeuw, "The Demand for Housing: A Review of Cross-Sectional Evidence," The Review of Economics and Statistics, February 1971, p. 1. Geoffrey Carliner subsequently arrived at much lower estimates of .5 to .75 based on new data; see "Income Elasticity of Housing Demand," Institute for Research on Poverty, Discussion Paper 144-72, November 1972. p. 8.*

that e_{GR} , the elasticity of the gross rent multiplier, very considerably exceeds zero, and probably falls in the range of .5 to .7.[21]

The joint values of e_{RY} and e_{GR} suggest that e_{TY}, the income elasticity of property taxes, is between 1.2 and 1.7 if one accepts deLeeuw's estimates and from .75 to 1.3 if one accepts Carliner's.[22] The values contrast sharply with an elasticity of property taxes with respect to measured income implied by ACIR of about 0.5.

Since the ACIR estimates, based on the Census Bureau's Survey of Residential Finances, uses reported property tax payments by homeowners and landlords, the primary distortion in these estimates (if one accepts their incidence theory) is reliance on measured income. That current measured income is inferior to permanent income in predicting housing expenditures and, therefore, in distributing tax burdens on housing expenditures seems beyond dispute. The continuation of empirical studies of property tax incidence based on current measured income must be due to the ready availability of data on current measured income and the ease of applying the incidence assumptions. There is certainly no theoretical justification.

Incentives Created by Circuit-Breakers
Among Local Governments and States

According to the argument of the preceding section, circuit-breaker aid is unrelated to the real burdens of the property tax. This conclusion is inescapable for renters even if the tax is forward shifted, since most states impute to all renters the same fraction of rent as property taxes despite intrastate variations in property taxes far larger than and imperfectly correlated with variations in other elements of housing cost.

If the conclusion of general equilibrium analysis is accepted that the property tax is borne substantially by owners of capital, then circuit-breakers are not compensation for tax burdens, but rather a form of negative income tax based on current income and property tax payments. Tables 8, 9, and 10 provide some information on which to judge the desirability of this form of negative income tax. Each must judge the attractiveness of an aid formula that provides increasing amounts of aid as net worth increases.

The question most advocates of circuit-breakers have failed to answer is why one relatively minor element of household expenditures should be singled out as an index for financial support. Property taxes may be viewed as an element of housing costs or of total

---

21. "The Regressivity of the Residential Property Tax," op. cit., pp. 15 ff.

22. Geoffrey Carliner, op. cit. See note 20.

tax payments, or as one of the many determinants of factor incomes. Viewed in these ways, one might argue for a housing allowance (if property taxes, along with other forces, affect housing costs), for relief of total taxes over a fraction of income (if property and other taxes "excessively" burden certain households), or for income supplements (if factor incomes of some households are unacceptably low).

The case for circuit-breakers over these alternatives seems to rest on only one very sturdy pillar—political acceptability. Moreover, since most aid under circuit-breakers does accrue to households with relatively low incomes,[23] even those who recognize the weakness of the supporting analysis may be prepared to support them and to endorse proposals such as the Muskie-Percy bill "to hurry history along." Before doing so, one should consider the incentives circuit-breakers create for local governments and that federal support of circuit-breakers creates for the states.

1. Circuit-breakers may increase relative and absolute reliance on property taxes. This result would come about to the extent that aid for low-income families induces them (or others) to support or accede to property taxes they might otherwise have opposed. Circuit-breakers may well change attitudes of the aged toward school financing. If the federal government supports state circuit-breakers, states will be encouraged to rely more heavily than they otherwise would on property taxes, since the federal government will bear part of the cost. This effect may be particularly powerful in the South because the proportion of households with incomes below any given level is greater than in other regions and because aid to few households will be constrained by maximums. All of these statements must be qualified to the extent that decisions in effect are made by the median voter or by other groups who are ineligible for aid. Furthermore, all circuit-breakers impose limits on maximum benefits that can be paid to any one household.

2. Local governments will be encouraged to impose property taxes rather than user charges. One common argument against user charges is that they are regressive. Circuit-breakers add weight to this objection. This effect of circuit-breakers will reinforce incentives, already present in the formula for general revenue sharing, which discourages user charges.

3. Federal support for circuit-breakers will encourage states to drop homestead exemptions and other systems of relief provided by all except four of the states now without circuit-breakers. To the

---

23. The new Michigan plan is an exception, since many families with above median incomes will probably qualify for support.

extent that the shift to circuit-breakers merely shifts the cost of aid from states to the federal government, federal support for state circuit-breakers is revenue sharing, not property tax relief.

4. Circuit-breakers create yet another marginal tax rate that some-what reduces work incentives of low income households. Although the implicit tax rate in circuit-breakers is modest—no higher than 6 per-cent under the Muskie-Percy bill, for example—it will combine with the implicit tax rate under public assistance, Medicaid, food stamps, housing subsidies, and other programs to reduce net benefits from work.[24] As a result, the task of designing an integrated system of support for low-income households that promotes work incentive will be made a bit harder.

Misgivings Should Outweigh Temptations

Although it is tempting to support politically acceptable circuit-breakers which promise, however imperfectly, to assist households of below average income, the temptation should be resisted for the following reasons:

—Many of the neediest households will not receive aid, while some households with substantial wealth will qualify for relief.

—Aid will be focused on regions that for historical reasons have relied disproportionately on property taxes and denied other regions which have used other tax instruments or have provided few public services.

—Circuit-breakers will set up incentives to reverse the trend of recent decades away from property taxes and toward state income and sales taxes.

—Circuit-breakers although not obviously related to the problem of reforming welfare will make just a bit harder the problem of de-signing an integrated system of support for low-income families.

24. For a discussion of these issues, see Henry Aaron, Why Is Welfare So Hard to Reform?, Washington, D.C., Brookings, 1973.

5

AN AGENDA FOR STRENGTHENING THE PROPERTY TAX

by Mason Gaffney

I have four points: we do *not* need property tax relief; we *do* need assessment reform; we *do* need to shift the property tax in part to the state level; and we *do* need to convert the general property tax into a tax on site value.

WE DO NOT NEED PROPERTY TAX RELIEF

To speak of property tax "relief" is tendentious. Property tax relief is sales tax aggravation, or income tax or payroll tax aggravation. True tax relief may be secured by making cities more compact, economical, and efficient; by cutting out boondoggling in public works and highways; by increasing employment and cutting the welfare rolls; by reducing military outlays; and so on. Insofar as tax policy may contribute to these ends it will indeed bring true tax relief, and one reason for favoring the site value approach to property taxation is to make cities more efficient and cut per capita social overhead costs. That is genuine tax relief.

The Property Tax in the Total Tax System

We need to view the property tax in the context of a total tax system. The personal income tax, which is larger than the property tax, shelters property income from the full impact of its rates, so that payrolls must bear the main brunt. The other payroll tax, the one once connected with social security, is also larger than the property tax—and not deductible, as property taxes are, from taxable income. The sum of all excise taxes is certainly larger. Only a small share of the total tax burden is comprised by the $45 billion paid in property taxes.

The other taxes are all activity-based—that is, they are based on some act, usually constructive, of enterprise, management, trade, turn-

MASON GAFFNEY, Senior Research Staff, Resources For The Future. (Since July 1973, Director, British Columbia Institute for Economic Policy Analysis, Victoria, British Columbia.)

65

over, consumption, and above all labor. The property tax is the only one based on passively owning, as opposed to doing. I submit that enterprise and labor are worth more to a nation than inert wealth. The property tax activates wealth. That is especially true of the part of the tax that falls on land—another reason, of course, for favoring the site value approach. In lesser measure, and in the short run, it is also true of the part that falls on capital, most notably in cartelized industries which are characterized by excess capacity.

In one sense the property tax cannot be progressive because it is simply proportional to value, without regard to size of ownership. However, a common tax rate applied to all property, regardless of the owner's total wealth, tends to be progressive for the basic reason that the use of property is generally regressive. That is, larger holdings are combined with less labor, and produce less volume per dollar of capital and more profit per dollar of volume than smaller properties do. This follows as a result of the tendency of interest rates to be regressive—the poor and the small must pay more to hire capital.

To illustrate I have calculated profits per dollar of sales for Fortune's 500 largest industrial corporations, ranked by net worth. For the top ten it is 9.6 percent; for all 500, 6.1 percent; and for the smallest ten, .8 percent.[1] The last figure should not be taken too literally because the top 500 were originally chosen by sales; then I reranked them by net worth, so the bottom ten are biased to include firms of high sales relative to net worth. Still, the contrast of 9.6 percent for the top and .8 percent for the bottom ten is hard to dismiss.

Wage rates on the other hand tend to be progressive—the rich pay more. So larger firms are more capital-intensive and land and resource-intensive; smaller firms are more labor-intensive. Larger capitals turn over more slowly; smaller ones more rapidly, thus generating more activity and volume per dollar of taxable property. Illustrating this, I calculated the profits per employee for Fortune's 500. For the top ten this was $3,291; for the whole group, $1,489; and for the smallest ten $297. Again, the last figure is biased downwards by the selection process, as described before. But the contrast of the top ten with the whole group is not materially biased, and the contrasts are hard to dismiss.

The meaning for tax policy is that a property tax tends to be progressive (among corporations) when compared with taxes on activity, such as sales, personal income, or payroll taxes.

There is an a priori reason to assume that the stock of the better cushioned corporations is held by wealthier individuals, on the whole,

---

1. The Fortune Directory, August 1964.

than the stock of the marginal corporations with low profit margins. The reason is that rentable assets everywhere gravitate to strong hands, while financially weaker individuals move into marginal situations with high turnover. Strong hands also enjoy a comparative advantage in holding appreciating assets for future liquidation, and the six oil companies in the top ten obviously represent that kind of situation, compared with firms in the bottom ten like Iowa Beef Packers, Olivetti-Underwood, and Jonathan Logan.

If this a *priori* reasoning is correct, then wealthier individuals are attracted to the stock of corporations whose income comes more from wealth than from activity, regardless of size. It follows that the property tax may zero in on wealth more accurately than even a corporate income tax; even a progressive one. Corporate size is correlated with high profit margins and low employment/wealth ratios but is not identical with them. It is incidental here rather than essential. However when we move from interpersonal equity to another question, the viability of a free market economy, then corporate size becomes more central. The property tax must earn good marks as a tax that hits bigger businesses harder than small. It also hits cartels harder because their hallmark is excess capacity.

The use of property tends to be regressive. Carrying this a step farther, larger ownerships tend to make more expansive use of land relative to capital. The top ten firms include six oil companies, heavily committed to gas stations, key refinery sites, tank farms, docks, yards for truck fleets, pipeline rights of way, and above all minerals in the ground. More systematically the *U.S. Census of Agriculture* from 1900-40 reported separately on land and building values. I calculated the ratio of building value to land value by size class for 1940, the latest year reported.[2] Three figures tell the story. For all farms this building/land ratio is .45; for farms of 20-49 acres, .68; for farms 1,000 acres and over, .14. The ratio declines without a break from the smallest to the largest class.

More recently, John Riew has found the same pattern in Wisconsin farming, using assessed values.[3] Other studies of this pattern are by Morton Paglin[4] and Albert Berry.[5] This pattern is of course another reason for favoring the site value approach to property taxa-

2. 1940 Census of Agriculture, *Vol. 3, Washington, D.C., p. 80.*

3. John Riew, *"Assigning Collections of a Statewide Uniform Rate Land Tax,"* to be published in Richard Lindholm, Property Taxation and the Finance of Education, Madison, University of Wisconsin Press, 1973.

4. Morton Paglin, *"Surplus Agricultural Labor and Development: Facts and Theories,"* American Economic Review, *September 1965, pp. 815-33.*

5. Albert Berry, *"Presumptive Income Tax on Agricultural Land: The Case of Colombia,"* National Tax Journal, *June 1972, pp. 169-81.*

tion. If factor proportions are skewed towards a greater relative use of land among wealthier producers, a tax on land value would be more progressive than a tax on all property value.

Property Income Differs from Labor Income

Yet another reason for favoring property taxation is that on welfare grounds, property income should be taxed at a higher rate than labor income.

Wealth itself is part of "ability to pay," regardless of current income. Wealth implies the ability to liquidate and, to avoid that, the ability to borrow, for wealth is the basis of credit ratings. With respect to the elderly, wealth is a reasonable basis for expecting one's heirs to cover his or her real estate taxes. The maudlin approach that is used in discussing the retired elderly seems to be premised on the idea that children do not care for their aged parents. It is an unusual condition, the more so when the parents are holding property for these same children. I invite your attention to the fact that many elderly property owners avoid selling homes and farms which are much too large for them, specifically to avoid payment of capital gains taxes. We know that when property changes hands at death, the entire capital gain up to that date escapes income tax, 100 percent. The heir begins with a new stepped-up basis, the value at death.

The principle that wealth is part of ability to pay is quite general, but in respect to the elderly specifically, some liquidation of wealth during retirement years is a normal part of the life cycle. It is unreasonable and misleading to judge the relative burden on the aged in terms of current income alone. The aged, in anticipation of death, have a greater ability to liquidate their wealth than others, and a much greater security in terms of support from middle-aged children. Most of us can supply illustrations from our own families.

An exaggerated concern to give special privileges to the elderly and the retired is part of the put-them-on-the-shelf syndrome toward the aged which should go the way of white racism and male chauvinism. The aged, like the rest of us, do not need to be patronized. They need the opportunity to be useful. Those that become welfare cases should be treated by the welfare system on an impartial basis, without special favor to property owners. To use property tax relief as a substitute for welfare is to distribute welfare in proportion to wealth, surely an odd notion. To shape the entire property tax for the benefit of one special age and class of people would not, on its face, be well-balanced policy making.

Worse, the preoccupation with the special short-run situation of a few aged property owners serves as a diversion to distract us from larger issues of property tax reform. It sounds suspiciously like the widows-and-orphans melodrama in new greasepaint. It lets senators on the Intergovernmental Relations Subcommittee sponsor bills called "property tax reform" when all they are doing is making a little loophole for one special group defined by age and adjusted gross income, avoiding the large and tough issues.

There is a maudlin appeal to aiding the helpless widow that should put us on guard by reflex: who is playing our emotions, and to what end? If there is a good case to be made it can be made soberly and without seeking to shame us into holding back sharp questions. The young have problems too. And in terms of maximizing *everyone's* welfare by allocating wealth efficiently, the major problem between youth and age is increasingly to pry loose the control of inert property from the old for the young before the young have *become* the old.

Property income puts one on a higher plane of well-being or welfare than labor income of the same amount, because one needn't work for it. Fifteen thousand dollars a year earned by working long shifts in a coal mine with black lung disease is not the same as $15,000 a year from property with a life of ease (plus the option of living off the wealth, or banking or parlaying it). The industrial accident and disease toll each year is frightful. So is the highway accident toll, most of which occurs during commutation. Income is not income, in terms of welfare: it depends on what you have to do to get it. Before 1942, there was an earned-income credit in the personal income tax in recognition of this. Today, income from labor is taxed much higher than income from property, because tax shelters and loopholes mainly involve property ownership. The main counterpoise to this is the property tax.

The Public Equity in Land

The property tax asserts a general public equity in land under private tenure. This is a counterpart to a system in which much of our land is committed to private tenure. Most of the United States was public domain not long ago—not long in the perspective of history. Everyone had an equal claim. Land was turned to private tenure in order that the land be put to a higher use than is possible or likely under direct public administration. It is not practical to give everyone an equal share. To compensate those who are left out, land in private tenure has been made subject to the property tax. The tax asserts the equity of nonholders.

This was all darkened over when the states relinquished the property tax to localities, which are not much interested in protecting the equity of the landless, especially as the latter become increasingly migratory. But it was at the same time reaffirmed by the states' requiring localities to provide public schools, and leaving the school districts dependent on the property tax. The right of every child to a free education is a form of social dividend, a way in which part of property income is shared with each citizen as a birthright.

This basic relationship and principle is forgotten in the catch-phrase, "Property should pay for services to property, but not for services to people." Property should pay for services to people because all people have an equity in property by virtue of birth and citizenship.

This is basic to Anglo-Saxon-Norman land law, taken into every state constitution when it adopted the English common law. It is enshrined in words like "real estate" which is the Norman "royal estate," the king's land; words like "eminent domain," and "fee" (as in feudal). It is enshrined in the priority that taxes enjoy over mortgages and over the fee-holder's equity. Land title chains generally hark back to some European monarch. All the fee-holder has is what the king gave away; and all the king gave away was tenure subject to taxes. The king never gave away his right to levy taxes, nor have the kings' successors, the sovereign states. Government is more than a convenience for fee-holders, who are the king's tenants; it is the protector of the rights of the landless.

In 16th century Europe, doctrines of this general stamp were known as the Anabaptist heresy, some of whose votaries were burned at the stake. But it came to the fore in England, and came to prevail strongly in the United States and other British settlements, largely via school finance. If that all sounds too radical, remember that the property tax is now being attacked for not being radical enough, i.e. not sufficiently progressive. Attitudes have changed a good deal since they burned Anabaptists. I invite you to entertain the entrancing possibility that a tax which is attacked at once for being too radical and too conservative might, for the great middle American, be about right.

But today the old equilibrium has been disturbed because localities have learned to wiggle out from under their educational servitude by exclusionary policies: large-lot zoning, restrictive building codes, sewer power, regressive assessment, and overassessing buildings relative to land. Also, most of them probably spend less on education than consumers would like, if by spending large amounts on schooling they did not make themselves more vulnerable to immigration by others.

The solution is not to abolish the property tax, for it is not the problem. The solution is to finance education at a higher level, state and/or federal. This can be done without sacrificing local or individual control of schools by following the pattern of the G.I. Bill and employing a voucher system, or any other system where state funds are proportional to attendance, or any other formula based on numbers of people. Conceivably such formulae might be modified for differential local costs and "needs," as some school finance people wish, but that is an option. The point here is that support should vary as a function of population, thus giving the distribution the character of a social dividend.

Regressivity

The propery tax is not regressive. I have written an article to this effect, which I cite here rather than recite.[6] I would underscore certain central points that have been omitted or overlooked in later discussion.

I have already mentioned here that income, and especially current cash or realized income, is no index to well-being or ability to pay, either. On top of that, the Adjusted Gross Income (AGI) calculated on Form 1040 is no index to income. AGI is what is left over after most of the loopholes. Most of the loopholes are related to owning property—a blue collar job has never been called a tax shelter.

Wendell Willkie once said that a good catchword can obscure analysis for fifty years. The catchword of the generation now pushing fifty has certainly been "income." The economics profession has practiced idolatry on it, and made the income tax a panacea. This comes to the surface when economists judge the property tax by comparing it with AGI.

Yet tax economists have long been up in arms against loopholes, and the public is, if anything, ahead of them. It is a popular campaign issue, near the top rating. AGI is neither intellectually respectable nor popularly credible. It is bad enough to stack the cards by judging the property tax on the basis of how closely it resembles an income tax. It is worse to judge it on the basis of how closely it resembles a tax based on AGI. AGI has gotten so bad, any public policy based on AGI is a fraud.

Consider the effect that a few wealthy persons with low AGI have on the data which we see on the property taxes of "low-income" people. Suppose one person has a million dollars in taxable property and, at 2 percent, pays $20,000 a year in property taxes but has managed to reach near zero AGI through a skillful use of loopholes.

6. Mason Gaffney, "The Property Tax Is a Progressive Tax," Proceedings of 64th Annual Conference on Taxation, *National Tax Association, 1971, pp. 408-26.*

It would take 100 genuine paupers in $10,000 dwelling units to have a million dollars of taxable property and pay $20,000 in property taxes. That one ringer in the crowd doubles the mean property tax burden.

Then the statistician takes the mean value and says poor people with income below $2,000 pay 10 percent of their income in property taxes, and it is a groaning burden. Talleyrand said "The masses want to believe in something; for their benefit, nothing is so easy to arrange as the facts." We had better massage the data some more and get rid of that enormity.

The ownership of property is incomparably more concentrated in a few hands than is the receipt of taxable income. The data are cited in my article mentioned above. In the lower brackets of income, most income comes from labor; in the higher brackets most comes from property, and much property income isn't even counted. I see no way to get away from these overpowering facts.

Even if the residential property tax were 100 percent shifted forward, that would not make it regressive. Almost everyone has overlooked the point that the poor live, by and large, in dwelling units whose capital value is low relative to the rent. Slums have a low price/earnings ratio, and besides that the earnings are a small share of the gross rent because of high operating and collection costs. The property tax is based on capital value, not on rent. Data cited on how rent relates to income are therefore not relevant. Even if all property taxes were shifted to tenants and included in rent, the property taxes levied on the dwellings of the poor are a small share of the rent.[7] It is true that some slums are located on land of high speculative value on the growing edges of business districts, but here it is only the land that is valuable. The buildings have little value remaining. And if any part of the property tax is shifted to tenants it is of course only the part on buildings.

In addition, the rich go in for second homes, summer homes, lakeside cottages, ski chalets, hobby farms, and the like. The rich travel more, and spend more on hotels and motels—all taxable property.

Homeowner Exemptions

There have been recurrent proposals in the wind to exempt homeowners. This group is now nominated to enjoy the mindless adulation and bottomless subsidy previously heaped on such fallen angels as farmers, motherhood, growth, and maybe even the Pentagon.

---

7. George Peterson, "The 'Regressivity' of the Residential Property Tax," *Working Paper 1207-10*, Washington, D.C., The Urban Institute, November 1972.

Americans need to spoil something, it seems, and home folks are good folks.

The definition problems are formidable. How much of a hobby farm is a "home," how much a speculative investment? You can imagine how much expensive fun the lawyers will make of that, and how counterproductive it all will be. But that is only a nit, next to the main fault.

I deplore the use of slanted catchphrases like "relief for the homeowners." There are other life-support systems besides owner-occupied homes, and it is single-minded to judge a policy on the basis of what it does for the homeowner or any other special class. The world is full of various kinds of fundamentalists. You name it, and I can find ten people who think the taxpayers should subsidize it: hunting and fishing, caribou in Alaska, fine arts, performing arts, highway transportation, the merchant marine, interplanetary exploration, education, religion, medicine, birth, birth control, burial, war, peace . . . it goes on and on. The world has invented the market to help arbitrate these competing claims, or some of them. Anyone who wants to substitute his judgment for the market's needs to face up to a certain burden of proof. For the market, with all its failings, does have a rationale.

Residential relief is not especially called for if it means more payroll taxes, for example. The imputed income from the capital value of the owner-occupied home is already exempt from the income tax, while payrolls are taxed both as payrolls and again as income, and again on retail purchases.

Homeowner relief is certainly uncalled for if it means sloughing the burden onto tenants. If regressivity is one's concern then he would certainly begin with tenant relief, not homeowner relief.

On the other hand, there is a place for residential relief—for example, by deBalkanizing the property tax base and bringing industrial and mineral tax enclaves into school districts with many poor children. We need to tax cars much more heavily than homes, for the homes now provide streets for the cars and suffer enormously from auto noise and fumes. But "relief for the homeowner" is not an end in itself. Fairness, overall balanced equity, and maximum social efficiency and well-being are more adequate statements of ultimate goals. They do not point to lowering the property tax.

Voters Overrule the Polls

Poll results are alleged to show that the property tax is the least popular tax. How are we to reconcile this with the direct messages we have from the voters? Proposals to cut down the property tax were defeated in California, Oregon, Michigan, Colorado, and New Jersey in 1972, by direct popular vote. It was not a partisan issue. Nixon and McGovern alike campaigned to lower property taxes. But faced with the issue itself, the voters saved the property tax. There is no tax over which the average voter has so much control as over the local property tax. The rapid rise of this tax testifies to its popularity, not the reverse. It is conventional rhetoric to grumble about property taxes, perhaps because large owners of property set fashions. When I was a graduate student twenty years ago in California, and ever since, it has been the style to condemn the property tax—and go right on raising it.

If indeed the property tax is so unpopular, it is fair to ask why many legislatures have made it harder for the voters to raise the property tax than other taxes: to set debt limits and tax limits for localities; to require two-thirds approval on bond issues; to require improvement districts to prove benefits received by property which they tax? There are no such handcuffs on other taxes. Ever since Alexander Hamilton, it has been a pattern of legislators protecting property against the irresponsible popular will.

I ask you to ponder the inconsistency in the deliberations following *Serrano v. Priest,* of postulating the unpopularity of the property tax while on the other hand raising the specter that localities, relieved from school finance, will move right in and raise property taxes for other purposes. This is more consistent with a hypothesis that the property tax is unpopular with a minority who would block the majority from making use of it. If it were really so unpopular it would go away by popular vote.

WE DO NEED ASSESSMENT REFORM

The U.S. Census of Governments' quinquennial report on assessment ratios is persuasive and general evidence that we need assessment reform, but it understates how much we need reform. In respect to industrial property, it omits ownerships whose value is judged to surpass a quarter of a million dollars: that is, most industrial property. It is unfortunate that this is pointed out in a part of the Census most users don't get around to reading, even though perhaps they should, so that it took Nader's Raiders to ferret this out.

So many economists are mistaken, I believe, to cite the Census to show that industrial property is not underassessed. The Census is simply not in on the action here, and Nader's data, non-random though they may be, have more to tell us than the Census.

Much of Nader's data are consistent with and supplement and

reaffirm the general principle that land is underassessed. He has focused on industrial landholdings: oil in Texas, coal in the Appalachians, copper in Montana, timber in Georgia and Maine. I know of no reason to doubt the generality of these findings, and many reasons to believe it.

Census Study Omission

The Census study omits the class of land most underassessed, that is unsubdivided acreage inside SMSAs. Much of that is speculative; much is in estates held by the very (and the very very) rich; and much is industrial.

I studied some of this industrial land in Milwaukee. It was not only underassessed, but regressively assessed. The large tracts were given a wholesale rate, allegedly because large tracts sell for less per unit. At the same time, the city was assembling and/or holding large tracts in an industrial land bank, allegedly because the market put a premium on large tracts. It makes an interesting contrast. I have published some of my findings on this question elsewhere.[8] Similar findings by Armin Jocz in Beloit, Wisconsin and by Alene Ammond in Cherry Hill, New Jersey, were published recently as testimony presented to the Senate Subcommittee on Intergovernmental Relations.[9]

Professor Samuel Loescher of Indiana University has written me that his students' study "confirms the substantial underassessment of industrial land relative to adjacent residential land, measured on a per-acre basis, in the area of every major industrial property in Monroe County, Indiana."[10]

Beyond Revenue Productivity

The value of assessment reform is much greater than the gain of revenue, however great or small that may be. Increased taxpayer confidence and acceptance are equally important. I do not think that people who countenance corruption and maladministration have any inkling of how destructive these are to the morale of citizens who are outraged first by the facts, and then outraged again by the complaisance and laxity of responsible officials who have the power and duty to act.

8. "What Is Property Tax Reform?" American Journal of Economics and Sociology, April 1972, and "Adequacy of Land as a Tax Base," in Daniel Holland, Ed., The Assessment of Land Value, Madison, University of Wisconsin Press, 1970.

9. Hearings before the Subcommittee on Intergovernmental Relations, The Impact and Administration of the Property Tax, Washington, D.C., Government Printing Office, 1973.

10. John Goss and Dave Hill, "An Examination of Property Tax Assessments in Monroe County," MS.

The revenue productivity of a tax is limited by the suffering of those most impacted, i.e. those overassessed and paying the highest effective rates. These become the widows and orphans trotted out to damn the entire system.

Easy Half Step

We can move halfway from here to the site value tax without changing any law, simply by obeying the laws we already have and assessing land at market the way we do buildings. I do not exaggerate. Listen to what people say when an assessor moves toward bringing assessed valuation up to market value. "The assessor has gone hog-wild." "He's trying to tell people how to use their land." "The assessor is taking over the planning function." "This vicious radical theory of market value." "Our community is unique." Sound familiar? It gives a notion how time has withered and custom staled the notion that all property should be assessed on the same basis according to law.

I invite your close attention to what has happened in a few jurisdictions whose assessors have brought land up to market: Rosslyn, Va.; Southfield, Michigan; Sacramento, California. I further invite your attention to the cities of Canada, especially western Canada, where assessors traditionally value land more heavily than they do here. These cities compare favorably in most respects with the remains of many of ours.

The underassessment of land is worse than the Census shows, at least in my experience. *Building the American City,* the final report of the Douglas Commission (National Commission on Urban Problems), cites Allen D. Manvel to the effect that 40 percent of urban real estate value is land value, and I believe the true figure is at least that high. But in most city assessment rolls it is down nearer 20 percent or 25 percent.

In sylvan areas, every forest owner likes to overstate the value of stumpage for federal tax purposes (to transfer profit to timber culture, which gets capital gains) and to understate it for state and local excise and property tax purposes. All that is needed here is for state and federal tax officers to exchange information and demand the same valuations be used, although of course immature timber must be discounted from its maturity value.

The most underassessed of all properties are mineral reserves. Producing properties are underassessed; reserve properties are not assessed as mineral-bearing land at all. This has something to do with the problem of measuring reserves, but not very much. It has more to do with differential political power and constitutes, in my opinion, one of the worst breakdowns of the democratic process that we suffer. If one *really* means to help those poor widows, here is a place to start. If the Watergate catharsis is used merely to review the way we play cops-and-robbers, the newsprint lavished on the affair will have been largely wasted. The point is rather how dependence on campaign contributions biases and subverts politicians of both parties at all levels in favor of large contributors. Federal income tax loopholes for mineral owners are matched by local assessors and courts who underassess mineral reserves to the point of exemption.

In West Virginia, for example, the United States Geological Survey maps of coal reserves have been available for a long time, but not used. Recently the State Department of Assessment has begun staff work to help local assessors use these maps, and to win the court cases that inevitably follow. They need help.

Congress should instruct the U.S.G.S., Bureau of Mines, and other federal agencies to cooperate actively with state and perhaps local agencies in the process of valuing mineral reserves. This entails not just ascertaining the physical volume and grade of the reserves; it entails valuation, an economic art.

If it be anticipated that states might not cooperate, I suggest that no state—until it shall have done so—be allowed to plead poverty in Washington. I predict few of them would have reason to plead poverty afterwards.

If it be anticipated that the agencies might not cooperate, or would represent the assessed parties instead of the public, then a new agency may be called for. Whether in a new or old agency, new personnel are needed with new skills and a sense of the new mission.

How Underassessing Land Bleeds U.S. Treasury

The Internal Revenue Service accepts the assessment of land by local assessors as prima facie evidence of land value in disputes over income taxes. Land is not depreciable for income tax; buildings are. Understating the share of land lets the taxpayer overstate the depreciable share of real estate. It lets the owner of income property depreciate land to write off against cash flow.

There is little useful incentive effect of this tax break. On the contrary, it is a reason for urban nonrenewal and decay. Ecologists will not smile on the wildlife it shelters, the *Rattus norvegicus, Rattus rattus,* and friends. The main shelter goes to owners of land with older buildings.

Every time an old building is sold the buyer may depreciate it again. For the new basis he uses the new purchase price, never mind how many times previous owners have written off the building, and part of the land value, too. It is bad enough to let an owner depreciate land once only. If you figure it out it is tantamount to exemption in perpetuity: all the Treasury gets thereafter is a return on its own investment.[11] But our tax system lets land be depreciated as many times as it is sold, or inherited. The income is not only exempt, it is supplemented by the Treasury, for each additional false depreciation is a gift.

This practice bleeds the Treasury. It affects most income property, nonresidential and residential both, and thus affects more than half of all the property there is. I have not tried to estimate how many billions of tax money hemorrhage from this ruptured artery, but it can hardly be inconsiderable. Two otherwise impressive quantitative studies of depreciation, one by Slitor for the Douglas Commission[12] and one by Aaron,[13] shed no light on this particular matter. Both were limited to housing. Both studies downplayed the quantity of tax subsidy in fast write-off (Aaron) and multiple write-off (Slitor). They did not come to grips with false write-off of land. I know of no study that has. It is past time that the Office of Tax Analysis and a hundred independent researchers jump into this issue with both feet. The ACIR recently suggested that such a study be made.[14] Would that it will soon follow through and devote some of its own resources to such a study.

I recommend that there be established in the Internal Revenue Service something like a Federal Board of Equalization, whose function would be to prevent local assessors from helping their constituents lower their income tax liability in this manner. Otherwise we never will get true assessment of land, for you need little imagination to see what pressure this inevitably brings on the local assessor, a

11. *Suppose in 1973 I write off $100 of land value, and my tax rate is 40 percent. I reduce my taxes by $40 in 1973. Thereafter the Treasury has a $40 or 40 percent investment in the land. It takes 40 percent of the ordinary income in perpetuity (maybe), thus getting only a return on its investment. The owner has a 60 percent investment in the land, and clears 60 percent of the ordinary income after taxes. Effective tax rate: zero. This is modified by liability for capital gains tax on excess of sales price over book value. But there are a dozen ways to cut that down, often to zero, and in every case it comes later than the write-off, and only half of it is taxable.*

12. Richard E. Slitor, The Federal Income Tax in Relation to Housing, *Research Report 5, National Commission on Urban Problems, Washington, D.C., Government Printing Office, 1968.*

13. Henry Aaron, "Income Taxes and Housing," *American Economic Review, Vol. 60, December 1970, pp. 789-806.*

14. *Advisory Commission on Intergovernmental Relations,* Financing Schools and Property Tax Relief: a State Responsibility, *Washington, ACIR, January 1973, p. 6.*

pressure that is all one-sided. What we have now is a modern variation of the old problem of competitive underassessment. States solve
that problem at low cost by the use of boards of equalization. The
federal government can and should do the same.

We keep hearing of public land purchases at prices far above
equalized assessed value. Each such case is evidence of malfeasance
on someone's part and should alert us to the need for full review,
disclosure, and perhaps criminal charges. Is such systematic violation
of the law less harmful than breaking and entering?

WE DO NEED TO SHIFT THE PROPERTY TAX
TO THE STATE LEVEL

Half the reasons one hears cited for damning the property
tax are not arguments against the property tax as such, but against
tax enclaves, against Balkanization, against fiscal zoning and havens
of high per capita tax base. These are arguments in favor of shifting
the financing of some public services, especially schools, to the state
level. The property tax is only incidental, because for the last few
decades it has been mainly local. It used to be a state level tax, and
could be again.

Serrano v. Priest and like decisions in other states have not outlawed the property tax for school finance. Rather they have outlawed
gross inequalities in the local tax base used for school finance. In
Rodriguez the U.S. Supreme Court did not say "forget it." It said
each state legislature should respond to its own courts and voters.
One way or another, the courts are saying tax bases must be equalized
at the state level.

It is not necessary, therefore, to relinquish the property tax, but
only to move it to the state level. Thus every local tax haven will
automatically be tapped for the benefit of every school child—and
without the need for families to move to invade the tax havens, either,
and I submit that when people start locating without being influenced
by this factor we will achieve a much more compact and rational
pattern of metropolitan settlement.

It is not just industrial tax enclaves like Emeryville, California,
West Milwaukee, Wisconsin, and Clearing, Illinois that will be tapped.
Butte, Montana, Hibbing, Minnesota, and Kern County, California
look like good candidates, too, with their mineral wealth. (Mineral
wealth is concentrated in a few places, usually remote from populous
school districts.) So do the undertaxed forest lands of Maine, Oregon,
and Florida, and the coal reserves of Appalachia.

The quality of property tax administration would probably improve at the state level. The optimal scale of assessors' work is larger than most jurisdictions presently going, although the optimal size would fall if we could spread the overhead over more frequent and careful assessments. The ideal arrangement involves a compromise between the advantages of scale and those of local intimacy, with staff work and research and training conducted at the state level, and nuts-and-bolts assessment at the county level, with equalization and review again at the state level.

However, this is only a mote next to the basic gain from state assumption of the property tax for schools. The quantum advance in the quality of American government that would result is the change of local incentives toward immigration. Now, every tax jurisdiction in the country, be it rural, sylvan, suburb or central city, is fighting to dump its fiscal deficit generators over its borders. Mayor Henry Maier of Milwaukee, President of the National Conference of Mayors, said in his presidential address in New Orleans that we must remove "whole square miles of people" from the cities, and this sums up the prevailing attitudes nicely. So everyone adopts exclusionary low density zoning and a host of allied policies to repel the poor and avoiding diluting the local tax base. But given state support of schools, local governments would be faced with a different set of incentives and become much more hospitable to the poor.

We had better move in that direction soon, or we will create a class of gypsies who have no place to park their trailers but on the Interstate Highway System. Anyone who thinks that is a good idea had better review the data on rising rates of crime and welfare dependency. For a democratic society to work, we need local governments that compete to attract people, not to exclude them.

WE DO NEED TO CONVERT THE PROPERTY TAX TO A SITE VALUE TAX

Dick Netzer, Lowell Harriss, Arthur Becker, I, and others have written a good deal about the advantages of the site value approach, and I will merely summarize here some major points, stressing a few which have been neglected.

The proposal is to exempt reproducible capital from the property tax base, and focus it on land value. There would be little or no loss of tax base. Untaxing buildings adds to site value an amount as great as the capitalized value of the building taxes, and this new value becomes part of the site value base.[15] Thus, we would be taxing the same real estate; we would just be taxing it in a different way.

15. "Adequacy of Land as a Tax Base," op. cit. (note 8), pp. 187-92.

For the same reason, there would be, in general, no invasion of the present owners' equity in land. There would be some reshuffling, and over a transition period there would be a recentralization of values because the redevelopment of inner lands would satisfy and pull in the demand now proliferating over peripheral areas. Judging by what one hears, most owners in peripheral areas would prefer it that way.

The market would become the judge of what is the best use of land, unswayed by tax bias, as now. When buildings are taxed, the tax biases the owner in favor of the use more lightly taxed.

Nowadays some people decry "highest and best use" as though it were a kind of morbidity. There may be a tendency for social critics to overstate the external effects of a land use and understate the basic internal purpose. Highest and best use simply means that use offering society the greatest net service flow, insofar as the market is able to judge it. Those not accepting the market's judgment need to show that their objection is based on something more substantial than, for example, a subjective esthetic reaction. It would only be a form of tyranny to let taste dictators judge the external effects of a building on the sort of emotive basis that is fashionable among architectural journalists.

A more objective method, I believe, would be to note the effect on land values across the street. In my studies of land values, I have almost always found that highrise buildings, even something like the Allen-Bradley building in Milwaukee, an eight-story factory that uses its land to the sidewalk, raise values around them. I cannot say the same for gas stations, junk yards, auto dealerships, and vacant lots—no, not even cemeteries—and I wish that those who are concerned with external effects of land uses would get more exercised about those that can be objectively demonstrated to harm their neighborhoods and communities.

Effects of Taxing Buildings

Taxing buildings slows down renewal and replacement of decayed and obsolete buildings by new. Taxing land does just the opposite. It drains cash from the holdout and the sleeping owner of underdeveloped land and presses him to improve, or sell.

We hear a lot about how the site value tax is economically "neutral," and lets the market alone to do its work. In an important sense that is true. But tax theorists have long noted that taxes have two kinds of effects. There is the marginal effect, and the wealth effect. Land taxes have no marginal effect, that is, the marginal increment of capital applied to land is not taxed, and that is a great virtue. But land

82

taxes do have a wealth effect. They drain wealth from holdouts and reduce their holdout power. It is not a small matter.

In some European colonies in Africa, the European governments once forced natives to work in the mines by levying a head tax. The natives, living happily in the bush, had to work in the mines to raise the money to pay the head tax—or else go to jail. That is a wealth effect. The land tax uses the same principle in favor of labor. It forces landowners to put land to use to pay the tax. But there is no jail in view. It is a carrot and stick thing. The carrot is the option of building on land free of building taxes. The carrot and stick together get results. The carrot balances the stick in terms of equity. And everyone gains.

That might seem too obvious to spell out were it not that the large Chicago-Virginia-UCLA axis has built an influential, highly reasoned philosophy that pretty well dismisses wealth effects. To this school of thought it doesn't matter who originally owns property or who begins the game with all the chips. Create good tenure rights, minimize transaction and information costs, and the market will lead to the same ideal results. For example, charging polluters an effluent tax leads to the same results as "bribing" them not to pollute so much. It is this kind of thinking that makes a tax on site value merely "neutral." There is far more in taxing the earth, Horatio, than is comprehended in this poor philosophy. In my opinion the wealth effects are at least as important as the marginal or trade-off effects.

Taxing Land Economizes on Public Capital

When public works are extended, land assessments rise, bringing in private buildings to match the public, nicely synchronized with it and with each other. Planning needs such a tool. And here at last is a way to tax relief—true tax relief achieved in the only possible way by economy in public spending, not by the childish dodge of substituting another tax and calling it relief.

Compact settlement reduces almost all public costs per capita since most of these, and many private costs as well, vary with the length of streets and lines. This important principle has been obscured in many comparative studies because they have lumped school costs with land-service costs.[16] High density does not reduce school costs, except in small ways. It does reduce street improvement costs, capital budgets, linkage and distribution costs, and all other costs that vary with area, like the costs of flood control and radio coverage, for example.

16. *Many studies comparing suburbs and central cities have also compared new suburbs and old cities, thus biasing the findings against high density.*

The share of wealth that is land tends to increase with total wealth, making the land tax very progressive. As discussed above, the use of land is regressive, making a land tax progressive relative to activity-based taxes. The land tax may be as heavy as the community likes without driving away capital, but only attracting it the more. No other tax can make that statement.

Stimulating Employment

By stimulating rebuilding and new building and putting land to full use, the site value tax stimulates employment. This in turn cuts down on welfare costs, affording true tax relief.

This has to be viewed in the national perspective. Many of us are hung up on viewing the property tax in provincial and particularistic terms, and think of employment as a pestilence, inviting problems and especially school taxes into our enclave. But here we are discussing the property tax as a national institution. The national effects of a national change in the character of the tax would be to increase the demand for labor nationwide, and abate the problem of unemployment and its derivative evils. It would not involve flooding any one particular jurisdiction with the rejects of all the others.

Looking at it this way, you can see why some have thought that the site value tax might tend to accomplish the goal that we once hoped Keynesian policies would achieve, to wit full employment. Society has now allowed this utopian dream to be entertained, and even legislated it as a national goal in the Full Employment Act of 1946. The Keynesian approaches seem to have been pushed past their load limit, but perhaps at least it is permissible to dream some more. It was unrealistic of the old Georgists to expect local jurisdictions to solve the national unemployment problem with local tools. But now that we have a national Full Employment Act, and an Advisory Commission on Intergovernmental Relations that is concerned with the property tax, could we not begin to think of the property tax in part as a tool to help achieve full employment?

EIGHT RECOMMENDATIONS

I have eight specific recommendations as my own agenda for property tax reform:

1. That the Bureau of Mines, the United States Geological Survey, and other appropriate federal agencies be instructed and funded to work actively with state and local assessors to help assess mineral reserves.

2. That the Internal Revenue Service be instructed to share in-

formation with local assessors in order to help improve the assessment product.

3. That federal acquisition of real estate at prices above its equalized assessed valuation be declared contrary to public policy. Either condemnation shall be at the equalized assessed value; or else the entire jurisdictional assessment shall be challengeable by any other affected party.

4. That timber valuations for income tax be made identical with assessed valuations for state and local taxation; and the same for mineral valuations at the time of severance. In each case, the value of immature reserves needs a discount, but I warn against a propensity to exaggerate the discount, especially for larger owners with slower schedules of harvest and extraction of reserves.

5. That there be established, presumably in the Internal Revenue Service and with the aid of the Census of Governments, a national Board of Equalization, whose function is to protect the federal revenues by preventing the underassessment of land and resulting depreciation of land.

6. That the federal influence be exerted to encourage shifting the property tax to the state level.

7. That the federal influence be exerted to encourage converting the property tax to a site value tax.

8. Finally, that the federal power to tax property be reviewed. The Constitution allows federal property taxation, and the federal government has used this power five times. The power was weakened by the requirement that the tax be apportioned among the states according to their respective populations as determined by the Census, just like Congressmen. Now, however, two changes have occurred.

One is the Sixteenth Amendment, allowing taxation of income from whatever source derived and without apportionment. It is reasonably certain that imputed income from property might be included, as Joseph Pechman and other advocates of a "comprehensive tax base" preach it should be. Imputed income and unrealized capital gains both tend to be in proportion to capital value, so a tax on these incomes could be levied just as the property tax is now on the base of capital value.

The second change is revenue sharing. A federal property tax could be apportioned by population, and the revenue then shared in the same way, or any way Congress decides. The Constitution tells us how taxes must be apportioned, but with spending, anything goes. So, as Professor Don Hagman of the U.C.L.A. law school has pointed out, apportionment is really no constitutional barrier to an effective use of the property tax by the federal government. There isn't any.

6

THE PROPERTY TAX AND THE COURTS: SCHOOL FINANCE AFTER RODRIGUEZ

by David C. Long

If the United States Supreme Court had affirmed the three-judge district court's judgment in *San Antonio Independent School District v. Rodriguez*,[1] we would now be contemplating what responses legislatures throughout the country would have to make to comply with the court's mandate—a mandate that could have included the requirement that state systems of funding public education be "fiscally neutral," the doctrine that educational expenditures cannot be made a function of a school district's taxable wealth. This of course did not happen. We do not have a federal constitutional standard governing the distribution, within a state, of tax revenues for education among school districts. The loss in *Rodriguez*, however, should not be viewed as setting the school finance reform movement back to where it was prior to the California Supreme Court's decision in *Serrano* v. *Priest*.[2] Nor does it signal the demise of the doctrine of fiscal neutrality. It does mean that the primary focus of litigation in this area, at least for the immediate future, will be on state constitutional provisions enforced by state courts.

The state supreme courts in California and Michigan have already held that the relationship between a district's property tax wealth per pupil and its educational expenditures must be broken in those states. To what extent the courts in other states will follow their lead is yet unknown. However, the recent decision of the New Jersey Supreme Court in *Robinson* v. *Cahill*[3] is an indication that we have entered a period of doctrinal pluralism in which fiscal neutrality will be one

DAVID C. LONG is Staff Attorney, Lawyers Committee for Civil Rights Under Law, Washington, D.C.

1. *337 F. Supp. 280 (1971), rev'd, —— U.S. ——, 36 L. Ed. 2d 16 (1973).*
2. *96 Cal. Rptr. 601, 487 P. 2d 1241 (1971).*
3. *Robinson* v. *Cahill, 118 N.J. Super 223, 287 A. 2d 187 (1972); aff'd, 303 A. 2d 273 (1973).*

among several doctrines on which the present schemes for financing education may be declared unconstitutional by state courts.

Although this chapter focuses on the property tax and the courts, it is important to bear in mind that the major suits in this area, challenging statewide school finance systems, have not been fashioned as property tax suits, nor has relief been granted, generally, because taxpayers are inequitably treated. The *Serrano-Rodriguez* line of cases has been largely brought on behalf of children, alleging that the primary harm is to their educational interests, i.e., that the present system results in less being spent on their education because their school district has little taxable wealth per pupil. Since, however, the harm complained of results from the inability of taxpayers in poor districts to raise sufficient educational funds at an acceptable property tax rate, the relief granted in these cases benefits taxpayers as much as children.

Another way of looking at these cases is that their concern is with how property taxes are distributed and not with how the tax is collected. Examples of cases dealing with tax collection issues are the multitude of suits in which taxpayers have alleged that their property has been assessed at a higher percentage of market value than other similar properties—assessment uniformity suits.[4] The school finance cases have not dealt with tax collection issues. However, without question, these cases do have implications for how the property tax is collected, since to eliminate the relationship between educational expenditures and taxable property wealth, one must be able to compare accurately the assessed valuations of different districts within a state. This, at a minimum, necessitates an adequate state assessment equalization program. The focus here, however, will be on the rapidly developing case law pertaining to educational finance, rather than on that involving property tax collection since the legal precedent in the collection area is comparatively well established.

This discussion will first consider the implications of the Supreme Court's decision in *San Antonio Independent School District* v. *Rodriguez,* especially as it affects the availability of the federal courts for future litigation in the school finance area. Then the role that state courts and state constitutional and statutory provisions are likely to play will be discussed.

THE RODRIGUEZ DECISION: WHAT FUTURE FOR SCHOOL FINANCE REFORM BY THE FEDERAL COURTS?

The decision of the three-judge federal district court in Texas

4. *See, e.g., Sioux City Bridge Co.* v. *Dakota County, 260 U.S. 44 (1923); Township of Hillsborough* v. *Cromwell, 326 U.S. 620 (1946). Hellerstein,* Judicial Review of Property Tax Assessments, *14 Tax L. Rev. 327 (1959); Note,* Inequality in Property Tax Assessments: New Cure for an Old Ill, *75 Harv. L. R. 1374 (1962).*

which declared that state's school finance system unconstitutional, on the ground that it discriminated between school districts on the basis of district wealth, was not the first judicial declaration that a state finance scheme for education was unlawful. The first was the California Supreme Court's August 1971 landmark decision in *Serrano* v. *Priest*. The California court held that the plaintiffs' claim, if proven, would result in the California system for funding public schools being declared unconstitutional under both state and federal constitutions. The court stated further:

> We have determined that [the California] funding scheme invidiously discriminates against the poor because it makes the quality of a child's education a function of the wealth of his parents and neighbors.

Following the date of that judgment, which declared the California system of funding public schools to be unconstitutional, nearly fifty similar suits were filed in state and federal courts throughout the country. And prior to March 21, 1973, the date the United States Supreme Court announced its decision in *Rodriguez*, state courts in Arizona,[5] Kansas,[6] Michigan[7] and New Jersey,[8] and federal courts in Minnesota[9] and Texas[10] followed the lead of *Serrano* by declaring their states' systems of public school finance to be unconstitutional.

The five to four decision of the United States Supreme Court in *Rodriguez*, which refused to declare the Texas school finance system unconstitutional, was a substantial setback for school finance and property tax reform. While an affirmative decision in *Rodriguez* would not have been viewed, even by those of us who supported the decision, as a panacea for all the financial ills of education, it probably would have eliminated the major reason for great variations in educational expenditures—the linkage between expenditures and the taxable wealth of the school district—and set the political process in motion to construct fairer allocation formulas which would be based on considerations of educational policy rather than wealth.

Rodriguez was brought by Mexican-American school children and their parents who lived in the Edgewood Independent School

5. *Hollins* v. *Shofstall*, No. C-253652, *Super. Ct., Maricopa County (decided June 5, 1972); appeal docketed, No. 11165, Ariz. Sup. Ct.*
6. *Caldwell* v. *Kansas*, No. 50616 (D.C. Johnson County, decided Aug. 30, 1972).
7. *Milliken* v. *Green*, —— Mich. ——, 203 N.W. 2d 457 (1972).
8. See note 3.
9. *Van Dusartz* v. *Hatfield*, 334 F. Supp. 870 (D. Minn. 1971).
10. *Rodriguez*, 337 F. Supp. 280 (W.D. Texas 1971).

District, a low-wealth, low-expenditure district in the San Antonio area. They challenged the Texas school finance system on the ground that it made the quality of education they received a function of the amount of taxable wealth per pupil available in their school district. The facts showed that Edgewood, which taxed at a higher rate than neighboring Alamo Heights, raised only about $60 per pupil while Alamo Heights raised over $300. Furthermore, state aid did little to mitigate these disparities. As a result Alamo Heights spent nearly twice as much per pupil on education as Edgewood. The facts also showed that the districts of lowest taxable wealth in Texas also had the highest percentages of poor people, while those districts of greatest wealth had the highest percentages of affluent residents.

Finding that education was a fundamental interest and that a suspect wealth classification was involved, the three-judge district court held that the state had to justify this discrimination on the basis of a compelling state interest. This Texas could not do. Additionally the court found there was not even a reasonable basis for these classifications. It held that the equal protection clause of the Fourteenth Amendment demanded "fiscal neutrality," i.e., "the quality of public education may not be a function of wealth, other than the wealth of the state as a whole."

The State of Texas appealed from this decision and the Supreme Court in June 1972 noted probable jurisdiction. Once the Supreme Court indicated that it would hear one of the many suits on file challenging state school finance systems, most state and federal courts with similar suits pending stayed further proceedings to await the Supreme Court's decision in *Rodriguez*.

The importance of the case for the reform of school finance was widely recognized. Briefs as amici curiae on behalf of the plaintiffs were filed by five state governors, nine national civil rights and religious organizations, a group of urban school districts, labor unions and other groups representing urban interests, the plaintiffs in the *Serrano* case, and the California controller, superintendent of education, and state board of education, among others. Amici curiae supporting the defendants were the attorneys general from twenty-eight states in which school finance suits were pending, the local school district defendants in the *Serrano* case, and the New Jersey defendants in *Robinson* v. *Cahill*. Because the questions which might be decided included such broad issues under the Fourteenth Amendment's equal protection clause as whether education is a fundamental interest and whether wealth is a suspect classification, the decision was recognized as likely to have great impact on many related cases as well.

Those close to the case were not highly optimistic that the Supreme Court would announce broad principles with respect to the fundamentality of education and the suspectness of wealth as a classifying factor. But, there was hope that the Court would continue its movement, evidenced in recent cases, toward a more flexible test for judging alleged equal protection violations than it had typically applied in the past. The Court has usually looked to see whether a fundamental constitutional interest was involved, such as the right to speak and the right to equal participation in the electoral process, and if so it would strictly scrutinize any discriminations respecting access to such rights. In such a case the state has usually been required to justify the discrimination on the basis of some compelling state interest.[11] Where discrimination was based on a suspect classification, such as by race, the Court has applied the same analysis.[12] Where the conditions for strict scrutiny were not met the Court traditionally applied a rational basis test. In the past there have been few occasions, once the Court has invoked this test, that it has found the classification scheme to be unreasonable. However, in more recent cases the Court has used a balancing test under which the Court weighs the state's interest promoted by the classification against the fundamental personal rights that the classification endangers.[13] In terms of the scrutiny applied, it falls somewhere between the other two.

Mr. Justice Powell's opinion for four members of the Court ignores this balancing test. Additionally, it refused to invoke the strict scrutiny test, which would have required the state to justify the discrimination by a compelling state interest, finding that education was not fundamental under the federal Constitution and that the classification by wealth here was not suspect. The Court then applied the rational basis test and accepted the state's assertion that the system was rationally related to the promotion of local control.

In discussing the wealth classifications involved in the case, the Court noted there were three possible ways of looking at the class discriminated against—first, as those whose incomes fall below some identifiable level of poverty; second, as those who are poor in comparison to others; and third as those who, irrespective of personal income, happen to live in relatively poor school districts. The Court interpreted its past decisions with respect to discrimination based on poverty as protecting only those who "were completely unable to

11. *E.g., Reynolds v. Sims, 377 U.S. 533 (1964); Shapiro v. Thompson, 394 U.S. 618 (1969).*

12. *E.g., Brown v. Board of Education, 347 U.S. 483 (1954).*

13. *For examples of the Court's application of the traditional rational basis test see: McGowan v. Maryland, 336 U.S. 420 (1961); Railway Express Agency v. New York, 336 U.S. 106 (1949). An example of "balancing" is found in Weber v. Aetna Casualty & Surety Co., 406 U.S. 164 (1972).*

pay for some desired benefit, and as a consequence . . . sustained an absolute deprivation of a meaningful opportunity to enjoy that benefit." The Court found this line of cases inapplicable to the facts here because there had been no showing that the Texas system operates "to the peculiar disadvantage" of those who are poor by reference to some level of "absolute impecunity." Additionally, the Court was unable to see that the Texas system resulted in any "absolute deprivation of education." Thus, the Court found the traditional analysis used in poverty-based cases inapplicable.

The Court found that it did not have to decide whether comparative or relative discrimination based on family income might be constitutionally suspect because the evidence in the case, according to the Court, did not show a relationship between district wealth and individual wealth over a broad enough range of district wealth differences.

The Court thus refused to view the case as one involving constitutionally significant discrimination based on personal poverty. While plaintiffs had argued discrimination against poor people, they had placed primary reliance on discrimination based on district wealth as measured by assessed property valuation per pupil. The Supreme Court clearly held that differences between school districts in the amounts of such wealth do not trigger a suspect classification analysis.

The Court also refused to find that education was fundamental as a matter of federal constitutional law. The Court rejected the notion of education's fundamentality on the ground that education is not one of the rights afforded protection under the federal Constitution. It did leave open the possibility, however, that a system which "fails to provide each child with an opportunity to acquire the basic minimal skills necessary for the enjoyment of the rights of speech and of full participation in the political process" might be subject to constitutional challenge.

Having thus found that the State of Texas did not have to justify the discrimination in its financing system on the basis of a compelling state interest, the Court then analyzed the system to determine whether it bore some "rational relationship to legitimate state purposes." The Supreme Court held, as a matter of federal constitutional law, that it did. The major consideration upon which the Court appears to rely in finding the Texas system rational is the system's alleged responsiveness to the state's interest in promoting local control. Conceding that poor districts probably had little local control due to their inability to raise significant extra funds from their local tax bases, the Court nevertheless held that since fundamental constitutional right were not at stake here, the state need not use the least restrictive alternative to further its legitimate state interest in local control. Additionally, the Court found at least plausible the state's arguments that alternatives to the present system which would meet the "fiscal neutrality" standard of the lower court's decision might diminish local control over educational policy.

The Court's concept of its role in a federal structure also loomed large in the decision. It asserted that the Supreme Court traditionally has deferred to state legislatures in the raising and disposition of public revenues, and that because of the complexity of the problems, states' efforts to deal with them should be given respect. Thus, although the Court recognizes that "the need is apparent for reform of tax systems which may well have relied too long and too heavily on the local property tax," it did not see its role as including the "consideration and initiation of fundamental reforms with respect to state taxation and education."

Justices Brennan, White, and Marshall all wrote dissenting opinions. Mr. Justice Brennan viewed education as constitutionally fundamental because of its link to speech and political participation and thus would have subjected the Texas school finance scheme to strict judicial scrutiny, which Texas conceded it could not survive. Mr. Justice Marshall also found education to be a fundamental interest, but focused primarily on his disagreement with the Court's "rigidified approach to equal protection analysis" which results in the Court's placement of all cases into two arbitrary categories, one of which receives strict scrutiny and the other of which only has to meet a rational basis test. He found a relaxation of this arbitrary categorization in the Court's past opinions and argued that the degree of scrutiny should depend upon the "character of the classification in question, the relative importance to the individuals in the class discriminated against of the government benefits they do not receive, and the asserted state interests in support of the classification." Mr. Justice White, in a dissent joined by Justices Douglas and Brennan, argued that the Texas scheme bears no rational relationship to the objective of local control which Texas argued that it furthered.

A majority of the Supreme Court has thus rejected the doctrine of fiscal neutrality as a constitutional standard. But because this doctrine is likely to remain viable in state courts, further discussion of its merits is warranted. Fiscal neutrality as it has been defined requires that the amount which a district spends on education cannot be made a function of the taxable wealth of the school district. The measure of wealth is the amount of assessed valuation per pupil within the school district. There has been much confusion about what the doctrine prohibits or requires. Its acceptance does not require the abolition of local property taxes. Furthermore, it does not require that equal dollars be spent on each pupil. It does not mandate any particular educational policy; for example, it does not require but would certainly permit more educational resources to be provided for educationally disadvantaged children. The standard essentially proscribes a current evil, without prescribing any particular educational policy. The elimination of local taxable wealth as a determinant of a school district's expenditures is all that it requires.

One argument made against fiscal neutrality is that it insures more equity for taxpayers than for school children. Another is that it would not necessarily require legislatures, in responding to the asserted unconstitutionality of present finance systems, to take into account the higher costs of educating central city children or the great proportion of central city taxes, as compared to taxes in suburban and rural areas, which must be used for noneducational costs ("municipal overburden"). Others have criticized it because poor people do not always live in poor districts and because some districts that have above average taxable wealth have large concentrations of poor people.[14] Nevertheless, almost no one has agreed that present finance systems are rational from an educational standpoint, i.e., that they distribute educational resources according to some rational educational criteria. The primary thrust of the criticisms is that the irrationality of the present system, in certain cases, benefits those that a rational system should benefit, e.g., the poor and central cities. Underlying some of the criticism appears to be the sentiment that if the courts will not force legislators to benefit those who should be benefited through school finance reform, then perhaps the status quo, irrational though it may be, may be preferable.

Support for the fiscal neutrality cases has been based on a number of considerations: Any benefits which some cities—because of their above average assessed valuation—get from the present system is of only short-run advantage since many presently "wealthy" cities are likely in the future to be of only average wealth or below due to the fact that their tax bases are remaining static or growing at a slow rate while the tax bases of surrounding communities in their metropolitan areas are rapidly growing.[15] Once the legislative log-

---

14. See, e.g., Goldstein, Interdistrict Inequalities in School Financing: a critical analysis of Serrano and its progeny, 120 U. Pa. L. Rev. 504 (1972); Note, A Statistical Analysis of the School Finance Divisions: On Winning Battles and Losing Wars, 81 Yale L.J. 1303 (1972).

15. See, Advisory Commission on Intergovernmental Relations, Metropolitan Disparities: A Second Reading (1970); ACIR, Urban America and the Federal System (1969); Staff of Senate Select Committee on Equal Educational Opportunity, 92d Cong., 1st Sess., Federal Aid to Education: Who Benefits? (Committee Print 1971).

jam with respect to school finance is broken by the courts, the high-wealth suburban districts, in order to prevent a substantial loss of resources, would have to bargain with the cities and other districts of low and average wealth to produce mutually acceptable reform. A funding system that is based on educationally relevant criteria is more likely in the long run, than one tied to district wealth, to channel benefits to children according to need. If the critics have no hope that the legislative process, with judicial prodding, would improve the allocation of educational resources within a state, what hope can there be for improvement without such prodding?

But another feature of the fiscal neutrality doctrine which has commended itself to its supporters is that it, among the variety of constitutional theories which have been considered, appeared to stand the greatest likelihood of being accepted by the courts. Fiscal neutrality is within established judicial tradition which accepts telling a legislature what it cannot do but avoids, where possible, detailed directives governing legislative action. Fiscal neutrality is essentially a negative doctrine which leaves a legislature great flexibility in responding to a declaration that the present system is unconstitutional. Furthermore, its legal standard is relatively clear—the amount of educational funding cannot be tied to the wealth of the local tax base; the variables here are dollars which are easily determinable rather than the more subjective variables of educational policy. That the Court was not being asked to enter the arena of educational policy was seen as one of the doctrine's major strengths.[16] Plaintiffs in the earlier federal court cases of *McGinnis v. Ogilvie*[17] and *Burrus v. Wilkerson*[18] had asked to have school finance systems declared unconstitutional because they did not distribute educational benefits according to the particular needs of students. Both suits were dismissed with the pronouncement that plaintiffs had provided no standards for measuring educational needs. The Supreme Court without opinion summarily affirmed the decisions of the lower courts dismissing these cases. While no one knew exactly what the Supreme Court had in mind when it affirmed these decisions, attorneys were reasonably certain that any constitutional theory which directly asserted that the general vice of a school finance system was the incongruity between educational needs and the amount of resources distributed would fail in federal court.

In short, the legal theory upon which *Rodriguez* was based did not guarantee that all of the goals of school finance reform would

16. See, Coons, J., W. Clune, S. Sugarman, Private Wealth and Public Education (1970) at 306 et seq.
17. 293 F.Supp. 327 (N.D. Ill. 1968); aff'd mem., 394 U.S. 322 (1969).
18. 310 F.Supp. 527 (W.D. Va. 1969); aff'd mem., 397 U.S. 44 (1970).

be met; it did, however, appear to stand the best chance of setting in motion a process that would be moving in the right direction.

After an adverse decision such as *Rodriguez*, there are always lingering questions about whether this was the best case to take to the Supreme Court, or whether another similar case could be distinguished from it and might stand a better chance of succeeding in the Supreme Court in the immediate future. First, those Texas plaintiffs and their attorneys who brought this suit had no choice about whether it got to the Supreme Court. They had won before a three-judge federal court below, and the defendants had an appeal as a matter of right to the United States Supreme Court. This was not, however, a weak case by any means. Not only are the Texas wealth and expenditure disparities among the greatest in the country, but there is also a significant positive correlation between district wealth and individual wealth in Texas. Furthermore, the plaintiffs and a good proportion of others most harmed by the Texas inequities are Mexican-Americans, a distinct ethnic minority in the American Southwest. While an equally strong case might stand a better chance of succeeding in the Supreme Court several years from now, assuming in the meantime that more state and lower federal courts will have ruled their school finance systems unconstitutional and that legislators will have had a chance to respond with acceptable alternative finance programs, this is by no means certain. In any case, we are left with the decision, and it is safe to predict that the strength of the Texas facts coupled with the broad sweep of the Supreme Court's opinion probably means that challenges to disparities in educational resources among school districts, at least as related to unequal local tax bases, are foreclosed in the federal courts for the next few years.

If we look to the precedent of the past, there is reason to hope that *Rodriguez* may, some time in the future, be overruled. You may recall that as recently as 1946 the Supreme Court, in *Colegrove* v. *Green*, ruled that the apportionment of representatives to a state legislature was a political matter and thus nonjusticiable.[19] *Colegrove* was overruled in the 1962 landmark reapportionment decision, *Baker v. Carr*.[20] In *Rodriguez*, the doctrinal inconsistency of the Court with respect to its analysis of equal protection claims provides some hope that a future Supreme Court may find it wrongly decided. Nowhere does the majority opinion acknowledge that the two tests for equal protection violation which it discusses—fundamental interest and rational basis—are not the only tests which the Court has used in this

19. *328 U.S. 549 (1946)*.
20. *369 U.S. 186 (1962)*.

area. Indeed the author of that opinion, Mr. Justice Powell, himself used another, a balancing test, in finding certain discrimination against illegitimate children unconstitutional during the previous term. Significantly, he totally ignored this test and any mention of his earlier opinion in *Weber v. Aetna Casualty & Surety Company*[21] in writing the *Rodriguez* opinion. It is this test which Mr. Justice Marshall, in his *Rodriguez* dissent, argues is the proper one for judging the constitutionality of the Texas system. His lengthy dissent, which points out this inconsistency of analysis, appears to be written for a Supreme Court of the future which might adopt his reasoning.

What, however, did the Supreme Court leave open for adjudication in the educational finance area? Are there other education or property tax inequities which the present Supreme Court may find unconstitutional? Although the Court was only deciding the case before it, there is a good deal of discussion in the *Rodriguez* opinion about closely related factual situations and legal issues. It is with these that I will now deal.

Cases of Actual or Constructive Exclusion from the Educational Process

As has been indicated, the court was not attracted to plaintiffs' theory of relative discrimination—by which richer districts or individuals get more educational resources than poorer ones, but where even the poor get something—albeit not very much. The court refused to decide whether, in some future case, a constitutional claim based on relative poverty might succeed, but did make clear that it did not wish to deal with the constitutional significance of relative poverty unless a perfect or near perfect correlation between wealth and benefits could be shown throughout the whole range of individuals affected.[22] However, the Court indicated that it might be more receptive to claims that a child was totally excluded from any educational opportunity.

Early in 1972 the Court granted certiorari in a case from New York in which such a claim was raised.[23] Students from poor families in that case challenged the requirement that elementary school pupils purchase their own textbooks; they claimed that their inability to afford textbooks meant that they had to sit in classes without them, not

21. *Weber v. Aetna Casualty & Surety Co., 406 U.S. 164 (1972)*.

22. *36 L. Ed. 2d at 81, et seq.* In Rodriguez the districts grouped at the highest and lowest ends of the assessed valuation per pupil scale also had the highest and lowest per capita median incomes respectively. The districts grouped in the middle showed a mixed pattern.

23. *Johnson v. New York State Education Dept., —— U.S. ——, 34 L. Ed. 2d 290 (1972)*.

comprehending or being able to prepare for their lessons, and were because of their poverty effectively excluded from an educational opportunity. The Supreme Court never reached the merits because, after agreeing to hear the case, the court dismissed it as moot due to the fact that the school district, while the case was on appeal, had voted to provide free textbooks to the students.

Lau v. *Nichols* presents a similar issue, and a petition for certiorari was granted by the Supreme Court in 1973.[24] There, non-English-speaking Chinese students claim that they have been effectively excluded from an education by the failure of the San Francisco Unified School District to provide any instruction which would enable them to benefit from their classes, which are taught in the English language. The United States Court of Appeals for the Ninth Circuit held that these Chinese students' constitutional rights were not violated since they received the same instruction as all other students—it made no difference that they could not comprehend what was going on in the classroom. A decision by the Supreme Court appeared likely in the 1973-74 term of the Court.

Additionally, there are a number of cases which have been decided by or are pending in federal district courts throughout the country which challenge the exclusion by school districts of children with various mental and physical handicaps.[25] These are appealing cases because it is common for school districts to provide no instruction whatsoever for many such students; in addition, educational strategies are now available which can provide handicapped students with the skills and understanding to live useful lives. It is likely that at least one of these "exclusion cases" will be heard by the Supreme Court within the next several years.

The exclusion cases will probably not play a direct role with respect to reform of school finance systems. Of course, if plaintiffs win, there will be additional educational costs which will have to be assumed by someone—in the first instance probably by school districts, who will then put pressure on their legislatures to increase state assistance for the education of nonEnglish-speaking and handicapped students. Since state and federal categorical assistance for the education of such students is already well established, it is likely that a state's response to a court order is more likely to take the form of the creation or the increased funding of categorical programs rather than a reassessment of the relationship between educational funding and taxable wealth.

---

24. No. 26155 (Court of Appeals, 9th Cir., Jan. 8, 1973); petition for cert. granted June 11, 1973, 37 L. Ed. 2d 397.
25. See, e.g., Mills v. Board of Education, Civ. No. 1939-71 (D.C. D.C.); Harrison v. Michigan, Civ. No. 38357 (D.C. E.D. Mich., October 30, 1972).

These cases may, however, tell us whether *Rodriguez* was intended to post the whole area of education and related finance issues as off-limits to the federal courts; or whether the Supreme Court was largely concerned about the magnitude of the upheaval that it believed an affirmance in *Rodriguez* would cause, but did not intend to say that such issues can never give rise to a constitutional claim on which relief may be granted.

Tax Limitation Cases

One property tax related education finance problem to which the *Rodriguez* majority opinion specifically refers and did not foreclose federal court relief in was that presented in *Hargrave* v. *Kirk*.[26] In that case Florida's local property tax rate limits for school support imposed a legal bar to school districts, with low assessed valuations per pupil, ever providing their pupils with the amount of educational resources that richer districts could provide by taxing at or below the maximum rate. Plaintiffs in *Hargrave* won before a three-judge federal court. The Supreme Court reversed and remanded the case because it believed the federal court should have abstained from reaching a decision until the impact of the new school finance system, of which the millage rollback law was a part, had been fully considered and the state courts had had an opportunity to construe it. Thus, the Supreme Court never reached the merits of the case.

It is possible that the federal courts may still hold unconstitutional such tax rate limits on school districts which seriously and permanently discriminate against children in poorer school districts, i.e., the rate limits are not just part of a millage rollback accompanying a plan for greater state aid to education. The basis for this view is the importance which the Supreme Court in *Rodriguez* places on local control of educational finance. The State of Texas had relied on this justification to defend its finance system, and the Supreme Court accepted this, noting that there had been no showing that the poorer districts in Texas were precluded by law from increasing their educational expenditures, as were the districts in *Hargrave*.[27]

A rate limit suit, while of potential benefit to school children, does nothing to eliminate property tax inequities. Indeed the unfairness to taxpayers of present school finance systems would be increased. This results from the fact that increasing the school tax rate in a tax-poor district could dramatically increase the burdens on the district's taxpayers with little to show in terms of increased per pupil expenditures. For example, if a district with $5,000 assessed valuation

---

26. *313 F.Supp. 944 (M.D. Fla. 1970); vacated 401 U.S. 479 (1971).*
27. *36 L. Ed. 2d at 53, n. 107.*

per pupil increases its tax rate by $1 per $100 of assessed valuation (10 mills), it would have increased the educational expenditures in the district by only $50 per pupil. The same tax rate increase in a district with $50,000 assessed valuation per pupil will raise $500 additional for each pupil in the wealthier districts. Taxpayers in the poorer district, to raise $500 additional per child, would have to pay ten times the tax rate of the richer district (100 mills).

Suits Challenging the Use of Unequalized Local Property Tax Assessments to Allocate State Education Aid

The Supreme Court showed great insensitivity to the effect of a situation which remains the subject of litigation in *Fort Worth Independent School District* v. *Edgar*, now pending in the federal district court in Texas.[28] This was thought to be a suit with some potential for bringing about school finance and property tax reform in those states that have no adequate statewide program for equalizing local assessments or which do not use equalized assessment data for distribution of state school aid. The case was filed by the three large school districts of Fort Worth, Houston, and Dallas against the superintendent of public instruction, among others. In apportioning state school aid in Texas a county economic index, one part of which consists of assessed property valuation per pupil, is used. Unequalized assessed valuation as reported by local assessors is taken as correct in making up the index. Since the three Texas cities assess at a much higher percentage of market value than many other areas in Texas, these cities look richer than they are and consequently get less state aid than they are entitled to.

Unfortunately Mr. Justice Powell's opinion in *Rodriguez*, while not considering whether an equalizing aid scheme which relies on unequalized assessed valuation is constitutional, showed great insensitivity to its irrationality, and there are statements in the opinion which arguably appear to condone this Texas practice.[29]

CHALLENGES TO SCHOOL FINANCE SYSTEMS IN STATE COURTS

The United States Supreme Court in *Rodriguez* in no way fore-

---

28. *Civ. No. 4-1405 (D.C. N.D. Tex.).*

29. *The Court says the amount Alamo Heights (a wealthy district) and Edgewood (a poor district) must pay into the state education fund reflects a "rough approximation of the relative taxpaying potential of each" (36 L. Ed. 2d at 32). The Court also notes that it has been suggested that the formula be altered "to promote a more accurate reflection of local taxpaying ability, especially of urban school districts" (Id. at 32 n. 37). Mr. Justice Marshall in dissent quotes a published criticism of the Economic Index that in "evaluating local ability [it] offers a little better measure than sheer chance but not much." (36 L. Ed. 2d at 69.)*

closes state court litigation challenging school finance systems on state constitutional and statutory grounds. *Rodriguez* only considered the constitutionality of the Texas finance scheme under the Fourteenth Amendment's equal protection clause. Its failure to find a violation of the federal Constitution means only that it refused to impose a federal constitutional standard for the distribution of educational resources on the states. The Court's opinion leaves state courts in similar cases, based on state constitutional and statutory provisions, perfectly free to find that school finance systems violate state law.

Moreover, the reasoning used by the *Rodriguez* Court and Mr. Justice Stewart in his concurring opinion, is supportive of state courts taking a much closer look at these educational inequities than the Supreme Court. The Supreme Court found that education is not a fundamental interest under the federal Constitution, which meant that the Court would not strictly scrutinize the discrimination resulting from the Texas finance system. The Court determined that it is not fundamental, in large part, because a right to an education is neither implicit nor explicit under the United States Constitution. Furthermore, the federal government has not undertaken to provide education to all children. In contrast, not only have the states undertaken this obligation, but they are compelled by their state constitutions to do so. Virtually every state constitution requires the state to maintain a system of free public schools, which many constitutions require to be "thorough and efficient" or "general and uniform" or to meet similar standards. If such language appeared in the federal Constitution, it can be said on the basis of *Rodriguez* that education probably would have been considered fundamental. Thus, even if state courts decide in interpreting their state constitutions to apply the reasoning used by the Supreme Court, education should be considered fundamental as a matter of state law.

This reasoning process to find education fundamental under state constitutions for purposes of analysis of state equal protection guarantees was explicitly used by the Michigan Supreme Court to invalidate the Michigan school finance system on the basis of state law.[30] It is implicit in the California Supreme Court's decision in *Serrano* v. *Priest*.[31] It was rejected by the New Jersey Supreme Court, which held New Jersey's school finance laws unconstitutional on other state grounds.[32] These three cases, the judicial and legislative sequels within those states, and the acceptance of their grounds for decision by the courts of other states appear to hold the key to the future of school finance litigation.

30. *See note 7.*

31. *See note 2.*

32. *See note 3.*

Serrano v. Priest: Does Money Make a Difference?

In *Serrano* v. *Priest* the Supreme Court of California held the state's school finance laws unconstitutional on the basis of facts alleged in the plaintiffs' complaint which had been dismissed by the trial court. The court said that it was a violation of both the federal and state constitutions to make the quality of a child's education depend on the wealth of his parents and neighbors. The case was then remanded for trial, since the court's decision had assumed the facts plaintiffs alleged were true. The trial, which lasted for five months, was completed in May 1973.

Since there was little disagreement between plaintiffs and defendants about disparities between school districts in assessed valuations per pupil, tax rates and educational expenditures, the trial focused primarily on the issues of a) whether expenditure inequalities injure children in poor districts, and b) whether a bill recently passed by the California Assembly sufficiently eliminates the inequities complained of.

For the first time in school finance litigation there has been a full airing of the "cost-achievement" issue—the relationship of educational inputs (and especially operating or total costs) to educational outputs as measured by achievement on standardized tests. The issue has been raised and evidence on it has been heard in other cases; but no case heretofore has so thoroughly explored both the factual contentions on either side and the legal relevance (or irrelevance) of the issue.

Defendants in *Serrano* contended that the plaintiffs had to prove a positive relationship between cost and achievement (holding socioeconomic status constant); furthermore, defendants sought to show that there was no such relationship. Plaintiffs took the position that this issue is irrelevant since all plaintiffs seek is that the state provide them with the same *opportunity* to benefit from a public education and are not asking the state to guarantee results. Furthermore, the school finance system has been structured by the state on the premise that money makes a difference, and it ill behooves the state and wealthy school districts, which benefit from its inequities, to defend this maldistribution of resources on the basis that it makes no difference. Indeed, if it does not, wealthy districts have no basis for defending the rationality of their own expenditures. Plaintiffs also argued that achievement scores on standardized reading and math tests only measure a small part of what education is all about. Additionally, plaintiffs challenged the research upon which defendants relied, pointing out that educational research is still at a primitive stage; that most of it does not deal with the effect of additional educational inputs received by given children on their achievement, i.e., most research has not measured the effect of providing particular children with increased educational resources; and that there are studies, other than those on which defendants rely, which show a significant relationship between cost and achievement.

The trial court's decision in *Serrano* was expected before the end of 1973. Whichever way this decision comes out, it is certain to be appealed again to the California Supreme Court. However, since the first *Serrano* decision relied, in addition to the federal Constitution, on the equal protection provision of the California Constitution, the California Supreme Court could reaffirm its earlier ruling irrespective of *Rodriguez*.

Milliken v. Green: Education's Importance Under the Michigan Constitution

Another state in which its supreme court has held the school finance provisions to be in violation of the state constitution is Michigan. This judgment, in *Milliken* v. *Green*, was handed down while *Rodriguez* was awaiting decision in the United States Supreme Court. The Michigan court held that education is a fundamental interest under the Michigan constitution. It determined that the cost-achievement issue was irrelevant as a matter of law to its constitutional analysis since the Michigan constitution requires the legislature to "maintain and support" a system of free public schools; thus, the only question that the court had to decide was "whether or not the legislature's action maintains and supports free public schools equally or, if not equally, with valid classifications." Based on the fundamentality of education and the suspectness of wealth as a basis for classification, the court held that there was no compelling interest served by the educational disparities stemming from taxable wealth differences between districts. Further, the court found no rational basis for the discrimination. Both holdings were based on the equal protection provision of the Michigan Constitution. The status of this decision is uncertain since a motion for rehearing was granted in February 1973 by the Michigan Supreme Court and two members of the court have retired, one each from the majority and dissenting opinions, in what was a four to three decision.

Robinson v. Cahill: Inputs and Outputs

A third state supreme court, in a most interesting decision, has held its school finance system unconstitutional, but on different grounds and with different results than the other two. The New Jersey court, in *Robinson* v. *Cahill,* found that the present method of financing schools violates the state constitutional provision pertaining to education which requires that:

> The legislature shall provide for the maintenance and support of a thorough and efficient system of free public schools for the instruction of all the children in the state between the ages of five and eighteen years.

The court said that an education which is thorough and efficient "must be understood to embrace that educational opportunity which is needed in the contemporary setting to equip a child for his role as a citizen and as a competitor in the labor market." This much of the opinion sounds like an output standard, and the trial court below had found that both educational inputs and outputs were inadequate in certain New Jersey school districts. However, the New Jersey Supreme Court goes on to say that it finds the constitutional demand not met "on the basis of discrepancies in dollar input per pupil." It thus appears that the court had both inputs and outputs in mind when it wrote its opinion. The court viewed the "thorough and efficient" requirement as mandating "an equal educational opportunity for children," and further found that the existing finance scheme was not "visibly geared to the mandate that there be a 'thorough and efficient system of free public schools' . . . ," and "has no apparent relation to the mandate for equal educational opportunity." The key to harmonizing these statements appears to be the court's finding that "the state has never spelled out the content of the educational opportunity the constitution requires." Thus, a major aspect of the constitutional violation appears to be the failure of the state to take its constitutional obligations seriously in funding public education and, indeed, in not establishing input and output criteria for judging whether a thorough and efficient education is being provided.

The *Robinson* case is also interesting on the taxpayers' side. The trial court below had ruled that the New Jersey school finance provisions were unconstitutional for the reason, among others, that taxpayers in poorer districts are forced to pay higher property taxes for education than taxpayers in wealthier districts—the lower court found that this violated the tax uniformity provision of the New Jersey constitution as well as the state's equal protection guarantee. Although the local district would normally be considered the jurisdiction within which local property tax rates would have to be uniform, the judge believed the state was the relevant jurisdiction for purposes of uniformity when the revenues raised served "common state educational purposes."

The New Jersey Supreme Court rejected the trial court's view of the state constitution's tax uniformity provision. It held that education is a state function, but when the state delegates the fiscal responsibility for education to local districts, the property tax raised by local districts is a local and not a state tax; thus, uniformity of rate is required only within each school district.

Furthermore, the New Jersey court diverged from the equal protection analysis used by the highest courts of California and Michigan. The trial court in *Robinson,* in part relying on *Serrano,* had found that under New Jersey and federal equal protection provisions the inequities to children and taxpayers should be subject to strict scrutiny because education is a fundamental interest of the state and classifications based on wealth are disfavored; and he could find no compelling justification for sustaining a finance system which discriminated in this manner. The New Jersey Supreme Court was reluctant to rest its decision on state equal protection grounds because it confessed an inability to determine what services were "fundamental" so as to require strict scrutiny of classifications respecting access thereto. Additionally, although the court viewed certain discrimination based on individual wealth as arbitrary and thus unlawful, it did not see differences in benefits and tax burdens resulting from unequal local tax bases as constituting a suspect wealth classification. The court expressed fear that the differences in educational expenditures that resulted from such district wealth differences could not be distinguished from differences in the provision of other services, and that a ruling based on an equal protection wealth analysis would change the state's political structure.

Perhaps the New Jersey Supreme Court has created a "straw man" when it asserts that for the purpose of an equal protection analysis it would not be able to confine a decision based on education's "fundamentality" and district wealth's "suspectness" to the provision of educational services. Courts are expert at drawing such lines. Indeed, the specific state constitutional obligation to provide education, which the court does enforce, belies education's indistinguishability from other services. In any event, the New Jersey decision clearly separates, at least for purposes of state constitutional analysis, the inequalities between children and between taxpayers under the state's current school finance system. The court says that the state, if it chooses to assign its education obligation to local government, "must compel the local school districts to raise the money necessary . . . ." Thus, the New Jersey court only requires that children be treated equally.

This difference between the New Jersey decision and those from

California and Michigan may not be that significant with respect to reform alternatives that are politically viable to state legislatures. This is because the New Jersey legislature, in developing a school finance program to comply with the court's order, is likely to be just as concerned with its effect on local taxpayers as on children, even though, unlike California and Michigan, it need only be concerned with children.

SHIFTING THE FORUM TO
STATE COURTS AND LEGISLATURES

The discussion to this point has focused upon the opinion of the Supreme Court of the United States in *Rodriguez* and the emerging state constitutional law pertaining to the inequities produced by present statewide systems of school finance. Little has been said about the likelihood of numerous state courts across the nation declaring their finance systems unconstitutional, and for good reason. *Rodriguez* was decided just two months before this writing. Only one state supreme court, New Jersey's, has spoken since that decision was rendered. Much research on state law and constitutional history remains to be done. More time must pass and more work must be done before any prediction in that regard would be anything more than speculation. One thing is clear, however—the momentum for reform of the inequitable allocation of educational resources and tax burdens that has accelerated since the *Serrano* decision was not stopped by *Rodriguez*. It undoubtedly has been slowed since federal courts will not be prodding legislatures to action. Happily though, many legislative bodies are already in action. Minnesota, Kansas and Utah have all passed significant reform legislation.[33] Most states have school finance commissions at work. I am hopeful that the legislative reform efforts under way will demonstrate to states which are slower to move that equity in the allocation of educational resources is politically viable, and will diminish the fear of change based on the spectre of untried alternatives.

The current legislative activity has great relevance to the course of school finance litigation in state courts. It is likely that the pace of litigation will slow significantly in the next few years, in large part to see whether legislatures, absent court orders, will come to grips with the inequities in their school finance systems. To the extent that they do, the need for litigation will be obviated.

There are also other reasons for believing that future litigation in

33. *Minnesota's legislation calls for a substantially increased level of state foundation aid; Kansas has adopted a form of district power equalizing; and Utah has moved toward full state funding of education.*

this area will proceed more slowly than in the past. After *Serrano* there were those who believed that a school finance case could be won by submitting to a court a single exhibit which showed on a per pupil basis the assessed valuation of school districts in the state, their property tax rates, and educational expenditures. As attorneys on both sides of these cases have become increasingly knowledgeable about the issues, the complexity and cost of the litigation have escalated. Indeed the legal and educational articles published since *Serrano* discussing these issues would fill many notebooks. Thus, I would anticipate that more preparation than in the past will have to be done prior to filing future school finance cases, and that these cases will take longer to get to trial after filing. The future decisions of the California courts in *Serrano* and of the Michigan Supreme Court in *Milliken* may provide guidance as to what issues are relevant. The supreme courts of other states may also in the near future render decisions in already filed school finance cases.

As is readily apparent, this is an area of judicial and legislative activity that is in great flux. The United States Supreme Court, by ordering the federal courts to avoid school finance inequity issues, has shifted the forum to state courts—it has by no means precluded these courts from playing a major role in making educational finance rational and breaking the link between the amount of assessed property valuation a school district has and the resources it can devote to public education.

7

THE PROPERTY TAX AND LOW-INCOME HOUSING MARKETS

by George E. Peterson

Among the charges leveled against the local property tax, one of the more serious is that it badly distorts the operation of housing markets. In particular, many experts have asserted that high levels of property taxation contribute significantly to deterioration of the housing stock in low-income urban neighborhoods. In this chapter, I want to evaluate the role that the property tax plays in creating or perpetuating central city blight.

A standard demand-supply diagram will illustrate the effect that the property tax is thought to have on the housing market.[1] In Figure 1 the heavy curve SS represents the supply of housing. As the diagram has been drawn, the supply of housing has a high price elasticity, indicating that the owners of the housing stock will add to or cut back on that stock in response to fairly small changes in rental rates. The heavy DD curve in the diagram represents tenants' demand for housing. As the demand curve is drawn, it shows that household demand for housing is moderately elastic with respect to price changes; i.e., that the amount of housing that families demand is moderately sensitive to changes in rent levels.

Now if the property tax is treated as roughly equivalent to a sales tax on housing services, imposition of the tax can be represented as an upward shift in the supply curve SS.[2] After imposition of the tax, in

GEORGE E. PETERSON, Senior Research Staff, The Urban Institute.

1. This type of analysis is presented in great detail by James Hielbrun, Real Estate Taxes and Urban Housing, Columbia University Press, 1966. Also, Joseph DeSalvo, "The Effects of the Property Tax on Operating and Investment Decisions of Rental Property Owners," National Tax Journal, March 1971.

2. The property tax differs from a uniform sales tax on housing services in several respects. First, to the extent that the tax is levied uniformly on all income-generating capital, it is really a tax on the factor, capital, rather than a tax on the commodity, housing. Second, to the extent that families' propery tax liabilities equal the cost of the public services provided to them, the property tax becomes equivalent to a user charge, or "price," for the local public service bundle, rather than an addition to the cost of housing. Third, if the market value/rent ratios of properties vary

order to break even landlords must recover in rents an additional amount equal to their tax payments, beyond the other costs of operating housing. Thus the price at which they are willing to supply housing will shift upward, by the amount t. The after-tax supply schedule is indicated by the broken line S'S'. With the elasticities as indicated in the diagram, the result of imposing a property tax is both to raise the effective price for housing services (the market price or rent shifts upward from P_0 to P_1) and to diminish the total quantity of housing (the amount of housing consumed falls from Q_0 to Q_1). Although the diagram represents the aggregate market response, it usually is assumed that individual household demand curves resemble the market demand curve, with the result that individual households also will cut back on their housing consumption because of the added tax.

Figure 1 thus illustrates how imposition of a property tax, or an increase in property tax rates, can contribute to deterioration of the

Figure 1.
EFFECT OF PROPERTY TAX ON HOUSING SUPPLY

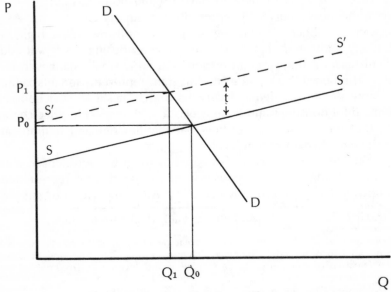

across neighborhoods—they tend to be much greater in affluent neighborhoods than in blighted neighborhoods—a uniform tax on the capital value of housing will not translate into a uniform sales tax on rentals, but into a graduated sales tax, which taxes more heavily the rents from expensive residences. Despite these possible divergences, as Dick Netzer points out in the second chapter in this volume, the residential property tax in practice retains many of the characteristics of a sales tax on housing.

housing stock or help to explain the low overall quality of housing in a city. The reduction in the "quantity" of housing that is caused by the tax actually will consist of a mixture of several changes: a possible reduction in the average size of housing accommodations for families, a reduction in the quality of housing enjoyed by each family, and a reduction in the total number of housing units on the market. For a low-income neighborhood, each of these adjustments usually signals deterioration. A reduction in the average size of housing quarters typically is accomplished by crowding more families into the same structures through subdivision of buildings into smaller rental units. A decline in "quality" typically is brought about by reduced expenditures on maintenance and upkeep by the operators of housing. And in low-income markets the easiest way to reduce the number of units in operation is through abandonment. While abandonment need not pose a severe problem for the displaced tenant, as long as there is an adequate supply of alternative accommodations available elsewhere in the metropolitan area, for the *neighborhood,* abandoned structures almost always produce multiple crises. For example, George Sternlieb reports that in Newark, New Jersey, severe fires in vacant residential buildings accounted for 21.2 percent of all severe fires in the city in 1970-71. Abandoned structures also provide a focal point for serious crime and drug usage.[3]

A demand-supply diagram illustrates the *equilibrium outcome* of a market where the price of housing has been distorted by property taxation. Unfortunately, any direct comparison between the actual $(P_1 \; Q_1)$ housing combination and the hypothetical one which would exist in the absence of a property tax is extremely difficult to carry out in empirical terms. More visible consequences of property taxation should occur during the process of adjustment to equilibrium. If the argument summarized in Figure 1 is right, a stiff property tax ought to discourage new housing investment (either in the form of rehabilitation or new construction) and should accelerate the rate of housing abandonment. It is these changes in investment behavior which ultimately produce the equilibrium stock differentials represented in Figure 1. In the rest of the chapter I shall examine such investment effects. However, since the magnitude of any housing market adjustment clearly depends on the size of the property tax liability that is imposed, I want first to consider the scale of the property tax burden that is borne by residential properties in the low-income neighborhoods of our major cities.

3. See *George Sternlieb and Robert W. Burchell,* Residential Abandonment: The Tenement Landlord Revisited, *Center for Urban Policy Research, Rutgers University, 1973; also, Sternlieb,* Some Aspects of the Abandoned House Problem, *Center for Urban Policy Research, Rutgers University, 1970.*

THE PROPERTY TAX BURDEN IN
LOW-INCOME NEIGHBORHOODS

By now it is a well established fact that property tax rates in the cities tend to be considerably greater than tax rates elsewhere in a state. In New Jersey, in 1972 the effective tax rates in Jersey City, Newark, and Hoboken were 7.3 percent, 7.4 percent, and 8.5 percent respectively, compared to a statewide median of 3.6 percent. Elsewhere in this volume, William Oakland has shown that Baltimore City's effective property tax is almost double the rate in Baltimore's suburbs. Boston's property tax rate is almost twice the average for Massachusetts. With few exceptions, the same pattern applies elsewhere. Property tax rates in the cities also are high enough to have a significant effect on the price of housing. Viewed in terms of its sales tax equivalent, the property tax burden on the average housing unit in a major city represents approximately 25 percent of gross rents. If the property tax were passed on to the consumer of housing in its entirety, this would represent a *one-third increase* in the price of housing, compared to what it would be in the absence of a tax.

The property tax burden in low-income urban neighborhoods is compounded by the fact that in many cities the effective rate of property taxation in such areas is even higher than it is for the city as a whole. A considerable amount of evidence has been accumulated, showing that residential properties in low-income neighborhoods tend to be assessed at a higher proportion of their market value than properties in more affluent neighborhoods. This, of course, is equivalent to levying a higher tax *rate* on blighted neighborhood properties. David Black recently demonstrated that Boston's census tracts with the lowest median family income are assessed at approximately a 50 percent higher proportion of market value than the highest income tracts, while the tracts with the greatest nonwhite population are assessed at almost 80 percent more than the citywide average. Similar results have been obtained for Hartford, Connecticut and the cities of New Jersey.[4]

Although the data on assessment bias are subject to several interpretations, one factor that undoubtedly plays a large role is the lag with which reassessments take place. Properties in low-income neighborhoods are overassessed in good part because of the failure to adjust

---

4. David E. Black, "The Nature and Extent of Effective *Property* Tax *Rate Variation within the City of Boston*," National Tax Journal, *June 1972. Oliver Oldman and Henry Aaron, "Assessment-Sales Ratios under the Boston Property Tax,"* National Tax Journal, *March 1965. Theodore Reynolds Smith,* Real Property Taxation and the Urban Center: A Case Study of Hartford, Connecticut, *John C. Lincoln Institute, 1972;* Report of the New Jersey Tax Policy Committee, Part II, Vol. 2, 1972.

assessed valuations downward as market values decline. In those cities where the collapse of the inner city housing market has been most severe and reassessment has been most delayed, assessment inequities can reach catastrophic proportions. Table 11 compares effective tax rates in blighted neighborhoods, downward transitional neighborhoods (where properties are declining into full-scale blight) and other neighborhoods for two sets of cities. The first set of cities (Baltimore, Chicago, Philadelphia, and Providence) have suffered greatly from deterioration of their poorer residential neighborhoods and also have exceedingly slow mechanisms for adjusting assessed valuations to changes in market value. The other group consists of cities which either are not old enough to have been hit by extreme urban decay (Atlanta; Nashville; Oklahoma City; Portland, Oregon; and San Francisco) or have taken explicit steps to reassess neighborhoods on an annual basis in order to keep current with changes in market values (Detroit, Portland, and San Francisco). As can be seen, effective tax rates in the former cities are as much as five times higher in blighted neighborhoods than in the rest of the city. By contrast, little systematic assessment bias is observable in the latter group. In the blighted neighborhoods of Chicago and Baltimore effective tax rates on low-income properties are more than 10 percent of true market value.

I conclude that, especially in the older industrial cities where the low-income housing problem is most acute, blighted neighborhoods

Table 11.

MEDIAN EFFECTIVE PROPERTY TAX RATE BY NEIGHBORHOOD AND CITY, 1970 (percent of market value)

City	Blighted Neighborhood	Downward Transitional Neighborhood	Rest of City
Baltimore	14.9	9.8	1.5
Chicago	10.7	4.7	3.0
Philadelphia	9.3	1.9	1.3
Providence	5.2	—	1.1
Atlanta	4.6	2.2	2.1
Detroit	3.0	3.5	3.0
Nashville	0.9	1.3	1.3
Oklahoma City	1.7	2.3	1.5
Portland	1.8	2.6	2.1
San Francisco	1.9	2.5	2.1

Source: George E. Peterson, Arthur P. Solomon, William C. Apgar, Jr., and Hadi Madjid, *Property Taxes, Housing, and the Cities*, D.C. Heath, 1973. Based on sample properties.

bear a very high property tax burden, which can substantially alter the price of housing.[5] Moreover, it is generally acknowledged that within the central city, a parcel's property tax burden bears little, if any, relation to the value of the public services which its occupants receive. As a result, property tax payments represent a genuine shift in the supply schedule for housing, rather than a disguised tax price which is charged for the bundle of local public services. The SS curve in Diagram 1 therefore experiences a sizable shift upward, which means that the potential exists for the property tax to cause a significant distortion in the quality of dwelling units on the low-income housing market.

THE DISINCENTIVE TO REHABILITATION

Perhaps the most frequently alleged harmful effect of the property tax is the discouragement it provides to improvement or rehabilitation of the existing housing stock in low-income neighborhoods. Coupled with this evaluation of the current, detrimental effect of property taxation is the claim that a skillful use of property tax abatements, or a sizable shifting of the tax burden from structures to land, would make it possible to improve the quality of the housing stock dramatically in low-income markets.[6]

The theory behind the property tax's disincentive effect is clear. According to the legal description of each city's tax system, residential

---

5. *To some degree, the high effective rates of property taxation in low-income neighborhoods are offset by much lower market value/rent ratios. Because of this second variation, the sales tax equivalent of the property tax—or tax payments as a percent of annual rental receipts—is much more evenly distributed across neighborhoods than is the property tax as a percentage of market value. See Peterson, "The Regressivity of the Residential Property Tax," Working Paper No. 1207-10, Washington, D.C., The Urban Institute, 1972.*

6. *For instance, Dick Netzer,* Impact of the Property Tax, *National Commission on Urban Problems, GPO, 1968, argues that "High property taxes effectively shrink the market for all types of improvement in the central city housing supply. This is perhaps most obvious for owner-occupants of unmodernized older housing considering rehabilitation; the rehabilitation is not only costly and difficult to finance, but in most cities, it also will result in some increase in assessment . . . . Fear of potential property tax increases can be a potent deterrent to improvements of central city residential properties." Netzer elsewhere emphasizes that many residential improvements in fact escape assessment. A less guarded statement can be found in Mary Rawson,* Property Taxation and Urban Development, *Urban Land Institute, 1961: "In the slum, the process of natural renewal by private action has come to a stop, hindered, among other things, by speculation in land, and by the taxation of improvements . . . . To exempt improvements and at the same time to tax land more heavily would provide a double incentive to the owners of derelict buildings to demolish them and to use the land more intensively. Here surely is a golden key to urban renewal . . . ."*

See also Walter Rybeck, How the Property Tax Can Be Modernized to Encourage Housing Construction, Rehabilitation, and Repair, *Working Paper 112-13, Washington, D.C., The Urban Institute, 1969.*

property is supposed to be taxed at a uniform proportion of its true value. If an improvement to a property augments its market value, this increment to value ought to be taxed at the overall property tax rate, just as if the value were attributable to the original portion of the property. Now a tax on the market value of an improvement represents an additional cost which the investor must take into account when deciding whether or not to upgrade his parcel. For an investor who requires a 10 percent rate of return on invested capital, the imposition of a 4 percent effective tax rate on a parcel's market value will effectively discourage all improvements whose original pre-tax rate of return lies between 10 percent and 14 percent, unless market conditions allow the investor to pass on the tax burden to his tenants.[7]

Whether the property tax actually discourages housing investment in this way will depend on whether improvements to the housing stock in fact result in reassessment, or at least are perceived to do so. In a study of property taxation in ten cities, several colleagues and I followed the case histories of some 420 central city parcels. As Table 12 shows, of all the improvements which cost less than $10,000 per unit to carry out, only 10 percent were reassessed within the four years following completion of the improvement, and these had their assessments raised by only a fraction of the cost of improvement. Of the 152 properties in the sample which had undergone private market rehabilitation or upgrading only 19 were reassessed within the four-year period.[8] While it is likely that some of the other improvements eventually will be reflected in assessed valuation—it is common practice, for instance, to reassess properties following a sale and the sale price indirectly incorporates the market value of improvements which the previous owner has made—the disincentive which the property tax provides to housing improvements may well have been exaggerated, for the simple reason that reassessment only infrequently occurs as a result of upgrading, and then with great lag.

More immediately to the point, this study found *no* instance where improvement to a property in a blighted neighborhood resulted in reassessment. As was pointed out earlier, residential properties in

7. The fact that property taxes can be counted as an operating cost for federal income tax purposes will modify this calculation somewhat. For example, if an investor is in the 30 percent marginal tax bracket, a 4 percent effective property tax rate is equivalent to a net (additional) tax of 2.8 percent.

8. It should be pointed out that assessors in all ten cities reported that they routinely make use of building permit data in deciding which properties to reassess. The Douglas Commission concluded from similar reports that the property tax must have a significant "deterrent effect" on housing investment. See Building the American City, Washington, D.C., Report of the National Commission on Urban Problems, GPO, 1968, p. 359. This inference from formal administrative procedures to economic effect seems not to be justified, however.

Table 12.
REASSESSMENT AS A RESULT OF PRIVATE MARKET REHABILITATION

Value of Rehab Per Unit	Number Properties Rehabilitated	Number Properties Reassessed as a Result of Rehab	Percent Reassessed
Less than $500	53	1	1.9%
$ 500 to $2,999	62	10	16.1
$ 3,000 to $9,999	30	4	13.3
$10,000 and over	7	4	57.1
ALL PROPERTIES	152	19	12.5

Source: Peterson et al., *Property Taxes, Housing, and the Cities.*

Table 13.
REASSESSMENT OF PRIVATE MARKET REHABILITATION BY NEIGHBORHOOD

	Less than $3000 Per Unit			More than $3000 Per Unit		
	Number of Properties Rehabilitated	Number of Properties Reassessed	Percentage Reassessed	Number of Properties Rehabilitated	Number of Properties Reassessed	Percentage Reassessed
Blighted	32	0	0.0	3	0	0.0
Transitional downward	30	5	16.7	3	0	0.0
Rest of City	53	6	11.0	31	8	26.0
ALL NEIGH-BORHOODS	115	11	9.6	37	8	21.6

Source: Peterson et al., *Property Taxes, Housing, and the Cities.*

blighted neighborhoods typically are overassessed, so that even a significant improvement to a building is unlikely to do more than bring the market value of the parcel into line with its assessed valuation. Assessors seem to recognize this fact, and refrain from penalizing improvements in blighted neighborhoods. (See Table 13.)

Investors' reports tend to confirm that fear of reassessment plays a small role in the decision whether or not to make improvements in blighted neighborhoods. As part of the above study, investors were asked to identify what they regarded as the principal obstacles to upgrading their parcels. Table 14 shows that only one owner in a blighted

Table 14.
OBSTACLES TO REHABILITATION OF RENTAL PROPERTIES
BY NEIGHBORHOOD

Obstacle	Blighted Neighborhoods	Downward Transitional	Rest of City
Difficulty of obtaining financing	24	14	35
Deterioration of neighborhood	27	21	12
Inability to raise rent	13	9	17
Unavailability of labor	3	6	13
Fear of reassessment	1	4	14

Note: Numbers refer to number of investors citing listed cause as "major obstacle" to rehabilitation.
Source: Peterson et al., *Property Taxes, Housing, and the Cities.*

neighborhood designated fear of reassessment as a "major obstacle" to upgrading. On the demand side, neighborhood deterioration and inability to raise rents were cited as the most important obstacles. On the supply side, investors assigned most importance to the lack of financing. Outside the blighted neighborhoods, fear of reassessment played a somewhat more important part in investors' calculations, but in low-income areas the prospect of increased property tax liability was the least important obstacle cited by those who thought their properties could benefit from upgrading.

One final piece of evidence has been adduced to support the view that property tax liability is an important factor in rehabilitation decisions. According to some authors,[9] cities which have experimented with property tax abatement plans have found them to provide a significant spur to investment in low-income housing. If exemption from property tax liability provides a significant incentive to investment, the argument runs, then tax liability itself must effectively discourage housing improvements in these markets.

A search of the literature reveals that the favorable impression of tax exemption schemes derives almost solely from reports of New York

9. *For example, Netzer,* Impact of the Property Tax, op. cit., *and Rybeck,* How the Property Tax Can be Modernized, op. cit.

City's success in encouraging rehabilitation by this means. Since this experience promises to become a precedent for other areas which are considering the adoption of abatement plans, it seems important to clarify just what can, and cannot, be concluded from New York's experience. The New York program is more accurately described as a large-scale *subsidy* for rehabilitation than as property tax abatement. It is true that as part of the encouragement to investment in rent-controlled units, New York provides exemption from local property taxes for a period of twelve years on the value of certified improvements. However, this is a relatively minor portion of the benefits which an investor obtains. He may, in addition, *reduce* his existing property tax liability by *90 percent* of the cost of an improvement, spread over a period of years. For example, if a landlord undertakes a $10,000 improvement, in addition to not being taxed on the increment to the parcel's value, he may reduce his existing property tax liability by $850 per year for almost eleven years, or until the total of his tax reduction reaches 90 percent of the improvement's cost. Given New York City's present property tax rate, the owner of a building worth $50,000 could wipe out his property tax obligation altogether for eleven years by making a $20,000 improvement to his property. On top of this, most improvements which qualify for tax exemption in New York City also qualify for reduced-rate municipal loans. In fact, almost all of the improvements which can be certified for tax exemption consist of investments undertaken to remove code or other legal violations. Hence, failure to make the subsidized investment renders the owner vulnerable to legal prosecution.

Given the welter of bureaucratic provisions which surround the investment decision in New York City, all of which conspire to lower the cost to the landlord of making improvements, or threaten legal action in case he fails to make such improvements, it is impossible to ascertain how important a spur to rehabilitation is the single factor of property tax abatement on the value of new investment. Admittedly, the combined effect of the various incentive programs has been impressive. For the twelve years ending March 1972 some 219,000 of New York's residential units were rehabilitated under the incentive program, at a cost of approximately $220 million. According to one estimate, however, in order to achieve this $220 million of rehabilitation investment, New York City will have to pay out more than $275 million in property tax reductions, most of this obligation derived from a period when the tax concessions were less generous than they now are. In other words, the city has granted property tax cuts which more than cover the total cost of the improvements which were effected. It is impossible, I believe, to judge from New York's experience with this type of subsidy program whether ordinary property tax abatement programs would significantly encourage housing investment, or, conversely, whether the presence of a property tax on improvements significantly discourages investment.[10]

Undoubtedly, in areas where property tax rates are extremely high, abatement schemes may succeed in inducing some *new* construction that otherwise would not take place. It seems that tax reduction has played a significant role in encouraging commercial construction in downtown Boston, and in making it possible for nonprofit and limited-profit sponsors to build moderate income housing in Newark. I know of no evidence, however, that property tax abatements anywhere have elicited a significant amount of private market investment in low-income neighborhoods, whether this investment consists of new construction or upgrading of the existing housing stock.

THE PROPERTY TAX AND HOUSING ABANDONMENT

Up to now, I have looked at the effect property taxation has on housing investment. At the other end of the scale, the decision whether or not to abandon a housing structure also affects the supply of inner-city housing, and also has been asserted to be sensitive to property tax policy.

In many cities, housing abandonment has reached crisis proportions. In *Newark*, no less than 7.5 percent of the total housing stock has been abandoned in the last four years alone. In *Chicago*, between 15 and 20 percent of the structures in Woodlawn and Lawndale which are older than ten years "have been demolished or boarded up, or stand vacant and vandalized." In *St. Louis* one-sixth of the structures in the Montgomery-Hyde Park, Murphy-Blair, and Yeatman areas are reported to have been abandoned. In *Philadelphia* some 20,000 units were abandoned as of 1970; in *Detroit* it is estimated that 20,000 structures under the FHA insurance program alone have been or will be abandoned.[11]

If housing abandonment represented just the discarding of capital whose economic life had been exhausted, it should occasion no more alarm than the scrapping of old automobiles or the junking of worn-

10. The description of New York City's program is taken from Price, Waterhouse & Co., A Study of the Effects of Real Estate Property Tax Incentive Programs upon Property Rehabilitation and New Construction, *Report to the Department of Housing and Urban Development, 1973.*

11. Data taken from Robert Powell Sangstar, "Abandonment of Inner-City Properties," *Federal Home Loan Bank Board Journal, Vol. 5, February 1972; National Urban League, The National Survey of Housing Abandonment, New York, The Center for Community Change, 1971; George Sternlieb and Robert W. Burchell, Residential Abandonment: The Tenement Landlord Revisited, Rutgers University, Center for Urban Policy Research, 1973; William Lilley, III and Timothy B. Clark, "Federal Programs Spur Abandonment of Housing in Major Cities," National Journal, January 1, 1972.*

out industrial machines, except for the fact that the social ills associated with vacant buildings would argue for an efficient policy of demolition. The dilemma is that by all reports much of the abandoned housing capital in low-income neighborhoods is still serviceable. If this is true, the massive rate at which abandonment is occurring in our older cities represents a serious loss of socially valuable capital as well as a tragedy for individual households. The question I now want to pose is: Does current property tax policy contribute to this premature scrapping of serviceable housing?

At least one link between property taxation and housing abandonment has been firmly established. Almost without exception, several years of property tax delinquency have been found to precede abandonment of a housing parcel.[12] In a typical scenario, the housing investor, once he sees that operating costs have risen to the level of rental receipts or soon will do so, enters into an end-game strategy, leading to the ultimate abandonment of his structure. With abandonment in mind, he squeezes the last rental income out of his units, while skimping on maintenance expenditures and defaulting on property tax payments. How long the landlord can operate his structure without making property tax payments depends on the delay involved in the *in rem* proceedings by which a city acquires title to delinquent parcels. Usually, however, these proceedings drag on for many years. In New York City, for example, more than six years elapse between the initiation of sustained property tax default and city takeover of property. During this time a landlord may continue to extract a positive cash flow from his property, even though he does not meet the legal obligations of ownership.

Now if property assessments were fairly and efficiently carried out, most of this linkage between tax delinquency and abandonment would not arise. Insofar as the abandonment of housing is a rational process, it occurs at the moment when the discounted net income that is generated by a property turns negative, with no substantial prospect for recovery. At this time the market value of the property also should become zero. If the assessed valuation accurately reflected market value, ownership of the structure then would carry no property tax liability at all since the property would have no value. In this case avoidance of property tax liability could never be the *cause* of abandoning a structure.

In the real world, of course, the stickiness of assessments makes for quite a different picture. In their studies of St. Louis and Chicago, the firm of Linton, Mields, and Coston showed that not only did vacant

---

12. *George Sternlieb and Robert W. Burchell, "Residential Tax Delinquency: A Forerunner to Residential Abandonment," Real Estate Law Journal, Spring 1973.*

structures go on accumulating tax liabilities, even after abandonment; but often, prior to abandonment, while the market value of these parcels was declining drastically, property tax bills actually were increasing.[13] George Sternlieb's analysis of abandonments in Newark reveals the same pattern of collapsing market values, accompanied by constant or increasing tax liabilities. In both of these studies, the authors imply that the property tax is a major cause of housing abandonment, since it is one of the principal costs that a landlord must face. Without property tax payments the operating statement of a landlord often would show a profit whereas, after tax payments, it shows a sizable loss. The owner, it is claimed, is forced to walk away from his property because of the tax burden.

Now it is worth pointing out the perceptions of property tax incidence which this analysis implies. Some opponents of the property tax have managed to argue that the tax is objectionable *both* because, viewed as a sales tax that is passed on to renters, the property tax is highly regressive, *and* because, viewed as a capital tax that is borne by landlords, it accelerates housing abandonment.[14] Such an analysis, of course, is self-contradictory. If it is legitimate to compute the tax burden of renters by assuming that tenants bear the full burden of the property tax, then it cannot be legitimate to turn around and argue that landlords abandon parcels, in part at least, because *they* bear the burden of the property tax. Any analysis of housing abandonment which assumes that landlords' operating profits are reduced by the full amount of their property tax payments almost certainly is in error, for the simple reason that part of this cost is passed on to tenants in the form of higher rents. If a *solitary* landlord had his property tax liability removed, he could go on charging tenants the same rents while paying no taxes. The tax reduction would boost his profits by the same amount. But if property tax liability were removed for all the parcels in the low-income housing market, landlord competition would force at least a portion of this cost-reduction to be passed on to tenants as rent reductions. For this reason one cannot conclude from the fact that a single cost item, such as property tax payments, figures prominently in investors' income statements that *removal* of the cost, for all investors, would boost profits commensurately.

Let us suppose, however, that a significant fraction of the total property tax burden is borne by landlords. Even so, a further look at the process of abandonment casts doubt on the conclusion that property tax liability importantly affects the abandonment decision. Hous-

---

13. *Linton, Mields, and Coston, Inc.,* A Study of the Problems of Abandoned Housing, *Report to the Department of Housing and Urban Development, 1971.*

14. *For example, Netzer,* Impact of the Property Tax, *op. cit.*

ing abandonment, above all, is a neighborhood phenomenon. In urban areas where rates of abandonment are high, bad neighborhood conditions—as evidenced by crime rates, poor quality public services, and dilapidated housing—typically place a ceiling on the rents a landlord can charge. If tenants are going to pay more than this amount for housing, they prefer to acquire neighborhood amenities that are available only by moving to another part of the city. Against this rent ceiling imposed by neighborhood conditions must be set the landlord's increasing operating costs—the higher costs of labor and maintenance, increasing utility charges, and increasing expenses due to vandalism that he must absorb, as well as possibly increasing property taxes. The property tax may well make the difference as to whether a building is *presently* profitable or not; but given the across-the-board nature of the landlord's cost squeeze in low-quality neighborhoods, once a building turns unprofitable net of property tax payments, it is generally only a matter of a few years until it turns unprofitable to operate, even without property taxes. In this case, the most the property tax does is advance the date of abandonment.

Given the delay with which cities acquire title to tax-delinquent parcels, however, the property tax may not affect even the date of abandonment. If an investor succeeds in estimating the date at which his net cash flow excluding property tax payment will hit zero, and can time his property tax defaults so that the city does not foreclose on his property while it still has income potential for him, the investor can simply cease paying his property taxes in advance and then abandon the parcel at the moment it is privately advantageous to him. In effect, the property tax obligation becomes irrelevant, since long before abandonment occurs the landlord has stopped paying his taxes. The empirical data show that very few properties are abandoned by their owners while still generating a positive cash flow, exclusive of tax liability, as would have to be the case if the property tax were a decisive influence on the timing of abandonment decisions.

Here again, the theoretical effect of the property tax is neutralized by the realities of its administration. Just as cities typically refrain from assessing private market rehabilitation in low-income areas, so they prove loath to take over properties which are laggard in their tax payments. The result is that at the margin, property tax considerations may scarcely enter into the owner's decision to upgrade or abandon a parcel.

It is true, though, that the accumulation of back property taxes on parcels can make it immensely more difficult to turn a *neighborhood* around through public policy. Once a landlord begins to default on property tax payments, even though he may continue to operate his parcel for some time, he in effect has made his abandonment decision. The necessity of paying off the back tax liability makes it much less likely that a change in public policy can convince an owner that it makes economic sense to restore his parcel to good operating condition. For this reason, any plan for neighborhood revitalization in areas where tax delinquency is high ought to include some provision for forgiveness of back tax liability, perhaps upon transfer of title to a new owner or adequate evidence of upgrading by the present owner.

THE PROPERTY TAX AND TRANSFER OF OWNERSHIP

The foregoing discussion suggests that at least in low-income urban housing markets, the property tax does not present the disincentive to housing investment, or the spur to housing abandonment, that is implied in many property tax discussions.

The property tax still may exert important indirect effects, however. A good deal of recent research suggests that purely economic models may have limited applicability in analyzing low-income housing markets. Much of the decision to maintain, upgrade, run down, or abandon low-income housing structures seems to depend upon what are usually classified as noneconomic factors. Several years ago George Sternlieb pointed out that owner-occupants maintain their parcels in far better condition, on average, than do absentee landlords, given the same neighborhood conditions. Franklin James and Robert Burchell have demonstrated that racial considerations play almost as large a part in abandonment decisions as do cash flow considerations. White landlords with black tenants are far more likely to abandon their buildings than are white landlords with white tenants or black landlords with black tenants, even though they face the same operating conditions. Sociologists at McGill University have gone even further. Their studies indicate that in low-income areas the personal compatibility of landlord and tenant does much to explain the level of maintenance which the landlord provides. In this respect, dealings between landlord and tenant resemble more the personal relations of "primitive" societies than the arm's length profit-loss calculations which most of our economic models build upon.[15]

One assumption of the rational economic model that seems especially inappropriate in the housing market is that investors are able to let bygones be bygones when deciding whether to invest further

---

15. *George Sternlieb,* The Tenement Landlord, *Rutgers-The State University, 1966. Franklin James and Robert Burchell, "Housing Abandonment" (unpublished paper); Roger Krohn and Ralph Tiller, "Landlord-Tenant Relations in a Declining Montreal Neighborhood," in Paul Halmus, Ed.,* Sociological Review Monograph, No. 14, *University of Keele, 1969; Roger Krohn and C. E. Berkeley Fleming, "Landlords and Tenants in a Working Class Montreal Neighborhood."*

Table 15.
CHANGE IN HOUSING QUALITY
BY LENGTH OF OWNERSHIP

	Type of Neighborhood	
	Blighted	Downward-Transitional
Improving Quality		
More than 5 years ownership	18.8%	19.1%
Less than 5 years ownership	56.5%	27.6%
Maintaining Quality		
More than 5 years ownership	37.5%	48.9%
Less than 5 years ownership	34.8%	44.8%
Deteriorating Quality		
More than 5 years ownership	43.8%	31.9%
Less than 5 years ownership	8.7%	27.6%

Based on stratified sample of 87 blighted-neighborhood properties and 76 downward-transitional properties. Quality classifications made on basis of visual inspection and analysis of five-year rehabilitation and maintenance histories for each property.

See Peterson et al., *Property Taxes, Housing, and the Cities.*

in the parcels they own. In the blighted neighborhoods of many cities, long-term owners are tied to vast capital losses which they suffered as inner-city neighborhoods collapsed during the 1960s. Many of these investors have held on to their parcels grudgingly, only because they are unable to find buyers for them.

Oftentimes, the profit-maximizing strategy for such investors would be to effect minor repairs or upgrading in order to fill vacancies in their units and boost their rent rolls. A new purchaser who has bought a building at a realistic, depreciated price may be able to see this profit opportunity, but it seems to require an excessively sanguine view of human nature to expect trapped investors, crippled by years of capital loss, to look upon their parcels in the same way, as objects of fresh investment.

Table 15 presents one illustration of the difference in behavior between recent purchasers of parcels in blighted and downward transitioned neighborhoods and long-time owners. As the table shows, the class of "new buyers" are far more likely to upgrade their parcels. When owners are further distinguished according to whether they express a desire to sell out their parcels at once (provided they can locate a buyer), the difference in operating behavior becomes even more striking. Long-time, unwilling holders of parcels (who also tend to be white, absentee owners) are far more likely to run down their properties than are recent buyers (who are disproportionately black landlords, and are more likely to live on the premises or in the neighborhood).

What does this difference in landlord behavior have to do with the property tax? It is possible that a one-time equalization of property tax burdens across the neighborhoods of a city, because it would substantially lower the effective tax rate on blighted properties, would provide just enough fillip to the market price of low-income parcels to encourage transfer of ownership from old, absentee owners, to new neighborhood owners.[16] After all, the price that is required to make sale preferable to abandonment is not very high. And in areas where property taxes currently run as high as 10 percent of market value, simply reducing the tax burden to its legally mandated rate should have a sizable capitalization effect, leading to an increase in the market value of parcels. This in turn could lead to a significant amount of unloading of properties, since the majority of long-term owners express a desire to sell out if they could only recover a portion of their investment. From the evidence currently available, such a transfer of ownership would lead to more investment in the low-income housing stock and better maintenance standards. Thus, one of the most important effects of current property tax policy may be that extremely high tax rates have helped to destroy the market in central-city low-income housing structures and therefore have discouraged the socially beneficial transfer of these properties to a new class of owners.

THE PROPERTY TAX AND LANDLORDS' CASH FLOW

A second, implausible assumption that appears in purely economic models of the housing market is that landlords will make the profit-maximizing expenditures on the housing they own, whatever their economic circumstance. In fact, most owners of properties in blighted neighborhoods find it extremely difficult to borrow capital. Small-scale owners tend to view their properties as anchors against bad fortune, and are reluctant to use them as security for going into debt even when financing is available. For these reasons, most landlords in low-income areas pay for maintenance and improvements

---

16. *It might be thought that some non-zero price must always clear the market in low-income housing structures, or at least those structures that have a remaining economic life. However, unless an owner can pay off his mortgage, he is unlikely to secure approval for sale from the mortgagor. As a result, an owner has only two options: either he sells his property at a high enough price to cover the mortgage, or he operates the parcel himself, eventually defaulting on the mortgage. Given the steep price declines that have taken place in low-income neighborhoods, numerous properties cannot be sold at a price equal to the outstanding principal on the mortgage debt. Unless governmental agencies intervene in some way, these parcels seem to be tied to their present owners.*

out of a building's cash flow. If this cash flow is limited, they allow the building to run down, even though in strictly economic terms it would be more profitable to use borrowed capital to maintain it better.

In low-income areas where effective property tax rates reach 6 to 10 percent, property tax liabilities can cut significantly into a small owner's cash flow, if even a portion of this tax burden falls on the owner. The predominant response is likely to be a lowering of upkeep standards as owners shrink their maintenance outlays to fit their cash receipts. In my judgment, high levels of property taxation probably exert their greatest influence on the low-income housing stock through the deterioration of maintenance standards that comes with a cash flow shortage.

CONCLUSION: PROPERTY TAX PERPETUATES URBAN BLIGHT—BUT NOT FOR REASONS GENERALLY CITED

Taxes of any sort have both a marginal incentive effect and a wealth effect. Traditionally, the property tax's effect on the housing market has been analyzed in terms of the disincentive it provides to housing investment. The prospect of additional property tax liability is thought to discourage investors from building new housing and from upgrading or repairing old housing. At the same time current tax liability is thought to encourage abandonment of otherwise profitable properties. In my view, these marginal incentive effects have been greatly exaggerated, at least as they concern the market for low-income housing.

More important are the wealth effects of the property tax. Maintenance expenditures by most blighted-area landlords are tied to the cash flow they receive. When property tax burdens increase, and the cash flow from a property declines, most owners react by cutting back on repairs and maintenance. The cumulative effect on the housing stock of this gradual disinvestment is at least as great as the more dramatic rehabilitation and abandonment decisions. In this way extremely high effective tax rates in low-income neighborhoods do contribute to housing deterioration.

Finally, the high property tax rates that burden some central city low-income neighborhoods appear to have contributed to the destruction of the transfer market for housing in these areas. As a result, new neighborhood ownership of low-income parcels becomes virtually impossible. To the extent that the property tax has contributed to the paralysis of market forces in low-income neighborhoods, it must also bear some of the responsibility for perpetuating urban blight.

8

PROPERTY TAXATION'S
INCENTIVE TO FISCAL ZONING

by Bruce W. Hamilton

The widespread reliance on property taxes to finance local public services in the United States causes a rational household to try to preserve or enhance the size of the property tax base in its community. The greater is the average taxable wealth per household in a community, the lower will be the property tax rate which a particular family must pay in order to finance a given level of local public services.

For this reason, households have an incentive to do what they can to increase the value of local taxable property. In the past, towns have competed with one another to attract industrial and commercial development on the expectation that the property tax contributions made by these establishments would outweigh the cost of providing services to them and any adverse influences industrial growth might have on the environment. Although such tax base competition persists today, the recently increased concern over environmental effects has diminished its vigor somewhat. At present, a more popular strategy for preserving the tax base, especially in relatively affluent suburbs, is the adoption of restrictive zoning ordinances. These are intended to exclude from a community households which would spend relatively little on housing, and therefore would require from the community more in the form of public service provision than they would contribute in the form of tax payments. Of course, there are other motivations for exclusionary zoning (such as the desire to avoid racial mixture), but the fiscal incentive to exclude poor people is strong enough to have marked effects on the way metropolitan areas are organized.

It is a widely held view among those interested in metropolitan development that zoning restrictions have been used by local govern-

BRUCE W. HAMILTON, Research Staff, The Urban Institute. (Since July 1973, Assistant Professor of Political Economy, Johns Hopkins University.)

ments to create several socially undesirable effects. In this chapter, I
want to consider four key questions:

1. Has fiscal zoning increased the income segregation of communities, as might be expected if jurisdictions are left free to engage
in competitive exclusion of poor families?

2. Have fiscal incentives affected the location of commercial
and industrial property, in turn affecting the taxable wealth of different communities?

3. Has the total supply of low-income housing been excessively
restricted by fiscal zoning?

4. What are the overall consequences for income distribution and
economic efficiency of the answers to the first three questions?

FISCAL ZONING AND INCOME SEGREGATION

Is there reason to believe that fiscal zoning has increased the
income segregation of communities?

Theory. It seems indisputable that if zoning boards seek to minimize the taxes current residents must pay for public services, they
will try to prohibit residential construction which depresses the per
household tax base. Furthermore, households will have at least some
incentive to avoid locating in a community with a particularly low
tax base. A contrary view is held by Babcock,[1] who believes that the
fiscal motivation for zoning is insignificant: "The resident of sub-
urbia('s) . . . wife spends more at the hairdresser in a month than the
apartment house will add to her husband's tax bill in a year." But
a simple calculation demonstrates that the orders of magnitude are
not nearly so trivial as Babcock would have us believe. Suppose that
the present tax burden on a household is $1,000 (or a 2.5 percent
effective tax rate on a $40,000 home). If through an aggressive zoning
policy the taxable wealth per family in the community could be
doubled, the household in question would save $500 per year. If the
discount rate is 10 percent this saving has a present value to the
household of $5,000. In other words, households and zoning boards
are playing for big stakes when they attempt to manipulate tax bases.

Now if fiscal considerations were the sole determinant of household decisions as to where to live, each family would try to move
into the jurisdiction which had the highest per household tax base,
since tax rates there would be lowest. Abstracting for the moment
from the influence of commercial and industrial property, the tax
base will be highest in the community which has the highest *average*
value of residential homes. Thus all households will try to take up

---

1. Richard Babcock, The Zoning Game, *Madison, University of Wisconsin Press, 1969.*

residence there. From the point of view of the community, however, an incentive exists to keep out households that would lower the average value of homes. In the extreme case where communities were able to adopt perfectly effective housing restrictions, such a combination of incentives eventually would lead to perfect stratification of jurisdictions by house value. No family voluntarily would take up residence in a jurisdiction with a low tax base. But the zoning restrictions in communities with high valued housing would effectively screen potential entrants. Thus households would move into the communities which had the highest tax bases (and hence the highest average home values and highest zoning restrictions) *consistent* with their own planned housing purchases. Families that wanted to buy $40,000 homes would move into communities that prohibited construction of lesser value, and families that wanted to buy $25,000 homes would move into areas that set $25,000 minimum housing levels. This parceling out of households by housing consumption would continue until perfect stratification was achieved.[2]

One clear consequence of fiscal zoning then ought to be a high degree of community segregation by house value. Since house values and family income are closely correlated, there ought also to be a discernible amount of community segregation by income. Of course, many other considerations besides tax rates enter into a household's location decision, and zoning regulations are far from perfectly effective as devices for determining minimum home values; but to the extent fiscal zoning is effective, it ought to lead to a visible degree of income segregation.

Note that this segregation is the consequence of fiscal incentives *in combination with* zoning powers. In terms of fiscal incentives alone, low-income households have the same reason to seek out residence in high-income communities that wealthy households do—namely, to save on their property tax rates. The existence of fiscal zoning, however, makes fulfillment of this objective possible only for the high-income group.

Empirical Evidence. There is only slender statistical evidence on the effects that local fiscal considerations have on residential location patterns.

In a recent study,[3] Edwin Mills, David Puryear and I measured the correlation between a set of explanatory variables related to local

---

2. See B. W. Hamilton, "Zoning and Property Taxation in a System of Local Governments," Urban Studies (forthcoming).

3. B. W. Hamilton, E. S. Mills, David Puryear, "The Tiebout Hypothesis and Residential Segregation," Working Paper 1207-20, Washington, D.C., The Urban Institute, April 1973.

fiscal considerations and the level of income-mixing[4] in census tracts drawn from the suburban sections of a sample of 21 major American cities. If local fiscal concerns are an important determinant of location patterns, we argued that census tract income homogeneity should increase as the number of school districts in the urban area increases. One of the crucial elements of the local fiscal model under consideration is that there is a wide range of choice of public service districts. If there are only a few school districts to choose from, the likelihood that their homogeneous development can be protected by zoning devices is much diminished. We also argued that the level of state and federal aid to education should be negatively correlated with local income homogeneity. The rationale for this is that, if education is financed largely through transfers from the state government, the advantage to current residents of protecting the local tax base is less. So they ought to be less vigilant in their zoning practices.

After correcting for many other determinants of the level of income homogeneity, we found that the number of school districts is positively correlated with the income homogeneity of census tracts.[5] With regard to intergovernmental aid, we found that not only the level, but also the *type* of state and federal aid to education makes a difference. If the aid is compensatory (based on the number of poor people or inversely related to the tax base), the most of admitting poor people to the community is greatly reduced. Almost all aid formulae are either of the compensatory type or flat—completely unrelated to any variable under the control of the local government.[6] We predict, then, that compensatory aid will lead to a substantial increase in income integration, and that an increase in the level of flat grants will lead to a lesser increase in integration. Again, these predictions are borne out by our statistical analysis. On average, an increase in compensatory aid brings about twice the reduction in our index of segregation that a similar increase in flat aid brings. And the compensatory aid coefficient is much more significant statistically than the flat aid coefficient.[7]

The measure of segregation we use is an index for which interpre-

---

4. *Our index of mixing was the Gini coefficient of per household income.*

5. *The estimated standard error for the correlation coefficient between these two variables enabled us to conclude that, with a probability of about .95, the observed correlation is nonrandom.*

6. *Many aid formulae contain matching provisions. But almost invariably these contain ceilings beyond which local effort will not be matched, and these ceilings are in fact binding in almost every case. So for our purposes these grants are flat.*

7. *For the compensatory aid variable, we are able to reject the random correlation "null" hypothesis with a probability of about .93, whereas we are able to reject the same random correlation hypothesis for the flat aid variable with only a confidence level of about 0.8.*

tation of magnitude is difficult. The notion that the Gini coefficient increases from 0.3 to 0.35 conveys little meaning except with regard to the direction of change. So our study, while it does tell us whether certain variables influence the level of segregation, does not convey in any intuitively meaningful sense the degree to which local fiscal considerations have influenced residential location patterns.

A similar study is that of E. J. Branfman, et. al.[8] They conducted a cross-sectional comparison of 30 Standard Metropolitan Statistical Areas (SMSAs), using standard statistical techniques to explain the geographic clustering of income groups. Aside from historical and racial factors, the authors found that the most important explanatory variable is the number of zoning authorities per million population. The proportion of local school budgets that is financed locally is somewhat less strongly correlated with the clustering index. And three other variables which the authors describe as local fiscal variables are completely insignificant. They are 1) local property tax as a percent of personal income, 2) local property tax as a percent of local revenue, and 3) an index of the strength of the state equalization formula for educational aid. The results on balance are similar to those of Mills, Puryear and myself, although the authors interpret them quite differently. They do not regard the number of zoning authorities as a fiscal variable, and hence find little evidence that fiscal considerations lead to income stratification; we interpret the number of school districts as a fiscal variable and find that it adds importantly to segregation by income. These variables are undoubtedly highly correlated. Further statistical work may enable us to distinguish between the segregation effect of additional school districts and additional zoning boards. My conjecture is that the fiscal incentive is being represented in both cases, partially because I do not see how a large number of zoning authorities would lead to more income clustering for non-fiscal reasons than would a small number of authorities.

I have one further bit of evidence that fragmentation, or "Balkanization," is a fiscal phenomenon. In my Ph.D. dissertation I calculated the correlation between the average number of suburban school districts per capita (by state) and the percent of school expenditure financed by the state. The level of state aid alone explained about 35 percent of the variation among states in the average size of school districts.[9] Although correlation does not prove causation, the most

8. E. J. Branfman, Benjamin I. Cohen, and David M. Trubeck, "Measuring the Invisible Wall: Land Use Controls and the Residential Patterns of the Poor," Yale Law Journal, January 1973.

9. I was able to reject with a probability of .99 the hypothesis that the correlation was random. B. W. Hamilton, "The Impact of Zoning and Property Taxes on Urban Structure and Housing Markets," unpublished doctoral dissertation, Princeton University, 1972.

plausible explanation to me of this finding is that a high level of state aid reduces the incentive to form a fragmented system of local governments.

In conclusion, I find that the two studies cited here lend considerable, though far from overwhelming, support to the notion that local fiscal incentives intensify income clustering.

ZONING AND THE LOCATION OF INDUSTRY

Has zoning influenced the location of commercial relative to residential property?

Theory. Assume provisionally that zoning boards maximize the welfare of current residents, and that firms regard local tax rates as given. Further, assume that the only effect that a firm has on a community is its contribution to the tax base. All of these assumptions will be relaxed in the course of the discussion.

Each community's zoning board will want to maximize the share of the tax base that is nonresidential, since increasing this share reduces the taxes that the household sector must pay for public services. A rational zoning board in a community with some nonresidential property would be willing to allow new residential construction only if the value of the new housing is at least equal to the per household total tax base (which will of course be higher than the per household residential tax base). In other words, the presence of nonresidential taxable property should cause communities to be more restrictive in their residential zoning than they would otherwise be. New low-income housing, assuming that it is not accompanied by growth in the commercial section, is undesirable even to a low-income community, since the new housing would cause the tax subsidy from industry to be spread among more households. New residents are welcome in a community only if they bring their own subsidies with them.

The location behavior of firms under this scheme also has important implications. We assume that firms are indifferent among communities except insofar as the property tax rate varies among communities. We can think of firms as single-mindedly trying to minimize their property tax liabilities. The communities with the lowest property tax rates are likely to be those with the highest average tax bases. Other things being equal, these will be communities which already have a large contingent of nonresidential property. So any average tax price differences among communities that arise due to the location of firms will tend to be magnified by subsequent location decisions of firms.[10]

The existence of commercial and industrial taxable property, given the assumptions we have made, gives rise to persistent, and possibly sizeable interjurisdictional differences in average tax bases, and gives rise to a motivation for restriction of the supply of low-income housing.

It seems likely that, if several communities are bidding for commercial and industrial property, firms will find a way of playing off one community against another, and that the size of the tax subsidy from firms to households will be reduced if not eliminated. For instance, a firm could request special tax assessment treatment in return for locating in a particular community. If, through competitive bidding, communities completely eliminate the tax subsidy paid by firms, then it will be a matter of indifference to zoning boards and households where firms locate.

The final assumption which needs to be relaxed is that the only way nonresidential property influences a community is through its tax contribution. It is generally believed that nonresidential property has undesirable side-effects. In a dissertation underway at Princeton, W. A. Fischel [11] examines the trade-off between desirable tax base effects and undesirable environmental effects of nonresidential property. For our purposes, his analysis yields two important results. First, after some point the desirable tax base effects are likely to be outweighed by increasing congestion and pollution costs. At this point the zoning board will prohibit further industrial development. So, contrary to the result derived above, there are forces which will tend to inhibit communities with large industrial tax bases from obtaining still larger industrial tax revenues. Second, the implicit demand price of a clean environment is likely to be higher in high-income communities than in low-income communities, so nonresidential property will not find itself zoned out of low-income communities as readily as from high-income communities. So there is at least some tendency for nonresidential wealth to be spread out among communities and among income classes.

Empirical evidence. Unfortunately, our knowledge about the relationship between industrial location and local fiscal variables is rather limited. Fischel [12] reports that, for a sample of New Jersey school districts, the fiscal dividend (the difference between resident-specific expenditures and property taxes, both per capita) is strongly and positively correlated with the value of commercial and industrial

10. If differential tax advantages are capitalized into nonresidential property values (as seems to be the case with residential property values), there will be no incentive for new firms to locate where the industrial tax base already is high, since any property tax advantage will be offset by higher land prices.

11. W. A. Fischel, "Firms, Zoning, and the Fiscal Dividend," unpublished, Princeton University, 1972.

12. Op. cit.

rateables per capita.[13] He further reports that the magnitude of the fiscal dividend is negatively correlated with mean per capita income in the community, lending support to the hypothesis that low-income communities are more willing to forsake environmental quality in return for taxable property. Local tax rates in Fischel's sample are not correlated with the level of nonresidential rateables per capita, indicating that the cumulative mutual attraction of nonresidential property discussed above is unimportant. Fischel's conclusion is that the location behavior of firms is strongly influenced by the actions of local governments, and that it is incorrect to view firms as freely locating in the community they find most desirable. It seems that communities carefully weigh the costs and benefits of nonresidential property.

Fischel's work provides some evidence that communities do not competitively bid the fiscal transfer from firms to residents down to zero, although it may still be true that competition substantially reduces the size of the transfer. There is also evidence that the transfer is merely a payment by firms to residents for the use of environmental services.[14]

ZONING AND LOW-INCOME HOUSING SUPPLY

Has the total supply of low-income housing (or possibly high-income housing) been excessively restricted due to the fiscal motivation for zoning?[15] There is widespread feeling, and some evidence, that low-income, high-density housing is restricted to central cities, that our growing suburban areas are almost the exclusive domain of low-density, high-income housing. The suburban land, being owned and occupied by the rich, appears to be unavailable to meet demanded increases in the supply of low-income housing.

Theory. There are several ways in which zoning might restrict the total supply of low-income housing in metropolitan areas.

---

13. *This bivariate regression measures the net effect of commercial and industrial location. It has been argued that some industry attracts low-income residents whose depressing effects on the tax base will offset the gains from the nonresidential property. Of course, this line of reasoning is based on the presumption that zoning is not used to prevent the in-migration of low-income workers as residents. At any rate, Fischel's results show that these second-round effects, if they exist, are not sufficient to offset the direct positive effect of industrial location.*

14. *This could be tested by seeing whether the transfer is capitalized into property values.*

15. *By "excessively restricted" we mean the following: Suppose there were no local public sector, and that all its functions were taken over by the federal government and financed by the income tax. Would the removal of the local fiscal incentive for zoning alter the relative supplies of various income classes of housing? The class of housing which would expand under such conditions is held to be inefficiently restricted in supply due to fiscal zoning. We utilize the standard result that, in the absence of inefficient distortions such as zoning and local taxes, competitive markets provide efficient allocation of resources.*

First, note that no zoning board pursuing the welfare of its residents will allow residential construction which lowers the per household tax base. This by itself might lead to an inefficient supply restriction of low-income housing. It may be that all the vacant land in an urban area is within the corporate limits of high-income communities, and that the zoning boards are unwilling to zone the property for low-income housing. But to the extent that the housing needs of the poor are satisfied by filtering rather than by new construction, this would seem to be a relatively unimportant consideration. The appropriate question is not whether vacant land is available, but whether zoning boards will allow housing to be converted from one use to another. It is quite possible that local zoning boards try to pass ordinances which restrict filtering (such as the prohibition of conversion of single-family homes to two-family or multi-family use) for *fiscal* reasons. It is not difficult to see how this would occur. As demand conditions change, and as the housing stock ages, the appropriate use of a given structure frequently changes, and it is most likely that it will pass to increasingly lower income households. If it were not for local fiscal effects, this process could take place, if not on a house-by-house basis, at least on a block-by-block basis. But the desire not to lower the *per-household* value of the tax base through more intensive use of the housing stock creates a fiscal interest in the filtering process.

Another possible source of distortion in the housing market is the zoning instrument itself. It is possible that through minimum lot-size requirements zoning boards have much greater control over the amount of land each household occupies than the value of its housing (land plus capital). If this is the case, each community will have to zone for very large lots in order to insure tax base protection. The same tax base protection could be achieved with smaller lot-size requirements if zoning boards could set minimum capital-consumption requirements as well. Widespread use of minimum lot-size requirements then might restrict the supply of land available for high-density construction. Such construction would be fiscally acceptable to the community if it had some assurance that a large amount of capital would be substituted for land. But in the absence of the appropriate zoning tools, no such assurance is forthcoming.[16]

Empirical evidence. Richard Muth [17] has found evidence that residential density patterns are somewhat different for suburban areas than for central cities. He calculated the rate at which population

---

16. Note that *restrictions based on the total value of housing might well do a "better" job of excluding low-income families, but would not create the distribution in factor use that minimum lot-size requirements can do.*

17. *Richard Muth,* Cities and Housing, *Chicago, University of Chicago Press, 1969.*

Figure 2.

RESIDENTIAL DENSITY IN CENTRAL CITY AND SUBURBS

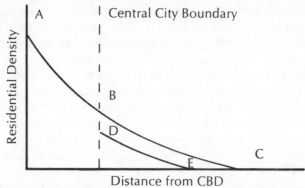

density falls off with distance from the Central Business District (CBD) for many large American central cities. He then extrapolated these "gradients" to the edge of the entire urban area. He discovered by comparing his calculated density results with actual population density that suburban population density is lower than he predicted. Referring to Figure 2, the section AB of the curve represents actual population density as a function of distance from the CBD within the central city. The section BC of the curve is an extrapolation of AB to the edge of the suburban fringe; it represents Muth's prediction of the suburban population density pattern. The curve DE represents actual suburban population density. He finds that the amount by which actual population density falls short of the predicted value depends upon two variables: the median income of the urban area and the population of the urban area. As median income grows, suburban population density grows (DE rises), but as the urban area population grows (income remaining constant) the central city population density grows relative to the suburban (the distance between BC and DE increases). This seems to indicate that there are income-related restrictions on suburban living. It seems likely that expansion of low-income housing is inhibited in the suburbs of many urban areas. Unfortunately, we do not know whether this restriction is due to local fiscal considerations.

There is also widespread evidence that, in many urban areas, land zoned for apartment dwellings is more valuable than land zoned for single-family dwellings. Land which is rezoned from single-family to apartment use frequently increases in value by a factor of as much as five or ten. Peter Mieszkowski[18] reports that land zoned for apart-

18. Peter Mieszkowski, "Notes on the Economic Effects of Land-Use Regulation," presented at International Institute of Public Finance Congress, New York, 1972.

ments in the New Haven area is about ten times as valuable as land zoned for single-family housing. And Ron Crowley[19] found that in Oshawa, Ontario, apartment-zoned land is about seven times as valuable as single-family land.

One seemingly apparent conclusion is that, relative to single-family dwellings, insufficient land is devoted to apartment buildings. But the evidence is difficult to interpret, for two reasons. First, land values vary within an urban area by perhaps as much as a factor of 1,000 for reasons unrelated to zoning. In general, land with good access to downtown is more valuable than other land. The natural response of developers to high priced land is to economize on its use, and one way of doing this is to construct apartment buildings rather than single-family housing. So we should in general expect to find land destined for apartment construction to be more valuable than land destined for single-family construction. The price difference might arise because there is a scarcity of land within one mile of Manhattan or because there is a scarcity of land within walking distance of a subway stop, rather than because there is a shortage of land zoned for apartment dwellings. In order to be sure that the price differentials are due to zoning, it is necessary to be extremely cautious in correcting for differences in the "natural" attributes of different parcels of land. For this reason, evidence on changes in land value as a given parcel is rezoned are important. Here we can conclude that the land value change is directly due to zoning, and not to some other cause. In other words, this is evidence that zoning has inhibited the construction of apartments.

Unfortunately, even having established that zoning constrains the supply of low-income housing and raises its price, we have not established that the supply is "inefficiently" restricted. Even with an efficient supply of low- and high-income housing, land zoned for the former activity would command a higher price than land zoned for the latter because of the fiscal advantages of buying the same public services through the lower total tax payments. I have done some rough calculations[20] indicating that land zoned for high density low-income housing could be as much as two or three times as valuable as land zoned for high-income housing strictly as a result of the fiscal transfer involved in financing public expenditures through the property tax, indicating that the seven-to-tenfold price difference reported here is probably too large to be explained by capitalization of relative tax advantages. There is some reason to believe, then, that the total

19. R. W. Crowley, "Benefit-Cost Analysis for Local Airports: A Case Study of Oshawa Airport," *Canadian Department of Transport*, March 1970.
20. B. W. Hamilton, "Capitalization of Intra-jurisdictional Differences in Local Tax Prices," *Working Paper 1207-26*, Washington, D.C., The Urban Institute, July 1973.

supply of low-income housing, particularly in the suburbs, has been inefficiently restricted by fiscally motivated zoning.

Some anecdotal support for the role of fiscal considerations in excluding low-income housing development comes from the State of Minnesota, where two important changes in the structure of local fiscal institutions were instituted recently. First, the state has taken over about 70 percent of the cost of financing education through an increase in the foundation school finance support program. Second, a nonresidential tax base sharing scheme has been instituted in the Minneapolis-St. Paul SMSA.[21] Thirty percent of the nonresidential tax revenues from property built after the passage of the law is to be shared among the jurisdictions within the area. Although statistical analysis of the effects of these changes has not yet been undertaken, there is some preliminary evidence. A nonprofit corporation in the Minneapolis area has been attempting to construct low-income housing in the suburban sections of the urban area. However, the corporation had been thwarted in its efforts by local government officials. After the changes in local finance institutions were promulgated, approval was obtained for construction of two large-scale developments in wealthy suburbs.

CONSEQUENCES FOR INCOME DISTRIBUTION AND EFFICIENCY

What are the efficiency and equity implications of our findings?

Theory. There is substantial evidence that interjurisdictional differences in fiscal attractiveness are capitalized into property values.[22] That is, if one community is in a more advantageous fiscal position than another, property values will adjust in such a manner that consumers are just indifferent as to which community they live in.[23] This means that a household pays the same amount for his housing-plus-local public service consumption regardless of where he lives. If he lives in a community with a particularly low tax price for public service, this will be offset by a higher price of housing.

So new buyers of housing do not benefit from a large nonresidential tax base. Prices will have adjusted such that the rate of return

---

21. *This provision was recently held to be unconstitutional by a Minnesota state court. The state is appealing.*

22. *W. E. Oates, "The Effects of Property Taxes and Local Public Spending on Property Values: An Empirical Study of Tax Capitalization and the Tiebout Hypothesis,"* Journal of Political Economy, *November/December 1969.*

23. *If there are differences besides fiscal attractiveness, some households will prefer the attributes of one community, and some the attributes of the other. Here the market will set prices such that the market for housing is just cleared in both communities. The analysis is not enriched by considering those complexities.*

from residential property does not depend on the size of the non-residential tax base. But a landlord does care about *changes* in the stock of nonresidential taxable property which might occur once he has purchased his property, since such changes will give rise to windfall changes in property values. The people who stand to gain or lose from nonresidential property are those who own residential property when firms are on the move. Whether a firm chooses to locate in a given community is a matter of great moment for landlords (be they owner-occupants or absentee landlords), but it is a matter of indifference to renters (assuming property markets equalize rates of return on real estate investment across communities). So interjurisdictional differences in average tax prices do not influence the distribution of income except when the differences change.

The distribution of wealth among consumers is not influenced by the fact that some housing units are located in communities with high or low tax bases. Only those who happen to own the properties when they change in value are affected.

But if differences in tax prices for public services and consequent differences in property values do not influence the distribution of wealth, they certainly do influence the way consumers allocate their wealth between housing and local public services. This is especially pronounced in the provision of education. In general, communities have the opportunity of taxing themselves separately for education and other services. Since the benefits of education accrue almost exclusively to residents, and the benefits of other types of expenditure (sewer, water, police) accrue in part to nonresidential property, a given increase in the nonresidential tax base gives rise to a much greater decline in the tax price of education than the tax price of other services. George Peterson[24] has demonstrated that large differences in the tax price of education exist among communities, and that the tax price is an important determinant of public school expenditure. It may well be considered wise as a national policy to subsidize education, in an effort to encourage people to buy more of this good. Peterson's results suggest that such a subsidy would indeed bring forth more expenditure on education. But it is difficult to make a case for a fiscal system where in some communities the cost to the average household of raising an additional dollar of local educational expenditure per pupil is $1.50 and in other communities it is less than ten cents. Regardless of whether there is a legitimate rationale for subsidizing education, we can only conclude that gross inefficiency results when consumers face prices which vary so widely, and differ so

---

24. G. E. Peterson, "The Demand for Public Schooling," *Working Paper 1207-21*, Washington, D.C., The Urban Institute, May 1973.

markedly from production costs. Although the evidence is far from complete, it seems likely that such tax price differences would be greatly diminished if it were impossible to use zoning to protect the land tax base.

We stated above that, if a given dwelling unit were moved from community to community, its value would change in such a manner that the occupant's total expenditure on housing plus public services would be invariant; that is, any changes in the tax liability would be just offset by changes in the value of the property.[25] But it is still possible that the poor pay a higher price per unit for housing plus public service than do the rich, regardless of where they live. Specifically, zoning may have restricted the supply of low-income housing in such a way that after accounting for the costs of public service, the poor pay a higher price per square foot of floor space than do the rich. Whether this is true depends upon the supply of low-income housing which has been permitted by zoning boards. The difficulties in gathering evidence on this question have been discussed above, and the evidence which is available lends fairly weak support to the notion that the poor pay more for housing. So we have some reason to believe that fiscal zoning discriminates against the poor through regulating the supply of low-income housing.

There is one other important result of zoning, with both equity and efficiency consequences. The theoretical and empirical evidence on the segregation effects of fiscal zoning indicates 1) that it makes neighborhoods more homogeneous, and 2) that it increases the concentration of poor people in central cities. In the absence of any restrictions on residential location, it is a frequent pattern for the rich to live farther from the central business district of a major city than do the poor. If there are strong incentives for zoning (either fiscal or other), this will tend to institutionalize and accentuate the separation of people by income class. As patterns of employment change over time, it is difficult for the lower-income classes to move around an urban area to take advantage of new employment opportunities. Manufacturing employment has been suburbanizing particularly quickly over the past decade or so, and there is evidence that at least some of the potential employees of these firms have not moved to the suburbs to take advantage of the employment opportunities there. A direct link among suburbanization of employment opportunities, inability of low-income people to suburbanize due to zoning, and unemployment rates among low-skill laborers has not been established,

---

25. *This statement is made on the assumption that the amount of local public service offered is the same in all communities. If a particular community offers more public service provision than another, the residents will have to pay more, either through higher taxes or through higher real estate prices.*

and indeed may not exist. It has been shown that residential segregation on the basis of race has reduced the availability of jobs to blacks,[26] but whether fiscally induced zoning, leading to segregation by income, puts the poor in general at the same disadvantage is, unfortunately, not known.

A PUBLIC FINANCE SOLUTION TO FISCAL ZONING

There is moderate evidence that fiscally motivated zoning is at least partially responsible for a large number of evils:

1. It restricts the total supply of low-income housing in an urban area.

2. It increases income segregation, possibly exacerbating the problems of the poor in finding employment and in commuting.

3. It helps to sustain a system of completely irrational price incentives for local public services, particularly education.

4. It gives rise to large and whimsical changes in the distribution of wealth as local tax bases change.

Reform, I believe, should not focus on the institution of zoning, but on the larger institution of local public finance. So long as local governments have a fiscal interest in manipulating land use, they will make a valiant effort to find a way of doing so. The tool can be zoning, building codes, selective granting of sewer permits, and so on. A legislative or judicial attack on local land use controls has two major defects in my view. First, local control over land use is so pervasive and ingrained that the probability of meaningful reform seems remote, particularly if it concentrates on a single exclusionary instrument like zoning. Second, local land use controls perform nonfiscal roles which may be useful. Prohibition of only fiscally motivated zoning strikes me as a futile exercise.

---

26. For instance, J. F. Kain, "Housing Segregation, Negro Employment, and Metropolitan Decentralization," Quarterly Journal of Economics, Vol. 82, May 1968, pp. 175-97.

9

USING THE PROPERTY TAX TO PAY FOR CITY GOVERNMENT: A CASE STUDY OF BALTIMORE

by William H. Oakland

Because the property tax is the principal source of locally raised public revenue, the future course of property taxation in the United States depends crucially on the revenue needs of local (and to a lesser degree, state) government.

The decade of the sixties witnessed a virtual explosion of government economic activity. Government expenditures, by all levels, increased by 150 percent between 1960 and 1970, rising from 28 percent to 36 percent of Gross National Product. Although growth occurred at all levels of government, it has been particularly rapid in the state-local sector. This is evidenced by the fact that the federal share of government expenditure decreased during the sixties from two-thirds to slightly over one-half. Over the same period state and local revenues increased from 8 percent of GNP to 10.5 percent. Since the tax receipts of state and local governments are not highly sensitive to economic growth, numerous tax *rate* increases were required to finance the increased state and local government spending.[1] Such increases have precipitated or threatened to precipitate financial crises for numerous state and local governments. The fiscal situation has been particularly problematic for this country's central cities, which, because of significant shifts in the socioeconomic characteristics of their residents, have experienced extraordinary increases in demands for public services while experiencing substandard growth in their ability to finance them. To some extent, this change in population

WILLIAM H. OAKLAND is Associate Professor, Department of Political Economy, Johns Hopkins University. (Since August 1973, Professor, Department of Economics, Ohio State University.) This chapter includes the author's work for a report by the Baltimore Urban Observatory, *Baltimore Municipal Finance Study,* July 1972. An earlier version was presented at the January 1973 conference of the Committee on Urban Economics (CUE).

1. *According to the Advisory Commission on Intergovernmental Relations there were 521 instances of tax rate increases at the state level alone during the 1959-71 period.*

composition is the *result* as well as the cause of central cities' financial difficulties. Deteriorating service levels and high taxes have contributed to the flight of middle-income residents to suburban communities. Thus, our central cities may be caught in the grip of a vicious spiral which threatens to strip them totally of means of fiscal support.

The deteriorating fiscal condition of our central cities has given rise to numerous proposals for reform, including metropolitan-wide government, tax base sharing of commercial and industrial property, increased state aid, and state assumption of the costs of certain programs now funded at the local level.

In order to assess the relative merits of such reform proposals, we need to know much more than we do about the nature of the fiscal crisis facing our central cities. Despite widespread agreement that such a crisis exists, we have had relatively little quantitative evidence concerning the dimensions of the problem. For example, little is known about the property tax differentials between cities and their suburbs. Nor do we have much evidence about the history of such differentials. As another example, it is often asserted that the central city is "exploited" by suburban commuters. However, we have virtually no information concerning the magnitude of the costs that are imposed by commuters.[2]

The paucity of information concerning city-suburban fiscal disparities is due in large measure to the fact that budgetary data are not published in a form suitable for such analysis. The primary source of budgetary information, the Census of Governments, provides data principally on a countywide basis, and when central city data are shown separately, the problems of overlapping jurisdictions make comparison with suburbs virtually impossible. It is only recently that attempts have been made, under the auspices of the ACIR, to disentangle census information for purposes of drawing city-suburban comparisons within SMSAs (Standard Metropolitan Statistical Areas).

Given the unavailability of suitable data for a comprehensive analysis, a case study of a representative metropolitan area may provide useful insights into the quantitative nature of the problem. The Baltimore SMSA is an excellent candidate for a case study. Its population, in excess of two million, ranks it as the ninth largest metropolitan area in the country. Hence, it is not so large as to give rise to the special problems of "super" SMSAs, such as New York or Chicago, yet it is large enough to exhibit those problems faced by the "typical"

2. *Some evidence of central city-suburban fiscal disparities are given in a forthcoming ACIR report entitled,* Financial Emergencies in American Cities. *Figures for earlier periods are shown in ACIR's* Fiscal Balance in the American Federal System, *Vol. 2, 1967.*

large SMSA, as will be shown below. More important, it is characterized by an extremely simple local government structure. The population resides in one of six nonoverlapping jurisdictions: five suburban
counties and the central city.[3] All local government functions, including education, are carried out by these jurisdictions. Thus, fiscal disparities between Baltimore City and its suburbs can be clearly identi-
fied.

A major conclusion of the study is that the property tax is totally
unsuitable as a primary means of central city finance, while it proves
more than adequate for suburban areas. A second finding is that most
reform proposals, including the recently enacted revenue sharing program, will not measurably affect existing and future disparities between
central cities and their suburbs. Their problem is that they simply do
not offer adequate *differential* relief to the central city.

COMPARISON WITH OTHER SMSAs

In terms of social, economic and fiscal characteristics, the Baltimore area is reasonably representative of large SMSAs in the United
States. Its per capita personal income in 1970 of $4167 is slightly be-
low the median value for the 38 largest SMSAs, $4247. In terms of
growth, Baltimore's performance has been average. Its population
growth and per capita income growth during the sixties were 81 percent and 20 percent respectively, while the median values for the 38
largest SMSAs were 76 percent and 20 percent respectively.

As shown by the Bureau of the Census report, "Local Government
Finances in Selected Metropolitan Areas in 1968-69," the combined
budgetary characteristics of all local governments in the Baltimore
area also resembled those of the typical large SMSA. For instance
(giving Baltimore SMSA data first, then data for 38 selected SMSAs in
parentheses), total per capita revenue was $403 ($448); of this amount,
per capita intergovernmental transfers amounted to $175 ($154) and
local property taxes amounted to $138 ($188). On the expenditure
side, total spending per capita was $433 ($499), of which spending
for education was $188 ($199), for public welfare and hospitals, $61
($76), for police and fire, $46 ($37), and for highways, $29 ($24). Debt
outstanding per capita was $490 ($591).

A few differences call for comment. The Baltimore area governments spent 15 percent less per capita than the average SMSA. However, more than half of this represents utility expenditure, reflecting
differences in institutional arrangements (e.g., private vs. public owner-

---

3. The Baltimore SMSA consists of Baltimore City and the following counties: *Anne
Arundel, Baltimore, Carroll, Harford,* and *Howard. Baltimore City and Baltimore
County do not overlap.*

ship of gas and electric companies). The remainder can be explained by differences in per capita income.

A significant difference also exists with respect to intergovernmental revenue; Baltimore obtains a higher fraction of revenue from this source. This results in a smaller share of the property tax in the revenue structure as well as a smaller property tax burden. As a fraction of personal income, property taxes in 1969 were 3.5 percent in Baltimore, while they stood at 4.6 percent in the other SMSAs. This means that the property tax is less oppressive in the Baltimore area than in the typical large SMSA.

Let us now turn to central city-suburban disparities. As Table 16 shows, Baltimore closely follows the pattern of large SMSAs. Baltimore City's population has declined absolutely and relatively. Despite the fact that the suburbs enjoyed rapid population growth, an overwhelming proportion of nonwhite population growth occurred in the city. Income growth in the city has failed to keep pace with the suburbs, resulting in a substantial widening of the gap in per capita income that existed over a decade earlier. The result is that a disproportionate number of poor are housed in the central city. Thus Baltimore conforms closely to what has become the "classic" pattern of urban development (decay)—a declining central city increasingly occupied by economically disadvantaged minorities, and surrounded by a growing and affluent white population.

These socioeconomic disparities carry over into the fiscal arena. While fiscal disparities in the Baltimore area will be discussed at greater length below, a few summary statistics are shown in Table 16 for purposes of comparison. With one exception, Baltimore conforms to the norm. The exception is intergovernmental aid. Unlike most large cities, Baltimore enjoys an advantage relative to its suburbs with respect to this revenue source. This reflects the fact that the state pays virtually all of the city's marginal welfare costs. Since 87 percent of SMSA's welfare cases reside in the city, it obtains a disproportionate share of such aid. Since state funding of welfare is often proposed as a partial solution to the fiscal crisis of central cities, a study of Baltimore can shed light on what problems will remain if such action is taken.

BALTIMORE SMSA FINANCES, 1960-70

Current expenditures by local governments in the Baltimore SMSA during the fiscal year 1970 amounted to $431 per capita. Of this amount, outlays for education absorbed 40 percent, while public safety, welfare, and debt service, taken together, account for another 33 percent. On the revenue side, 40 percent of current revenues were obtained from higher level governments. Less than one-third of current revenues were provided by the property tax, while a local income tax and charges provided slightly more than 20 percent.

Table 16.
CENTRAL CITY–SUBURBAN DISPARITIES:
BALTIMORE AND SELECTED SMSAs

	Median of 37 Largest SMSAs	Baltimore
Central City population as a percentage of SMSA, 1960	46.1	52.1
1970	40.4	43.7
Percent nonwhite in CC[a], 1970	21	46
Central City's share of nonwhite population growth, 1960-1970	82	91
Percent population growth, 1960-1970, CC	−2.2	−3.1
OCC[b]	34.3	34.7
Median house vales, CC/OCC ratio, 1970	81	53
Percentage increase in median house value, 1960-1970 CC	29	11
OCC	45	51
Percentage of owner-occupied housing valued at over $25,000, ratio, 1970	56	19
Crime rate per 100,000 population, CC/OCC ratio, 1970	245	282
Per capita income CC/OCC ratio, 1970	96	73
Percentage of households with incomes less than $3,000 CC/OCC ratio, 1970	180	286
Per capita expenditures, CC/OCC ratio, 1957	132	140
1970	138	183
Per capita tax collections, CC/OCC, 1957	152	169
1970	139	113
Per capita noneducational expenditures, CC/OCC, 1957	193	197
1970	212	310
Per capita educational expenditures, CC/OCC, 1957	69	83
1970	86	103
Educational expenditures as a percentage of total expenditures, CC/OCC ratio, 1957	59	56
1970	63	60
Current expenditures per pupil, CC/OCC ratio, 1970	107	108
Per capita state and federal aid, CC/OCC ratio, 1957	95	145
1970	117	259
State and federal aid as a percentage of total expenditure, CC/OCC ratio, 1957	75	103
1970	85	144
Per capita educational aid, state and federal, CC/OCC, 1970	76	93
Per capita noneducational aid, state and federal, CC/OCC ratio, 1970	180	552

Source: Advisory Commission on Intergovernmental Relations, *Financial Emergencies in American Cities.*
a. CC: Central Cities.
b. OCC: Outside Central Cities.

Table 17.

LOCAL GOVERNMENT REVENUES, EXPENDITURES, AND DEBT, BALTIMORE SMSA, 1960-1970

	1960				1970				Changes 1960 to 1970		
	Levels (thousands $)	Percent of Total	$ Per Capita	Percent of Personal Income	Levels (thousands $)	Percent of Total	$ Per Capita	Percent of Personal Income	Annual Rate of Growth of Level	Percent of Total Change	Annual Rate of Growth of Per Capita
	1	2	3	4	5	6	7	8	9	10	11
Revenues:											
Taxes—Local	163,199	55.1	90.5	3.7	420,492	46.5	203.7	4.9	9.5	42.3	8.5
Property	149,916	50.6	83.1	3.4	293,831	32.5	141.9	3.4	6.7	23.7	5.5
Income	(13,283)	(4.5)	(7.4)	(.3)	95,951	10.6	46.3	1.1	(24.1)	(18.6)	(22.4)
Other					30,710	3.4	14.8	.4			
Licenses and Permits	9,615	3.3	5.3	.2	8,322	.9	4.0	.1	-1.5	-.2	-2.9
Fines and Forfeitures	1,286	.4	.7	.0	3,118	.3	1.5	.1	9.0	.3	7.9
Charges for Current Services	29,170	9.9	16.2	.7	89,955	10.0	43.4	1.0	11.0	10.0	10.4
Revenue from the Use of Money and Property	2,275	.8	1.3	.1	16,020	1.8	7.7	.2	20.0	2.3	19.5
Own Revenue	205,545	69.5	114.0	4.7	537,907	59.5	259.8	6.2	9.6	54.7	8.2
Current Grants	52,010	17.6	28.8	1.2	295,241	32.7	142.6	3.4	18.1	40.0	16.5
State-shared taxes	37,917	12.8	21.0	.7	66,750	7.4	32.2	.8	5.5	4.7	4.4
Revenues from higher governments	89,927	30.4	49.9	2.1	361,991	40.1	174.8	4.2	14.2	44.8	12.8
Other Revenue	590	.2	.3	.0	4,123	.5	2.0	.0	15.4	.6	—
Revenues Available for Current Operations	296,062	100.0	164.1	6.8	904,021	100.0	436.6	10.4	11.3	100.0	9.8
Grants available for Capital Outlays	14,322	n.a.	7.9	.3	38,481	n.a.	28.2	.7	15.1	n.a.	13.6
TOTAL REVENUE	310,384	n.a.	171.8	7.1	962,502	n.a.	664.8	11.1	11.4	n.a.	10.0

Table 17. (continued)

	1960				1970				Changes 1960 to 1970		
	Levels (thousands $)	Percent of Total	$ Per Capita	Percent of Personal Income	Levels (thousands $)	Percent of Total	$ Per Capita	Percent of Personal Income	Annual Rate of Growth of Level	Percent of Total Change	Annual Rate of Growth of Per Capita
	1	2	3	4	5	6	7	8	9	10	11
Current Expenditure and Debt Service:											
General Government	13,871	4.7	7.7	.3	44,510	5.0	21.5	.5	12.0	5.2	10.8
Public Safety	39,024	13.1	21.6	.9	121,960	13.7	58.9	1.4	12.0	14.0	10.6
Highways	14,232	4.8	7.9	.3	28,469	3.2	13.7	.3	7.0	2.4	5.7
Sanitation and Waste Removal	11,013	3.7	6.1	.3	26,505	3.0	12.8	.3	9.0	2.6	7.7
Health	4,980	1.7	2.8	.1	23,069	2.6	11.1	.3	16.5	3.0	14.8
Hospitals	8,208	2.8	4.6	.2	22,839	2.6	11.0	.3	10.5	2.5	9.1
Public Welfare	24,472	8.2	13.6	.6	103,059	11.6	49.8	1.2	15.0	13.2	13.9
Correction	1,668	.6	.9	.0	3,961	.4	1.9	.0	8.5	.4	7.8
Schools	106,466	35.7	59.0	2.4	349,130	39.2	168.6	4.0	12.0	40.9	11.1
Recreation	8,994	3.0	5.0	.2	27,345	3.1	13.2	.3	11.0	3.1	10.2
Public Service Enterprises	6,970	2.3	3.9	.2	19,491	2.2	9.4	.2	10.5	2.1	9.2
Miscellaneous	18,087	6.1	10.0	.4	33,837	3.8	16.3	.4	6.0	2.7	5.0
Total Current Expense	257,980	86.7	143.0	5.9	304,176	90.4	388.4	9.3	11.5	92.0	10.5
Debt Service	40,168	13.5	22.3	.9	87,511	9.8	42.3	1.0	7.5	8.0	6.6
TOTAL	298,148	100.0	165.3	6.8	891,687	100.0	430.6	10.3	11.0	100.0	10.0
Items:											
Outstanding Debt	588,083	n.a.	326.0	13.5	1,097,674	n.a.	530.1	12.7	6.1	n.a.	4.8
Capital Outlay	64,487	n.a.	35.8	1.5	204,646	n.a.	98.8	2.4	11.5	n.a.	10.7
Personal Income	4,351,053	n.a.	2,418.0	100.0	8,650,001	n.a.	4,181.0	100.0	6.8	n.a.	5.4
Assessable Base	8,954,777	n.a.	4,964.2	n.a.	14,222,984	n.a.	6,868.2	n.a.	4.5	n.a.	3.2

n.a.—Not applicable.
Sources: *Baltimore Municipal Finance Study*, W. H. Oakland, E. Borukhov, F. T. Sparrow, and A. M. Teplin, Baltimore, 1972.

Table 17 summarizes many of the important features of local government finance for the SMSA taken as a whole for the years 1960 and 1970. While the figures in the table speak largely for themselves, certain features deserve special note. First, the role of the property tax in the local revenue structure diminished sharply during the sixties, dropping from more than half of local revenue to less than a third. This was the result of two important developments: 1) the introduction of a local income tax in 1967, and 2) a rapid expansion of intergovernmental aid. The latter is reflected in the fact that grants accounted for nearly 45 percent of all revenue increases over the period.

Second, it will be noted that, relative to income, property taxes did not increase during the sixties. Hence, the popularly held notion that property taxes have grown increasingly burdensome does not stand up for the Baltimore area as a whole. This observation must be tempered by the fact that the effective tax rate on real property advanced by 23 percent during the sixties, rising from 1.67 percent to 2.06 percent. Thus, Baltimore did not escape the problems associated with rising property tax rates. Furthermore, the fraction of income paid in all local taxes rose by nearly one-third. Like most large metropolitan areas, therefore, Baltimore substantially increased its revenue effort during the sixties.

Third, it will be noted that per capita current expenditure grew at nearly twice the rate of personal income, indicating a very rapid expansion of local government during the sixties. The most important source of expenditure growth was education, accounting for over 40 percent of the total increase in current spending. However, the growth of school expenditure only slightly exceeded that of local expenditure, indicating that other categories also played an important role in budget growth. In what follows, we attempt to identify the forces underlying the rapid expansion of local government expenditure.

Although there is no generally accepted theory of growth for local government activity, in virtually every discussion of the problem the following factors are present: growth of population, growth of income, and growth of costs. Table 18 shows the rate of growth of each of these factors. Our hypothesis is that local government expenditure can be expected to grow at a rate equal to the sum of the separate rates of growth. This is shown in line 7 of the table. It will be noted that we considered only two-thirds of the growth of real wages (line 5); this is because wages amount to that fraction of total expenditure (line 1). It will also be noted that we must add an interaction term (line 6) in arriving at the sum (line 7).

The table reveals that the four factors discussed above explain over 90 percent of the total growth in local expenditure in the Balti-

Table 18.
SOURCES OF GROWTH IN LOCAL GOVERNMENT EXPENDITURE, BALTIMORE SMSA, 1960 TO 1970

	Annual Rate of Growth 1960-1970 (percent)
1. Current Expenditure and Debt Service	11.0
2. Population	1.4
3. Real Personal Income Per Capita	3.4
4. Prices	2.7
5. Real Wages—Baltimore SMSA local government employees	3.4
6. Interaction of 2, 3, 4, and 5	.4
7. Total (2 + 3 + 4 [2/3] 5)	10.2
8. Residual (1-7)	.8
9. Addition to 1 caused by higher public welfare share	.5
10. Addition to 1 caused by higher proportion of students in population	.3

more SMSA during the sixties. Hence, at the aggregate level at least, the forces giving rise to expenditure growth are relatively straight-forward.

The residual, .8 percent per year, can be explained by two shifts that occurred during the sixties: a rising proportion of the population on welfare, and a rising proportion of the population in schools. Our calculations reveal these shifts to have expanded current outlay growth by .5 percent and .3 percent, respectively.

CITY AND REST OF SMSA DIFFERENCES

The most interesting features of the fiscal landscape lie in the disparities that exist within the Baltimore SMSA itself. Underlying these fiscal disparities are the differences in the socioeconomic charac-teristics of the population discussed above. In Table 19, we display certain properties of the budgets of Baltimore City and its suburbs: per capita budget figures for 1970, budget structure as indicated by a percentage breakdown for 1970, sources of budget growth for the period 1960 to 1970, and growth rates of budgetary items in both per capita and absolute terms during the period 1960 to 1970. A cursory inspection of the table reveals considerable differences between the two areas.

Perhaps the most striking difference between Baltimore City and its suburbs is the fact that, in 1970, the city government spent nearly

Table 19.
BALTIMORE CITY VS. REST OF SMSA: REVENUES AND EXPENDITURES 1970

| | 1970: Percent of Total | | 1960-1970: Percent of Total Change | | 1970: Per Capita ($) | | Annual Growth Rate | | | | | |
| | | | | | | | 1960-1970: Per Capita Change | | 1970: Percent of Total Income | | 1960-1970: Annual Rate of Growth | |
	Baltimore City	Rest of SMSA	Baltimore City	Rest of SMSA	Baltimore City	Rest of SMSA	Baltimore City	Rest of SMSA	Baltimore City	Rest of SMSA	Baltimore City	Rest of SMSA
	1	2	3	4	5	6	7	8	9	10	11	12
Revenues:												
Taxes—Local	37.0	59.7	26.3	61.0	214.3	194.3	6.4	11.8	6.0	4.2	5.5	14.5
Property	28.0	38.7	15.0	33.8	162.3	126.0	4.3	7.4	4.5	2.7	4.0	10.4
Income	6.4	16.4	(11.3)	(27.2)	37.2	53.4	(16.1)	(48.3)	1.0	1.2	15.7	68.5
Other	2.6	4.6	-.3	-.1	14.7	14.9	-1.9	-3.5	.4	.3	15.7	68.5
Licenses and Permits	.8	1.0	.4	.2	4.8	3.4	10.3	-4.8	.1	.1	-2.3	-.4
Fines and Forfeitures	.4	.3	.3		2.4	.8	11.0		.1	.0	8.5	9.0
Charges for Current Services	11.4	7.9	11.6	8.1	66.2	25.8	22.2	12.0	1.8	.6	10.0	14.5
Use of Money and Property	1.3	3.5	1.8	2.8	7.4	8.0	7.0	17.5	.2	.2	20.5	20.3
Own Revenue	50.9	71.4	39.7	72.1	295.1	232.4	21.1	10.9	8.2	5.0	6.6	14.1
Current Grants	39.9	22.6	54.1	23.6	231.2	73.7	5.3	12.5	6.4	1.6	19.5	15.2
State-shared Taxes	8.4	5.9	5.1	4.3	48.9	19.3	15.3	4.9	1.4	.4	4.5	7.7
Revenue from Higher Government	48.3	28.6	59.2	27.9	280.1	93.0	21.2	9.9	7.8	2.0	14.8	13.1
Other Revenue	.8	.0	1.1	.0	4.5	.0		.0	.1	.0	21.2	-9.1
Revenues Available for Current Operations	100.0	100.0	100.0	100.0	579.7	325.3	10.7	11.1	16.1	7.0	9.8	13.8
Grants Available for Capital Outlays	n.a.	n.a.	n.a.	n.a.	32.4	25.0	14.7	12.5	.9	.5	13.7	15.9
TOTAL REVENUES	n.a.	n.a.	n.a.	n.a.	612.0	350.4	10.4	11.2	17.0	7.6	9.9	14.6
Current Expenditure and Debt Service:												
General Government	5.4	4.4	5.6	4.6	31.2	14.0	11.5	11.8	.9	.3	10.5	14.5
Public Safety	17.2	8.6	18.1	8.9	99.8	27.1	11.6	11.8	2.8	.6	10.5	14.5
Highways	2.8	3.8	1.9	3.0	16.0	12.0	6.0	5.8	.4	.3	5.5	8.5
Sanitation and Waste Removal	3.1	2.8	2.6	2.6	18.0	8.8	8.2	8.5	.5	.2	7.5	11.0
Health	3.0	2.0	3.8	2.2	17.4	6.3	16.7	14.0	.5	.1	15.5	16.0
Hospitals	4.3	.1	4.5	.0	24.8	.3	11.6	-2.9	.7	.0	10.5	-.3
Public Welfare	17.0	3.8	20.8	4.0	98.5	11.9	15.8	12.7	2.7	.3	14.5	15.0
Correction	.6	.2	.6	.2	3.4	.7	10.1	3.4	.1	.0	9.0	7.0
Schools	29.2	53.4	30.1	54.1	169.2	168.1	11.2	11.0	4.7	3.6	10.0	13.5
Recreation	3.6	2.3	3.4	2.7	20.7	7.4	9.7	17.3	.6	.2	9.0	20.0
Public Service Enterprises	2.6	1.6	2.2	2.0	15.2	4.9	8.2	23.4	.4	.1	7.5	27.0
Miscellaneous	4.1	3.4	1.6	3.9	23.6	10.7	3.2	16.6	.7	.2	2.8	19.5
Total Current Expense	92.8	86.5	95.1	88.3	537.7	272.3	11.1	11.2	15.0	5.9	10.0	13.5
Debt Service	7.2	13.5	4.9	11.7	42.0	42.5	6.0	7.3	1.2	.9	5.5	10.0
TOTAL	100.0	100.0	100.0	100.0	579.7	314.7	10.6	10.6	16.1	6.4	9.5	13.0

85 percent ($265) more per citizen for current outlays than did its suburbs. Even allowing for differences in the costs of public welfare, the city spent 59 percent ($178) more per person. While the relative gap between city and suburbs has remained relatively constant over the sixties, the absolute gap in per capita expenditures has grown from $95 to $265. Table 19 also reveals that, with the exception of schools, highways, and debt service, the city spends more than twice as much per person on all categories. The greatest differences occur in public safety (4x), correction (5x), health and hospitals (7x), and welfare (9x). The magnitude of these figures reflect the considerable difference in the socioeconomic composition of the citizens of the two regions—particularly the fact that most of the region's poor reside in the city.

Important differences also exist with respect to the fraction of the budget devoted to various expenditure categories. The major differences are in public safety (17.2 percent for the city, 8.6 percent for the suburbs), health and hospitals (7.3 percent vs. 2.1 percent), public welfare (17.0 percent vs. 3.8 percent), schools (29.2 percent vs. 53.4 percent), and debt service (7.2 percent vs. 13.5 percent). It is interesting to note that despite the considerable difference in the school category, the city spends about the same amount per capita on education as does its suburbs. A large part of the difference in the budgetary structure of the regions owes to the city's greater activities in the health, safety, and welfare fields.

The difference in expenditure levels is made even more striking by the facts that, in 1970, per capita personal income in the city was only two-thirds that of the suburbs and per capita assessed valuation in the city was only 72 percent of the suburban figure (see Table 20).

Table 20.
BALTIMORE CITY AND SUBURBS, SELECTED CHARACTERISTICS

	1960		1970	
	City	Suburbs	City	Suburbs
Income per capita	2,278	2,558	3,594	4,631
Assessable base per capita	4,933	4,998	5,727	8,409
Local taxes as percent of income	5.1	2.5	6.0	4.2
Property taxes as percent of income	4.6	2.3	4.5	2.7
Property tax rate (effective percent)	2.11	1.20	2.83	1.50
Current expenditure as a percent of income	9.3	4.5	16.1	6.8

This means that relative to the income of its citizens, the city spends nearly three times as much as its suburbs upon public services, and relative to its taxable wealth more than two and a half times as much.

The city does not finance all of this difference in expenditure from its own sources. Indeed, the city raised only 51 percent of all its current revenues. This compares with 72.1 percent for the suburbs. Because of intergovernmental revenue, the gap between the city and suburbs is only $63 on the revenue side, as opposed to $265 on the expenditure side. Nevertheless, as a fraction of income, city-raised revenue amounts to 8.2 percent as compared to 5.0 percent for the suburbs. Since not all of the revenue raised by the city is paid by its residents and similarly for the suburbs, we cannot interpret the latter figures as indices of tax burden. For example, charges for current services include major payments by suburban residents to the city government. If we consider only taxes, we find that the above figures change to 6.0 percent and 4.2 percent respectively, which is still a sizeable differential. Further evidence of a greater tax effort by the city is the difference in the effective property tax rate; in 1970, the city rate was 2.83 percent whereas in the suburbs it was only 1.50 percent (see Table 20).

Turning to the growth of expenditures in the two areas, we find that, in per capita terms, current outlays grew at the same rate during the sixties. However, the composition of expenditure growth differed markedly between the city and its suburbs. Columns 3 and 4 of Table 19 show that schools accounted for more than half of all increases in expenditure between 1960 and 1970 in the suburbs, while in the city the figure was approximately 30 percent. This difference in part is due to the difference in the growth of enrollments in the two areas, but more significantly it reflects the fact that the city increased its expenditures on other categories to a much greater extent, thus reducing the *share* attributable to schools. Other than schools, the only category which absorbed a larger share of growth in the suburbs than in the city was debt service. This reflects the tremendous need for new capital facilities to accommodate the burgeoning suburban population.

Turning to the revenue side we find that revenues from higher levels of government financed nearly 60 percent of additional expenditures made by the city while the corresponding figure for the suburbs was 28 percent. As a result the suburbs had to finance more than twice as high (61 percent vs. 26 percent) a fraction of expenditure increases from local taxes as the city. This differential in aid was more than sufficient to finance the differential in expenditure growth in the social welfare category. This suggests that the fiscal disadvantage which the city suffers because of such expenditures did not worsen during the sixties. Indeed, as Table 20 shows, the fraction of income paid in local taxes increased much more in the suburbs than in the city (55 percent vs. 18 percent). Thus, the gap between city and suburban tax burden narrowed considerably during the sixties. This is also evidenced by the fact that property taxes, as a fraction of income, declined slightly in the city, while experiencing a modest increase in the suburbs. Curiously enough, however, the spread between city and suburban effective property tax rates actually *widened* during the decade. This suggests that the income elasticity of the property tax base is lower in the city than in the suburbs, a point to which we shall later return.

To summarize, the rapid expansion of city revenue from higher levels of governments during the sixties enabled it to maintain a growth rate of total expenditures comparable to the suburbs and, at the same time, enabled it to narrow its tax burden differential relative to the suburbs.

SOURCES OF CITY-SUBURBAN FISCAL DIFFERENTIALS

As the preceding section amply documents, the fiscal characteristics of Baltimore City and its suburbs differ. In the discussion to follow we shall examine some of the leading factors underlying these differences.

Expenditure Levels

First of all consider the differences in level of current expense per capita. Table 19 revealed this to be $265. To account for such a difference we examine the following dimensions: 1) differences in the welfare population or poverty population of the two regions; 2) differences in the compensation rate of public employees in the two areas; 3) fiscal burdens imposed by residents of one jurisdiction who are employed in another jurisdiction; and 4) services provided by one jurisdiction to residents of another jurisdiction.

With respect to the incidence of poverty, we find a tremendous difference between the two areas. In Baltimore City, nearly 13 percent of its citizens are receiving some form of public assistance, whereas in the suburbs the figure is less than 1.5 percent. Looked at somewhat differently, although the city has only 44 percent of the region's population it has 88 percent of the region's welfare case load. Since expenditures on welfare alone amount to nearly $100 per capita in the city, such a difference in welfare load directly accounts for nearly 40 percent of the gap in current expenditure. Indirectly, the difference in welfare load also contributes to the expenditure differential since outlays for public health, public safety, and hospitals (among others) are also considerably increased.

If we find that the city has to pay its employees more on the average than do the suburbs then we will have uncovered another reason for the higher per capita expenditures. However, in fact, this is not the case. According to the Bureau of the Census, Baltimore City pays its full time employees an average of $704 per month (as of October 1970) as compared with $742 for the SMSA as a whole. This should tend to lower city expenditures relative to the suburbs.

The 1970 Census of population has provided valuable information on commuting patterns in SMSAs. The data for the Baltimore region show that 136,000 suburban residents worked in the city, while 73,000 city residents were employed in the suburbs. Hence, the city experienced a net commuter inflow in excess of 60,000. Clearly the presence of commuters places financial costs upon the recipient locality. Expenditures upon transportation, public safety, sanitation, and utilities are among the expenditure categories increased by commuters. These "overburdens" are exacerbated by the fact that many commuters to the city work in the central business district where, because of congestion, the costs of providing services are considerably higher.

Finally, we consider those costs borne by the city for services which are enjoyed not only by city residents but suburban residents as well—irrespective of whether the suburbanites work in the city or not. Included here are the costs of water supply and sewage disposal services rendered to suburban areas. Although the city, in recent years, has been reimbursed for such services, they nonetheless are included in the expenditure per capita differentials mentioned above, to the extent that payment is made directly to the city by suburban citizens, which is the case for the bulk of water and sewer services. Also in this category are the cultural and sports facilities subsidized to varying degrees by Baltimore City. The costs of operating such facilities are included in total in the expenditure figure for the city even though they are at least partially offset by charges to users; hence, they serve to widen the expenditure differential. The above does not exhaust the list of services rendered by the city to the suburbs. For example many of the services provided by the city to its own residents also benefit the suburbs. This is clearly the case of public health activity, police activities related to criminal cases, correctional institutions, and so forth. However, the same could be said for similar activities performed by suburban governments—namely, they benefit city residents as well. Whether or not such spillover benefits offset one another has not been determined here. However, studies of other areas suggest that although the suburbs are net beneficiaries, the net costs on the central city are small.[4]

4. *See for example,* William B. Neenan, Political Economy of Urban Areas, *Chicago, Markham, 1972.*

What is the effect of allowing for the above factors upon the city-suburban expenditure differential? Table 21 sets out a crude calcula-

Table 21.
ADJUSTMENTS TO CITY–SUBURBAN EXPENDITURE DIFFERENTIAL
(per capita, 1970)

1. Unadjusted differential			$265.00
2. Allowance for poverty			
Public assistance	$86.60		
Health	11.10		
Hospitals	24.50		
		$132.20	
3. Allowance for services rendered to commuters: 17.3 percent of safety, highway, and sanitation expenditures		23.10	
4. Allowance for SMSA services provided by city: 51.3 percent of recreation and public service enterprises		18.30	
5. Allowance for lower salaries 55 percent of $597.70 times 1.054		−17.70	
6. Total adjustments			$155.90
7. Adjusted differential			$109.10

tion. In making the adjustments we have tried to keep errors on the liberal side. This offsets somewhat the downward bias in our adjustments caused by ignoring net spillovers.

On line 1 of the table, we show the unadjusted per capita expenditure differential between Baltimore City and its suburbs—$265. On line 2 we adjust for the fact that the city has larger direct and indirect expenditures relating to poverty. These expenditures, measured as the differences in per capita spending for public assistance, health, and hospitals, reveal that 50 percent of the overall differential is due to poverty.

On line 3 of the table, we attempt to allow for the effects of commutation into the city. This is done by taking the proportion of the city's employment which is accounted for by commuters (net); this amounts to 17.3 percent of total employment. Hence 17.3 percent of all expenditures made by the city upon public safety, sanitation, and highways were assumed to be caused by the net inflow of workers into the city.

On line 4, we adjust for the services rendered to all SMSA citizens by the city. The share of such outlays attributable to suburban dwellers is assumed to be their share of the SMSA's population. The outlays thus shared are assumed to be those upon recreation (including libraries) and upon public service enterprises (including water supply, the stadium, and so forth).

Finally, we adjust for the fact that the city pays less for its workers than the suburbs. If the city were to have paid the same wages to its employees its total expenditure would have been $17.70 per capita greater than they actually were. This figure was arrived at by multiplying the ratio of suburban wages to city wages by the fraction of city expenditures for employees, and multiplying the result by total expenditure in the city.

The net result of these adjustments is to account for all but $109 of the expenditure differential. This residual amounts to nearly 40 percent of the suburban expenditure figure. An explanation for a differential of such a magnitude must come from elsewhere. Perhaps it is due to the greater demands placed upon the city government by its residents because of the different socioeconomic composition of its population. Since city residents are much poorer with respect to private goods and services, they may attempt to offset this by greater public expenditures. Other explanations suggest themselves, the most credible being that we have not adequately reflected the cost differentials associated with items 2 through 4 of Table 21. This may most clearly be the case with respect to public safety and its relation to poverty. Clearly the poor place a heavier burden upon fire protection services since their housing is relatively dense and old; the cost of fire protection will thus be correspondingly higher. Perhaps most significant is the fact that the crime rate in the city is nearly three times that of the suburbs. This explanation takes greater force when it is recognized that, apart from welfare, the most important source of expenditure differential is the public safety category—amounting to nearly $72 per person. Thus, the explanation of the $109 differential is likely to lie in this area.

Revenues

Since Baltimore City spends nearly twice as much per capita on current services as its suburbs, it follows that it must also obtain twice as much revenue. The interesting contrast is not with respect to revenue *levels* but rather to the *composition* of revenues. As observed earlier, in 1970 the city obtained 48.3 percent of its revenue from higher levels of government while the suburbs obtained only 28.3 percent of its revenue in this fashion. On the other hand, the city derived only 37 percent of its revenues from local taxes while the suburbs raised 60 percent of their revenues in this way.

Grants-in-Aid. A large share (65 percent) of aid to the city is in support of social welfare programs such as public assistance, health, and anti-poverty programs. Since the city has a disproportionate share of the area's poor, it follows that it will get a disproportionate share of the intergovernmental grants for programs designed to alleviate and eliminate poverty. Furthermore, the character of most aid programs in the social welfare area is to provide for some equalization, i.e., greater aid to poorer regions per case than in wealthier regions. This is particularly true of the grant formula for public assistance. The city receives a larger grant per welfare case than do the suburban governments. This owes to the effect of a provision of state law which restricts local contributions to 10 mills on the property tax rate. Baltimore City has long been at the maximum contribution and since its property tax base has been virtually stagnant, its marginal cost of welfare is zero. Thus the city's fiscal difficulties are not due to crippling expenses for public welfare as is often alleged, and which is often the case in other large metropolitan areas.

A second important source of intergovernmental aid to Baltimore City but not to the suburbs is police aid. In 1970, the city received nearly $18 million, or nearly $20 per capita, from the state for police protection. This must be offset to some extent by the fact that the suburbs received indirect aid from the state via protection rendered by the state police, which does not operate within the city. While it is not possible to ascertain the quantitative significance of such indirect aid, it is our judgment that it provides only a small offset to the direct aid given the city.

A third area where the city receives a disproportionate amount of intergovernmental aid is with respect to highways. The city receives 20 percent of the State Motor Vehicle Fund, while the suburbs share 20 percent with all of the other counties in the state in proportion to their share of highway mileage and vehicular registrations. The share allocated to the city under the present formula is much higher than would be obtained if it were treated in the same fashion as the suburbs. The result is that the city receives $38.50 per capita in highway aid while the suburbs receive $10.39 per capita. This discrepancy between city and suburban highway aid cannot be interpreted as representing more generous state funding of city highways, however. The city is not served by state-built nor state-maintained highways but is totally responsible for its highway system. The suburbs on the other hand enjoy state construction and maintenance of a large majority of the primary roads passing through them. Furthermore, as already noted, responsibility for policing state highways is shared by the state police, which does not patrol city streets. The issue of whether the additional direct state aid to the city provides an adequate offset to the services provided to the suburbs cannot be determined here. Suffice it to say for our purposes, however, that the greater per capita highway aid provided the city substantially overstates any advantage (if any) the city may enjoy relative to the suburbs.

The final important category of intergovernmental aid is grants for education. This is of overwhelming importance for the suburbs, amounting to 62 percent of all aid they receive. Even in the city, where other programs loom important, education aid amounts to 25 percent of all aid. In this area, the city fares somewhat better than the suburbs. In terms of aid from the state and federal governments combined, the city received $471 per pupil in 1971 while the suburbs received $343 per pupil. The breakdown of state and federal aid, shown in Table 22,

Table 22.
GRANTS FOR CURRENT EDUCATION EXPENSES,
BALTIMORE SMSA, 1971

	State	Federal	Total
Suburbs	$72,201,620	$13,358,463	$89,560,083
Baltimore City	67,312,878	19,773,492	87,086,370
Suburbs (per student)	291.42	51.08	342.50
Baltimore City (per student)	364.05	106.94	470.99

Source: State Department of Education

reveals that the city receives nearly twice as much federal aid as its suburbs. This is understandable since the federal money is focussed upon disadvantaged youth who for reasons already discussed are concentrated in the inner city. The difference in state aid per pupil is surprisingly small—only $73 per pupil, or less than 10 percent of the amount spent per pupil. This is surprising because the state ostensibly pursues an aggressive equalization program in education, with aid presumably distributed in an inverse relation to taxable wealth and income in the various subdivisions. However, the aid formula contains a minimum state grant per pupil which is independent of wealth or income. This effectively serves to wipe out the equalizing effect of the program.

Summing up, the picture portrayed by the aggregated data on intergovernmental grants is that the city enjoys a wide edge over its suburban communities with respect to this source. A conclusion one might draw from such data is that the higher levels of government are pursuing vigorously a program of equalization. Closer scrutiny of the data reveals, however, that much of the city's advantage is apparent rather than real. A major reason for larger grant flows into the city is the concentration of poverty in the city—giving rise to more welfare and welfare related grants. Another major source of discrepancy is due to the differences in the division of responsibility between locality and state as between the city and suburbs.

The preceding remarks notwithstanding, it is clear that the city's financial plight would have been much more severe had it not been for a rapid expansion of intergovernmental aid. In 1960, such revenues financed 30 percent of current expenditures; by 1970, the figure had risen to 48 percent. Such a rapid expansion cannot be explained by the growth of programs eligible for aid alone. In Baltimore City, those programs which tend to account for much of the grant revenue— education, public safety, health, and public welfare—increased as a share of total expenditure between 1960 and 1970 from 60.3 percent to 69.2 percent. If, in 1970, such expenditures had maintained their 1960 relationship to total expenditures, and grants had financed the same fraction of expenditure, grant revenue would have accounted for 30.3 percent of revenue increases (suburban revenue would have increased 30.5 percent on the same basis). However, because the share of such city expenditure programs advanced by 15 percent, we would have expected grant revenue to account for approximately 42.5 percent of all revenue increases (while suburban grant revenues would account for 31.5 percent of their total revenue increases). Since grants actually accounted for 59.2 percent of all city revenue increases, the balance must be due to greater participation of higher levels of governments in financing city programs. (In the suburbs intergovernmental grants accounted for only 27.9 percent of all revenue increases.) In other words 75 percent (42.5/52.9) of all of the city growth in grant revenue is attributable to the expansion of expenditures which are subject to aid, while 25 percent is due to a larger share of expenditure being borne by higher levels of government. If no increase in expenditures had occurred between 1960 and 1970, the intergovernmental grants in 1970 still would have risen by 16.7 percent for the city, but they would have fallen 3.6 percent for the suburbs.

Differences in Taxes. We turn next to differences in local taxes. Table 19 revealed that local taxes amounted to $214 per capita for Baltimore City and $194 per capita for the suburbs. It would appear that taxes in the city are only marginally higher (10 percent) than in the suburbs. Expressed as a fraction of income, however, the difference appears much greater; 6 percent in the city vs. 4.2 percent in the suburbs. Nevertheless, the narrow differential in per capita taxes is quite surprising given the wide difference in effective property tax rate between the two areas. While the property tax rate stood at 53 percent of the city level in the suburban jurisdictions, they were able to raise 90 percent as much revenue per capita. We shall explore this discrepancy in what follows.

The discrepancy between tax effort and tax yield is due to two main factors: first, the incomes of city residents are considerably lower than those of suburban residents, and second, the suburbs enjoy a wide advantage with respect to the amount of taxable commercial, industrial, and agricultural property contained within their boundaries. We shall treat these in turn. (See Table 23.)

The difference in per capita income influences local taxes directly via its impact upon personal income taxes and indirectly via its effect upon the amount of residential real property available for taxation. In 1969, city per capita income was 78 percent of that in the suburbs. In 1970, however, the city collected only 70 percent as much income tax per capita as the suburbs—$37 vs. $53. This discrepancy owes to the fact that the income tax is mildly progressive and because a larger fraction of income in the city derives from nontaxable transfer payments.

The gap in per capita income also contributes to a discrepancy in property tax collections, since a major determinant of a family's expenditure upon housing is its income. The median value of owner-occupied housing in 1970 was $10,000 in Baltimore compared with $16,000 for the suburbs. This, in turn, affects the amount of real estate taxes the family pays. In addition, the city, unlike its suburbs, has a great deal of substandard housing. While the rents on such units are comparable with rents in nonslum areas, property values are much lower. The result is that housing expenditure is not translated into taxable property value.[5] Thus, in 1970 the city showed *taxable* residential real estate (at market value) of $2,653 per capita while the corresponding figure for the suburbs was $4,487. At any given tax rate, therefore, the suburbs would raise nearly 70 percent more per capita in residential real estate taxes than the city.

Now consider nonresidential real and personal property. In 1970, the suburbs had $3,922 per capita of such property while the city had only $3,074. This is extremely surprising, given the fact that the com-

---

5. See Michael A. Stegman, Housing Investment in the Inner City: The Dynamics of Decline, Cambridge-MIT Press, 1972.

mercial heart of the region lies in Baltimore City. As recently as 1959 the city enjoyed an advantage in this area—$2,580 vs. $2,236. Thus, the advantage of the suburbs with respect to business property is quite recent in origin and has grown extremely rapidly during the sixties. (Why such a reversal occurred is the subject of much discussion and is beyond the scope of this study.)

The significance of nonresidential property taxes is that they cannot be assumed to bear only upon the residents of the jurisdiction in which the business is located. Rather they are shared by the residents of the entire region or are exported to residents outside of the region. In either event, tax receipts from such sources can be spent on local services along with the tax receipts from residential property. Thus, suburban governments can enjoy a given level of tax support with a lower tax rate than the city. This can be illustrated by assuming that the city and suburbs have the same amount of residential real estate per capita: $3,685, the average for the region as a whole. Then, if the city government wants to raise a given amount of revenue per capita, its tax rate must be one-eighth higher than that required for the suburbs. Since the city actually has a lower residential real estate value per capita than the suburbs, the combined differentials will tend to discourage the growth of the nonresidential tax base of the city.

The greater income base, the greater residential property tax base, and the greater nonresidential property tax base enjoyed by the suburbs join to produce considerably greater revenues for them from a given tax structure. For example, if the suburbs had adopted the same effective property tax rate in 1970 as the city, local taxes would have increased $112 per capita—an increase in excess of 50 percent. Furthermore, local taxes per capita in the suburbs would have been $102 higher than in the city. Put another way, in 1970 the suburbs needed to exert only two-thirds as much tax effort as the city in order to raise a comparable amount of local revenue per capita. However one looks at it, the city revenue system is considerably less productive than that of the suburbs, so the city, to achieve the same level of services, would have to impose much higher tax rates. The latter in turn leads to a flight to the suburbs, further weakening the city's fiscal disadvantage.

Additional important insights into the relative burden of taxes on the citizens of the city and suburbs are developed in Table 23. Recall, it is not correct to assume that business taxes rest only upon the residents of the community in which the business resides. To some extent these taxes are shifted to the consumers of the products produced by the business and to the workers employed by these businesses. To some extent they fall upon the owners of the business enterprise. Since shoppers, workers, and owners need not reside in the same jurisdiction as the business, it would be incorrect to impute the business taxes to the citizens of the taxing jurisdiction.

The importance of business taxes to the measurement of local tax burden is shown in item 3 of the table. If we ignore business taxes completely, taxes per capita are higher on suburbanites than in the city. Indeed, even as a fraction of income, city taxes are lower than the suburbs. Since this is completely opposite to the result if business taxes are counted in full, the importance of how the burden of business taxes are distributed is evident.

The question of business tax incidence cannot be dealt with here in detail. However, Table 23 shows the effect of assuming that suburban residents bear a portion of the city's business taxes, and vice versa. The remainder is assumed to fall upon the residents of the community in which the business resides. The result of this calculation, line 2, shows that suburban residents bear a greater absolute amount of local taxes than city residents. As line 4 shows, the fraction of income paid in local taxes is only slightly higher in the city than in the suburbs. Under this plausible set of assumptions, tax burdens are no higher on city residents than on suburban residents, due to the fact that the city derives a larger fraction of its tax revenues from the business community.

How can we square these remarks with our earlier conclusion that the city is at a considerable disadvantage with respect to the productivity of its revenue structure? The answer is that, although the city resident is not more heavily burdened by local taxes than his suburban counterpart, attempts on the part of the city to further raise its effective property rate is to make investment in new business and residential real property more attractive in the suburbs. What prevents the city from taxing more heavily is not the *level* of the burden on its citizens but its fear of losing its tax base. This suggests that the city, in seeking to increase revenues, should rely on nonproperty sources such as the income tax. It is small wonder, then, that the city immediately adopted the maximum piggy-back income tax rate when the option was introduced in 1967. Indeed, such considerations presumably underlie the city's interest in levying earnings taxes—which do not fall directly on real property.

Growth of local taxes. Since the city of Baltimore and its suburbs differ markedly with respect to the proportion of revenue growth accounted for by grants, it follows they must differ sharply with respect to their use of local taxes. Indeed, over the decade, local taxes per capita tripled in the suburbs while not even doubling in Baltimore City. What is of major interest, however, is that the suburbs were able to accomplish this by increasing their property tax rates only margin-

Table 23.
COMPARISON OF LOCAL TAXES PER CAPITA,
BALTIMORE CITY AND SUBURBS, 1970

	City	Suburbs	Difference [a]
1. Local taxes	$ 214.3	$ 194.3	$ 10.3
Property	162.3	126.0	36.3
Residential	75.2	67.2	8.0
Nonresidential	87.1	58.8	28.3
Income	37.2	53.4	**16.2**
Other	14.7	14.9	.2
2. Local taxes borne by			
residents: Assumption I*	$ 192.6	$ 240.6	$ **64.9**
Property	136.8	176.6	**39.8**
Residential	75.2	67.2	8.0
Nonresidential	66.2	75.1	**17.8**
Income	37.2	53.4	**16.2**
Other	14.7	14.9	.2
3. Local taxes borne by			
residents: Assumption II**	$ 126.4	$ 165.5	$ **39.1**
4. Local taxes borne by			
residents as a percent of			
income			
Assumption I	5.36%	5.19%	.17%
Assumption II	3.51%	3.57%	.06%
5. Personal income, per capita	$3,594	$4,631	**$1,037**
6. Taxable property per capita	$5,727.5	$8,408.6	**$2,683.1**
Residential	2,653.3	4,486.8	**1,833.5**
Nonresidential	3,074.2	3,921.9	847.7
7. Exempt property per capita	$ 759.6	$ 756.3	$ 3.3
Other than local government			
exempt property	385.1	537.0	**151.9**
8. Effective property tax rate	2.83%	1.50%	**1.33%**
9. Local taxes if both use city			
effective property tax rate	$ 214.3	$ 316.3	$ **102.0**
10. Local taxes if both use suburb			
effective property tax rate	$ 137.9	$ 194.3	$ **56.4**

* Assumption I: All industrial and utility taxes and one-half of commercial and agricultural taxes are shared by residents of the SMSA in proportion to their income.
** Assumption II: No business taxes are borne by the residents of the region.
a. Regular type, positive difference. **Bold type, negative difference.**

ally higher (40 percent vs. 34 percent) than Baltimore City. In this section we attempt to explain this interesting fact.

One of the major factors enabling the suburbs to keep their property tax growing at rates similar to that of the city was the introduction of the local income tax option in 1967. Since incomes in the suburbs are considerably higher than in the city, the suburbs were able to obtain more revenue per capita from this source.

Of greater importance, however, has been the relative performance of the assessable base in the two regions. In Baltimore City, the assessable base increased at an annual rate of 1.0 percent per year during the sixties. This is despite the fact that per capita income during the decade increased by more than 60 percent. This meant that virtually all of the increase in property taxes which occurred during the sixties was the result of *rate* increases as opposed to base increases. The suburbs, on the other hand, experienced base increases averaging 7.4 percent per year during the sixties. The growth in assessable base approximated the increase in personal income during the period, suggesting an income elasticity close to one. Since their tax rates increased at a rate of only 3.5 percent per year, nearly 75 percent of all of their property tax increases occurred as a result of the expansion in the taxable base.

We now examine the forces underlying the expansion of the property tax base in the two regions. This will provide greater understanding of the future prospects of the property tax as an adequate source of local revenue.

Changes in the assessable base can be broken down into three categories: 1) new improvements, 2) new business personal property and utility property, and 3) changing values of existing property. The first category includes newly constructed residential and business real property. The second category includes other taxable business assets. The final category includes the result of two opposing forces on existing real property: upward reassessments, and downward reassessments or removals from the tax rolls because of demolition or other causes. We shall refer to this third category as revaluation, for short.

In Table 24 we show the contribution of each of these factors during various subperiods of the 1959 to 1972 period to the growth of the assessable base. The table clearly brings out the difference in the growth of the overall tax base discussed above. It also shows that new improvements were much larger in absolute terms in the suburbs than in the city. This reflects the greater growth of population in the suburbs as well as its attraction of a greater share of new area business. However, the most striking feature of the table is the fact that revaluation is of negligible proportions in the city but has been re-

Table 24.

PERCENT CHANGES IN THE VALUE OF THE ASSESSABLE PROPERTY TAX BASE, 1959-1972

(Annual Rates of Change)

	Baltimore City				Suburbs			
	New Improvements	Personal Property	Revaluation	Total	New Improvements	Personal Property	Revaluation	Total
1959-64	1.2%	−.8%	.3%	.7%	4.4%	1.5%	1.5%	6.9%
1964-69	.6%	.8%	.1%	1.5%	4.5%	1.7%	3.2%	8.5%
1969-72	.5%	.4%	.1%	.9%	4.2%	1.8%	2.2%	9.3%

Note: Figures should not necessarily add to total because each growth rate was calculated independently.

sponsible for considerable growth in the suburbs. This suggests that property values in the suburbs have consistently been on the upswing while in the city they have remained stable. The lack of revaluation gains in the city means that as city costs rise, revenues from the property tax do not respond. The contrary is true for the suburbs, where in spite of evidence that reassessment occurs with a long lag, rising property values have provided a more than negligible source of property tax revenue increase.

Several important conclusions can be drawn from this discussion. First is that the relative lack of revenue growth in the city was due to a lack of property values in the city to keep pace with those in the suburbs. Usually, attention is confined to the new improvements category. The second conclusion is that the property tax base has shown considerable growth in the suburbs and may be an adequate source of growth of revenues in the future. However, the stagnant behavior of the city base suggests that the property tax is wholly unsuited to meet the rising costs of government. Some other revenue source, preferably one which reflects income growth, is in order. This follows from the fact that disparities in per capita income growth are much smaller than for per capita taxable property.

PROJECTIONS TO 1975

We turn now to short-term budgetary forecasts for local governments in the Baltimore region. Specifically, budget projections were prepared for Baltimore City and its suburbs for fiscal year 1975.

The projections are made under two diametrically opposite premises concerning the behavior of government expenditure. We feel that these hypotheses enclose the limits of what reasonably can be expected to happen by 1975. The first is that the quality of government services will remain at their 1972 level. Alternatively, we assume that the quality of services will continue to increase at the rate experienced between 1965 and 1970. We refer to these as "conservative" and "trend" projections, respectively.

The measurement of the "quality" of government services is fraught with difficulties. Lacking a better alternative, our procedure is to use measures of input as indices of the "quality" of government services. Thus, though we cannot measure the quality of education services, we can measure the degree to which resources are put to this use.

We recognize the dangers inherent in using cost as an index of government output. Clearly increases in cost can represent other phenomena—particularly inflation and waste. While we can adjust for inflationary forces we can make no allowance for waste. To the extent that the percentage of waste increases over time, our measure of the quality of government services will be upward biased. This caveat should be kept in mind when interpreting our results.

We should also like to stress that the estimates of local tax revenues are based upon the rate structure prevailing in 1972. Thus, whatever deficit is uncovered by our projections can conceivably be eliminated by an upward adjustment of local tax rates. With regard to revenues from higher levels of government, it is assumed that the degree of participation which prevailed in 1972 will be continued to 1975.

In order to make the projections, assumptions regarding the overall economic environment had to be made. Our procedure was to use projections of employment, real personal income, and population for the entire SMSA prepared by the National Planning Association. These totals were then broken down between the city and suburbs on the basis of the pattern observed during the sixties. Inflation was projected to occur at a 3.5 percent rate during the 1972-1975 period.

Projections for Baltimore City are shown in Table 25. A quick glance reveals that, under the conservative projection, expenditures outstrip revenues by over $36 million. Under the trend assumption the gap widens to $96 million. To erase these deficits would require property tax rate increases at 20 percent and 55 percent, respectively. At the 1972 nominal tax rate of $5.64 per $100 of assessed value, this implies tax rate increases of $1.12 and $3.10 respectively. Clearly the latter is well outside the realm of possibility, while the former would require an average annual increase of 37 cents—a change frequently experienced in recent years. Thus it would appear that the city, under present arrangements, could at best maintain the quality of its services. Turning to columns (4) through (6) we find 80 percent of all new revenues to come from higher governmental levels—largely in the form of higher grants for social welfare programs. This compares with 60 percent for the sixties. Major reductions in the share from property and income taxes are anticipated; this lies at the heart of the city's financial difficulties.

On the expenditure side we find nearly 80 percent of the change to occur in the areas of education, public safety and social welfare. This is a continuation of the pattern experienced in the sixties. The composition of this 80 percent varies according to the estimates— particularly with respect to public welfare and public safety. In both cases, education is projected to absorb a considerably smaller fraction than during the sixties, anticipating a slowdown in school enrollments because of recent demographic trends.

Summing up, the data in columns (4) through (6) show a dis-

Table 25.
REVENUE AND EXPENDITURE PROJECTIONS, BALTIMORE CITY

	Change in Level (thousands $)			Percent of Total Change			Annual Rate of Growth			Percent of Total Level		
	1970	Conservative 1970-1975	Trend 1970-1975	1960-1970	Conservative 1970-1975	Trend 1970-1975	1960-1970	Conservative 1970-1975	Trend 1970-1975	1970	Conservative 1975	Trend 1975
	1	2	3	4	5	6	7	8	9	10	11	12
Revenues:												
Taxes—Local	194,094	41,685	41,685	26.3	15.6	12.8	5.5	4.1	4.1	37.0	29.7	27.7
Property	147,016	27,154	27,154	15.0	10.1	8.3	4.0	3.5	3.5	28.0	22.0	20.5
Income	33,735	9,565	9,565	(11.3)	3.6	2.9	(15.7)	5.1	5.1	6.4	5.5	5.1
Other	13,343	4,966	4,966	-.3	1.9	1.5	4.0	6.5	6.5	2.6	2.3	2.1
Licenses and Permits	4,354	932	932	.4	.3	.3	-2.3	4.0	4.0	.8	.7	.6
Fines and Forfeitures	2,154	-497	-497	-.3	-.2	-.2	8.5	-5.4	-5.4	.4	.2	.2
Charges for Current Services	59,917	8,983	25,519	11.6	3.4	7.8	10.0	2.8	7.2	11.4	8.7	10.0
Use of Money and Property	6,691	2,414	3,780	1.8	.9	1.2	20.5	6.3	9.4	1.3	1.1	1.2
Own Revenue	267,210	53,517	71,419	39.7	20.0	21.9	6.6	3.7	4.9	50.9	40.4	39.7
Current Grants	209,441	206,120	246,320	54.1	77.0	75.6	19.5	14.5	16.5	39.9	52.4	53.6
State-shared Taxes	44,277	9,155	9,155	5.1	3.4	2.8	4.5	3.7	3.7	8.4	6.7	6.3
Revenue from Higher Governments	253,718	215,275	255,475	59.2	80.4	78.4	14.8	13.1	15.0	48.3	59.1	59.9
Other Revenue	4,106	-947	-947	1.1	-.4	-.3	21.2	-5.4	-5.4	.8	.4	.4
Revenues Available for Current Operations	525,034	267,845	325,947	100.0	100.0	100.0	9.8	7.5	9.0	100.0	100.0	100.0
Current Expenditure and Debt Service:												
General Government	28,225	15,215	30,419	5.6	5.0	7.2	10.5	9.0	13.0	5.4	5.2	6.2
Public Safety	90,396	31,413	77,091	18.1	10.3	18.3	10.5	6.2	13.1	17.2	14.7	17.7
Highways	14,485	5,231	7,340	1.9	1.7	1.7	5.5	6.3	8.5	2.8	2.4	2.3
Sanitation and Waste Removal	16,275	5,883	11,645	2.6	1.9	2.8	7.5	6.3	11.4	3.1	2.7	2.9
Health	15,757	20,015	20,015	3.8	6.6	4.7	15.5	17.8	17.8	3.0	4.3	3.8
Hospitals	22,464	12,591	20,653	4.5	4.1	4.9	10.5	9.4	14.0	4.3	4.2	4.6
Public Welfare	89,204	122,621	122,621	20.8	40.3	29.1	14.5	18.9	18.9	17.0	25.5	22.4
Correction	3,106	1,968	2,779	.6	.7	.7	9.0	8.5	13.5	.6	.6	.6
Schools	153,265	57,556	87,070	30.1	18.9	20.6	10.0	6.6	9.4	29.2	25.4	25.4
Recreation	18,758	7,655	15,052	3.4	2.5	3.6	9.0	7.1	12.5	3.6	3.2	3.6
Public Service Enterprises	13,744	640	4,092	2.2	.2	1.0	7.5	.9	4.3	2.6	1.7	1.9
Miscellaneous	21,348	8,964	8,964	1.6	3.0	2.1	2.8	7.3	7.3	4.1	3.7	3.2
Total Current Expense	487,028	289,951	407,740	95.1	95.3	96.6	10.0	9.8	13.0	92.8	93.7	94.5
Debt Service	38,014	14,354	14,354	4.9	4.7	3.4	5.5	6.7	6.7	7.2	6.3	5.5
Total	525,042	304,115	422,095	100.0	100.0	100.0	9.5	9.5	12.5	100.0	100.0	100.0

proportionate share of city revenues to come from higher levels of government, primarily in response to rising welfare demands. The deficit faced by the city is thus not directly attributable to rising welfare outlays, since such outlays bring their own revenues. The problem is the failure of the city's tax structure to provide even modest increase in tax revenue for maintaining the quality of existing services.

The latter point is clearly brought out in columns (7) through (9). The local revenue system is expected to provide revenue increases of only 4.1 percent per year just to maintain quality. Matters are even worse than the table indicates, since much of the additional revenues under the property tax are the result of rate increases *already* enacted. Beyond 1972, the property tax, at constant rates, will exhibit growth of less than 1 percent per year. Thus, the growth of city tax revenues will be so slow as to make difficult the task of maintaining the quality of government services, let alone continue to improve it.

The figures for the suburbs are presented in Table 26. A cursory inspection of the first three columns reveals the situation for the suburbs to be radically different than for the city. According to the projections, the suburbs will be able to enjoy the same quality of services in 1975 as in 1972 at *lower* property tax rates than prevailed in 1972. To a large measure, this owes to the responsiveness of the suburban property tax base to changes in income and population. The suburbs could enjoy a property tax rate reduction in excess of 11 percent if they chose to adopt the conservative strategy. If, on the other hand, they choose the trend strategy, revenue increase at existing rates will fall marginally short (5 percent) of requirements for budgetary balance. This would require a property tax increase of slightly more than 6 percent over present levels—a figure well within the reach of the suburban governments.

An examination of the composition of budgetary growth in the suburbs also reveals considerable differences from the city. School expenditure increases are far and away the dominant force in expenditure growth in the suburbs with no other category, save public safety, worthy of note. With the exception of education, budgetary growth is relatively uniform across expenditure categories. In the city, social welfare and public safety were of disproportionate magnitude. On the revenue side, it is seen that, with unchanged rates, local taxes will provide approximately the same share of additional revenue as they did during the sixties. Only 30 percent of added revenue is projected to come from higher governmental levels.

Moving to an examination of growth rates, we find the relative ranking of expenditure categories to differ according to the underlying premise concerning quality improvement. In general, the trend esti-

Table 26.
REVENUE AND EXPENDITURE PROJECTIONS, REST OF SMSA (Excluding Baltimore City)

	Change in Level			Percent of Total Change			Annual Rate of Growth			Percent of Total Level		
	1970	Conservative 1970-1975	Trend 1970-1975	1960-1970	Conservative 1970-1975	Trend 1970-1975	1960-1970	Conservative 1970-1975	Trend 1970-1975	1970	Conservative 1975	Trend 1975
	1	2	3	4	5	6	7	8	9	10	11	12
Revenues:												
Taxes—Local	226,398	148,808	148,808	61.0	61.0	56.4	14.5	10.6	10.6	59.7	60.2	58.4
Property	146,815	90,256	90,256	33.8	37.0	34.2	10.4	10.1	10.1	38.7	38.1	36.9
Income	62,216	41,209	41,209	(27.2)	16.9	15.6	(68.5)	10.7	10.7	16.4	16.6	16.1
Other	17,367	17,343	17,343	-.1	7.1	6.6	-.4	14.9	14.9	4.6	5.6	5.4
Licenses and Permits	3,968	2,134	2,134	.2	.9	.8	9.0	9.0	9.0	1.0	1.0	.9
Fines and Forfeitures	964	-487	-487		-.2	-.2		-15.0	-15.0	.3	.1	.1
Charges for Current Services	30,038	15,925	25,762	8.1	6.5	9.8	14.5	8.9	13.2	7.9	7.4	8.7
Use of Money and Property	9,329	2,528	3,749	2.8	1.0	1.4	20.5	4.9	7.0	2.5	1.9	2.0
Own Revenue	270,697	168,908	179,966	72.1	69.3	68.2	14.1	10.2	10.7	71.4	70.6	70.1
Current Grants	85,800	70,236	79,072	23.6	28.8	30.0	15.2	12.7	14.0	22.6	25.1	25.7
State-shared Taxes	22,473	4,734	4,734	4.3	1.9	1.8	7.7	3.9	3.9	5.9	4.4	4.2
Revenue from Higher Governments	108,273	74,970	83,806	27.9	30.7	31.8	13.1	11.1	12.1	28.6	29.5	29.9
Other Revenue	1717	0	0	.0	.0	.0	-9.1	.0	.0	.0	.0	.0
Revenues Available for Current Operations	378,987	243,878	263,772	100.0	100.0	100.0	13.8	10.4	11.1	100.0	100.1	100.0
Grants Available for Capital Outlays	29,164						15.9	n.a.				
TOTAL REVENUE	408,151						14.6	n.a.				
Current Expenditure and Debt Service:												
General Government	16,285	9,346	17,471	4.6	4.1	6.0	14.5	9.5	15.0	4.4	4.3	5.1
Public Safety	31,564	18,911	35,266	8.9	8.3	12.1	14.5	10.0	16.0	8.6	8.5	10.2
Highways	13,984	8,365	8,365	3.0	3.7	2.9	8.5	10.0	10.0	3.8	3.8	3.4
Sanitation and Waste Removal	10,230	10,304	13,405	2.6	4.5	4.6	11.0	15.0	18.2	2.8	3.4	3.6
Health	7,312	6,504	10,193	2.2	2.8	3.5	16.0	13.5	19.0	2.0	2.3	2.7
Hospitals	375	170	170	.0	.1	.1	-.3	2.8	2.8	.1	.1	.1
Public Welfare	13,855	19,201	19,201	4.0	8.4	6.6	15.0	19.0	19.0	3.8	5.5	5.0
Correction	855	187	187	.2	.1	.1	7.0	4.0	4.0	.2	.2	.2
Schools	195,865	126,457	148,053	54.1	55.2	50.9	13.5	10.5	12.0	53.4	54.1	52.3
Recreation	8,587	5,087	10,980	2.7	2.2	3.8	20.0	9.8	18.0	2.3	2.3	3.0
Public Service Enterprises	5,747	6,859	9,557	2.0	3.0	3.3	27.0	17.0	21.0	1.6	2.1	2.3
Miscellaneous	12,489	795	795	3.9	.4	.3	19.5	2.0	2.0	3.4	2.2	2.0
Total Current Expense	317,148	212,176	273,633	88.3	92.6	94.1	13.5	11.0	13.3	86.5	88.8	89.9
Debt Service	49,497	17,028	17,028	11.7	7.4	5.9	10.0	6.0	6.0	13.5	11.2	10.1
TOTAL	366,645	229,204	290,661	100.0	100.0	100.0	13.0	10.0	12.5	100.0	100.0	100.0

n.a.—Not available

mates are much more similar to the experience of the sixties, both in terms of magnitudes and in terms of relative importance. This suggests that improvement in quality was very important in the sixties.

POSSIBLE SOLUTIONS

We consider now the impact upon our projections of certain changes in institutional arrangements which have occured or might take place before 1975. We shall consider three alternatives: federal revenue sharing, expansion of the local income tax, and state assumption of the costs of education.

Federal Revenue Sharing

When the projections were made in 1972, the passage and the nature of the program were in doubt. However by 1973 we had relatively precise estimates of the annual distribution of funds under the newly enacted general revenue sharing program: Baltimore City—$26.3 million; suburbs—$21.1 million for fiscal year 1975. This narrow differential is surprising since the allocation formula for local communities contains a tax effort parameter. However, there is also a ceiling which limits the per capita amount any locality can get to 150 percent of the statewide average. This ceiling cost Baltimore City nearly $14 million. Since the suburbs share in this amount, the impact on the differential is greater still, perhaps as much as $17 million.

Revenue sharing funds would enable Baltimore City to finance a constant quality (conservative) program with only a modest increase in tax rates. However, they would make only a small dent in the deficit created by the projected trend program. The suburbs, on the other hand, would be able to carry out their trend program without any increase, on average, in the local property tax rate, and if they chose the constant quality strategy, the entire amount could be used to reduce taxes.

However the city and suburbs choose to spend revenue sharing funds, it is clear that the program will make little inroads in the projected growth of tax or expenditure disparities. A differential relief of only $5.2 million is simply too small. Indeed, it is possible that no differential relief whatever will be forthcoming. Recall that the projections were made under the assumption that the federal government would continue to participate in local funding at present levels. To the extent that revenue sharing is used as a substitute for existing aid programs, the apparent revenue sharing differential in favor of the city may be purely illusory.

Expanding the Piggyback Option

This reform to permit greater use of the state income tax mechanism has been widely advocated by local government officials in Maryland. Besides providing additional revenue, it provides greater built-in growth than the property tax, particularly in Baltimore City. If the piggyback option were raised to 100 percent from its present ceiling of 50 percent, Baltimore City would enjoy additional revenues of $43 million while the suburbs would obtain $103 million extra. Since the suburbs do not require more than $15 million to close the revenue gap even under the trend assumption, it is doubtful that they will make immediate use of all of their new revenue potential. Nevertheless, local suburban government officials have expressed a desire for a higher piggyback tax. Thus, it is likely that it will be used to some extent—likely as a replacement for the property tax.

The additional revenue to Baltimore City will enable it to sustain, and even to improve somewhat, the quality of their services. However, they will be constrained from making greater use of the property tax if suburban governments lower their rates as suggested above. The city will feel tremendous competitive pressure to keep its property tax rate low. Thus, as with revenue sharing, an expenditure quality gap will likely emerge even if local income taxes are expanded. The main benefit to the city will be that its revenues will exhibit much greater built-in growth than with the present tax structure.

State Assumption of the Cost of Education

This program is often advanced as providing the greatest relief of fiscal disparities within large SMSAs. As we shall demonstrate, this is not the case. Under present arrangements the suburbs stand to gain much more through state finance of education.

We are able to offer only crude quantitative estimates of the impact of full state assumption of education costs. In 1975 we estimate that the city would spend $210.8 million on education under the conservative premise and $240.3 million under the trend premise. Not all of this would be saved by the city since they would lose aid to education on the revenue side. These amount to roughly $100 million and $113 million for the two premises, respectively. Thus the gross saving to the city would be from $110 million to $127 million. The corresponding figures for the suburbs are $215 million and $230 million respectively. Thus, the savings to the suburbs are nearly double those of the city. This is the result of two considerations: enrollments will continue to grow in the suburbs, while exhibiting a decline in the city; and the city currently enjoys in excess of 35 percent more state aid per pupil than the suburbs.

Changes of the above magnitude would enable both governments to maintain their trend variant expenditure programs. In addition, the city would be able to afford a small property tax decrease while the suburbs would be able to virtually eliminate the property tax. This suggests that the city would be forced to lower its property tax rates in order to remain competitive. Hence it would still not be fully able to maintain its trend variant program. The basic fact is that the *differential* between city and suburban property tax rates must be reckoned with. The proposed program, which saves the suburbs much more than the city, simply does not move in that direction. Hence, its effectiveness as a solution to local fiscal disparities is brought seriously into question. What is needed is some reform which provides *differential* relief to the city.

10
RATIONALIZING THE ASSESSMENT PROCESS

by Richard R. Almy

Criticism of property tax administration and calls for its reform have become a familiar litany. Interestingly, about two-thirds of the early respondents to a recent survey of the members of the International Association of Assessing Officers have agreed with their critics and have characterized the overall quality of assessment administration as either "relatively poor" or "very poor."[1] In view of the apparent unanimity of informed opinion regarding the need and opportunities for improving the assessment process, one might well ask why the efforts at reform have so far been ineffectual.

IMPEDIMENTS TO ASSESSMENT REFORM

Perhaps the greatest obstacle to assessment reform is the complexity and nebulousness of the property tax itself. In the United States, "the" property tax is comprised of fifty-one separate state-level property tax systems, each subject to numerous legal and extra-legal local variations and each changing in some fashion over time—through constitutional revision, enactment of statutes and ordinances, changes in administrative procedures, court decisions and changes in the capabilities of tax administrators. This phenomenon creates a problem for the serious and irresponsible critic alike—it is humanly impossible to comprehend all the variations in law, economic impact and assessment practices that do exist, much less keep up with the changes.[2] One is then forced to speak of assessment administration in terms of one's own experience and perspective. As a result of this,

RICHARD R. ALMY is Director, Research and Technical Services, International Association of Assessing Officers. (The views expressed are not necessarily those of the IAAO.)

1. *International Association of Assessing Officers, Research and Technical Service Department, "Questionnaire on Assessment Reform," IAAO Newsletter, April 1973, Supplement.*

2. *Compare, for example, two contemporary surveys of property tax administration: United States Senate, Committee on Government Operations, Subcommittee on Intergovernmental Relations, Status of Property Tax Administration in the States, Washington, D.C., Government Printing Office, 1973, and Alan C. Stauffer, Property Assessment and Exemptions: They Need Reform, Denver, Education Commission of the States, 1973.*

many generalizations and oversimplifications concerning assessment administration are found which, in the final analysis, may not be harmful but certainly contribute little to a better understanding of the assessment process. Equally troublesome is the tendency to recommend a particular solution or course of action as a panacea for all because it has proven satisfactory in a given jurisdiction or state—a "what's good for GM is good for the country" line of reasoning. Obviously, the import of what one person says can be lost on another whose experiences are quite different, but, as Rackham has observed, a sharing of views is a starting point for property tax reform.[3]

The rhetoric of property tax reform itself appears to be counterproductive. It is almost *de rigeur* for candidates for local public office and the popular press to list the alleged evils of the property tax, to invoke the "taxpayers' revolt," and to characterize assessment personnel in such terms as "ill-trained, poorly paid political creatures"[4] who operate in a "wasteland of ignorance and incompetence."[5] One assessor expressed his feelings about this in the following manner:

> I would lambaste every mayor, manager and city councilman with enough of the straight dope on proper assessment procedure so that they would be able to at least assume an intelligent look when confronted by the assessor and his problems.[6]

Another significant barrier to assessment reform, which John Shannon has ably described, is the pervasive pattern of misdirected political responsibility inherent in underassessment.[7] By the simple expedient of selective underassessment, an assessor can gain considerable, though extra-legal, influence over local public finance decision making.

The other side of this coin is that most of the 70,000 taxing jurisdictions have avoided responsibility for the performance of the 14,000 local assessment jurisdictions. One wonders whether a more direct involvement by taxing jurisdictions in the assessment process might not help alleviate this problem. In Iowa, for example, county

3. John B. Rackham, "Aspects of Property Taxation," Assessors Journal, Vol. 7, July 1972, p. 15.

4. "Trying to Change an Unfair Tax," Time, May 3, 1971, p. 81.

5. Mary Rawson, "The TRED-Mill Does It Again," Land and Liberty, Vol. 78, March-April, 1971, p. 36.

6. Alfred G. Drew, Assessing Officer, Barrington, Rhode Island, in a letter to IAAO dated May 8, 1973.

7. John Shannon, "Conflict Between State Assessment Law and Local Assessment Practice," in Richward W. Lindholm, Ed., Property Taxation—USA, Madison, University of Wisconsin Press, 1967, pp. 49-53.

assessors and their deputies are appointed by "conference boards" from lists of candidates certified by the Iowa Department of Revenue. County conference boards are composed of the mayors of all incorporated cities and towns in the county whose property is assessed by the county assessor, members of the county boards of education, and members of the board of supervisors. Similarly, cities over 10,000 population may appoint a city assessor who is appointed by a city conference board which is comprised of the city council, the school board, and the county board of supervisors. Oklahoma adopted a similar strategy in its recent statewide revaluation program whereby all taxing districts were required to share in the costs of the revaluation.[8]

The taxpaying public seems to share local government officials' apathy regarding assessment reform. Doubtless this is caused in part by a misunderstanding of the role of assessment personnel in the property tax system. To a taxpayer, an assessor's protestations that he is merely a valuer and that councilmen, commissioners, and board members are responsible for property taxes appear abstract—practical experience suggests that as assessments increase, taxes increase. Likewise most taxpayers are apt to equate assessment reform with revaluation which, in turn, is equated with higher taxes. The assessor is also the most accessible element of the property tax system. In the assessment appeal process a taxpayer has an opportunity to establish a one-to-one relationship with the system, and an individual effort can alter a taxpayer's tax bill. It must be remembered that in virtually all cases an assessment appeal is motivated by a desire to reduce one's tax burden, and the quality of an assessment vis-à-vis all other assessments is often of only incidental concern. In an analysis of over 2,000 residential property tax appeals in Detroit, for example, fully 40 percent of the complaints did not mention valuation factors.[9] Moreover,

---

8. Section 2481.4 of the 1969 Oklahoma Revaluation Act provides: The cost of the comprehensive program of revaluation shall be paid by those who receive the revenues of the mill rates levied on the property of the county in the following manner: The county assessor shall prepare a special budget for such comprehensive program of revaluation and file the same with the county equalization and excise board. That board shall apportion such cost among the various recipients of revenues from the mill rates levied, including the county, all cities and towns, all school districts, and all sinking funds of such recipients, in the ratio which each recipient's total tax proceeds collected from its mill rates levied for the preceding year bears to the total tax proceeds of all recipients from all their mill rates levied for the preceding year. Such amounts shall be included in or added to the budgets of each such recipient; including sinking funds, and the mill rates to be established by the board for each such recipient for the current year shall include and be based upon such amounts. Then the board and each such recipient shall appropriate the said amounts to the county assessor for expenditure for the comprehensive program of revaluation.

9. Detroit Board of Assessors, Research Division, "Summary of 1968 Assessor's Review of Residential Appeals," Detroit, 1968, p. 1.

many of the "high tax" appeals were from areas with low effective tax rates while few appeals were received from areas with high effective tax rates. Regrettably, many assessment appeal systems operate in a similarly arbitrary fashion and do not necessarily protect the legitimate interests of either taxpayers or the community as a whole.

Perhaps because of all of the problems described here, government policymakers appear to view assessment administration as a necessary evil—making it easy to allocate scarce government funds elsewhere. In any case, assessment administrators generally suffer from a shortage of both personnel and material resources. A 1971 study of 246 assessment jurisdictions disclosed that assessment expenditures averaged 0.88 percent of property tax revenues with the greatest concentration of administrative cost rates falling between 0.60 and 0.79 percent.[10] Only 24 percent of those jurisdictions studied spent more than the 1 to 1.5 percent of revenues that has been suggested as a reasonable range of expenditure for assessment administration, and in a number of those the cost of collection is included. By comparison, the cost of administering sales taxes averaged 0.98 percent in 1969-70.[11] Relating assessment expenditures to population and real property parcels also produces some interesting units of comparison. For the population groups in the study cited above, median assessment expenditures ranged between $1.03 and $2.33 per capita, while median per parcel expenditures ranged between $2.38 and $6.13. When one considers that residential appraisals for other purposes are usually in the $50 to $150 range, the statement by property tax experts that "making assessment administration good should cost less than the tax loss from doing the job too cheap" makes sense.[12]

In the face of the many conflicting and contradictory political pressures, apathy, and antipathy, an assessment administrator is apt to adopt a somewhat narrow and defensive posture: that of being merely an appraiser. The trouble with this posture is that an assessment appraiser, no matter how well qualified he may be, is usually regarded as somehow inferior to a fee appraiser—despite the fact that there is virtually no evidence to suggest that an expert fee appraiser could satisfactorily perform the assessment function.[13] Happily, there is an

---

10. International Association of Assessing Officers, Research and Technical Services Department, "Report on Assessment Expenditures, 1971," Chicago, 1972 (unpublished).

11. John F. Due, State and Local Sales Taxation, Chicago, Public Administration Service, 1971, p. 311.

12. "Better Assessments for Better Cities," Nation's Cities, May 1970, p. 24.

13. "Professional" appraisers themselves recently had to respond to questions of their allegedly inadequate performance. See American Institute of Real Estate Appraisers, Divergencies in Right-of-Way Valuations, National Cooperative Highway Research Program No. 126, Washington, D.C., Highway Research Board, 1972.

emerging breed of professional assessment administrators who have developed a sense of identity of their own.[14] As expressed by Rackham, even these, however, tend to view their role within the property tax system in relatively restricted terms:

> To him, the tax is static and single-dimensioned. He simply has to be a legalist. If the fundamental and statutory law covering the subject sets down the requirement that all individual properties should, for assessment purposes, be valued uniformly, he will strike his goal as program development and execution enabling the discovery of the current market value of every property represented on the assessment roll. That is a tall order and he knows it. It will require lots of competent, well paid help; so he will be trying to get more staff and higher salaries. In larger jurisdictions, it will require the application of computer technology; so he will be after increased data processing capacity and some complex and expensive computer programs.[15]

Such a position, however, does not come to terms with what might be called the political realities of property taxation. Shannon was grappling with this problem when he said:

> Those political barriers [to full value assessment], in turn, raise serious doubts concerning the basic theoretical premise underpinning full-value assessment laws—that the assessment process in all its aspects is simply a ministerial or technical task of market value estimation which can be divorced completely from the policy function of tax-load determination.[16]

BROADER ASSESSOR ROLE: CUSTODIAN OF PROPERTY INFORMATION SYSTEM

Without suggesting that the assessment function includes a policy making role in public finance or that it should serve as a check on the duly constituted policy makers, it seems that the assessment function has been viewed in too narrow a context. Attention has been

---

14. See, for example, Camille R. Godin, "The Municipal Assessor 'Evaluator' of the Future," trans. by H. L. Daudet, Appraisal Institute Magazine, Vol. 12, Fall 1968, pp. 27-31.

15. John B. Rackham, "Aspects of Property Taxation," op. cit. (note 4), p. 4.

16. John Shannon, "Conflict Between State Assessment Law and Local Assessment Practice," op. cit. (note 7), p. 49.

focused on the failures of the appraisal or valuation aspect of the assessment process, and there has been a tendency to overlook the two other major activities traditionally considered a part of the assessment process: discovery and listing. When the byproducts of the entire assessment process (e.g., cadastral maps, an inventory of structures and land improvements, sales lists, investment property rental and expense experience reports, and land development and building construction activity records) are taken into account, a different picture of the assessment process and of the possibilities for improving it begins to emerge. The information compiled in the assessment process, provided that it is accurate and accessible, would be of considerable usefulness to a wide variety of nonassessment users. In essence, the assessor could be viewed as the custodian of a land or property information system.

If the assessment process could be restructured to serve this larger information function, a number of benefits would accrue:

Accurate Property Valuations as Key to Taxpayer Confidence

Taxpayer confidence in assessment administration could be restored if they were provided with reasonably accurate estimates of their property values, together with the information necessary to compare their assessments with others similarly situated. This information would be useful not only in insuring that a person's property tax burden is equitable but also in real estate transactions and decision making where it would not be feasible to engage a fee appraiser.

Assessment Efficiency

Efficiency of assessment operations could be enhanced if valuation information were aggregated and analyzed by neighborhood, land use category, type of construction, age of improvements, etc., to refine the assessment product and to assign priorities to revaluation efforts. This would increase the cost-effectiveness of mass appraisal programs. Through statistical techniques such as assessment ratio and multiple regression analysis, greater use could be made of market data.

Tax Base Data to Aid Political Policy Makers

The major cause of the political impediments to assessment reform probably has been the absence of accurate information on the real potential of the tax base and an analysis of the economic consequences of fully utilizing the tax base. With valuation information aggregated at the taxing jurisdiction level, tax policy makers would have an opportunity to employ more facts and would be able to rely less on intuition.

Assessing would remain ministerial in nature. As implementers of tax policy and suppliers of information, assessment administrators could also be asked to supply advice as to the consequences of a particular proposed tax policy, but they would not be in a position to make a policy decision.

Harmonizing Planning with Property Value Patterns

Overall efficiency of local governmental operations could be enhanced if planners and various other governmental service agencies would make use of information compiled by assessors. Duplications of effort could be avoided. A notable example of this is the Urban Development Information System (UDIS) in Fairfax County, Virginia.[17] UDIS is designed to enable public officials, private developers, and others to monitor the urban growth process and facilitate the decision-making process as it relates to land use and urban planning. One report on UDIS contained the following conclusion:

> The Urban Development Information System in Fairfax County has assisted citizens and elected and appointed officials in solving many pressing problems. Most significant, the residents of Fairfax County and their elected county supervisors have had an opportunity to participate in the planning process of their county. At relatively small costs, the citizens have access to information that was once regarded as "secret." In Fairfax County, growth now occurs where public policy suggests, not merely where economics or real estate development is expedient.[18]

With the development of a General Urban Model (GUM), an even greater integration of assessment and planning processes has been envisioned.[19] With a GUM, land values could be generated which would be in harmony with planning objectives.

Serving State, National, and Private Sector Needs

If information systems were compatible, and they presumably would be within states at least, state and national government information needs could be met. At this level of aggregation of data,

17. J. L. Hysom, Jr., et al, Urban Development Information System, *Springfield, Virginia, National Technical Information Service,* 1972.

18. International City Management Association, "Computerized Urban Development Information System," Urban Data Service, September 1972, **p. 11.**

19. Theodore Reynolds Smith, "Physical Land Use Planning and Real Property Taxation" (paper presented at the 28th Congress of the International Institute of Public Finance, New York, September 14, 1972), pp. 27-29.

additional information on statutory provisions and administrative practices would also be extremely helpful.

Private sector needs also could be met. Former Orange County Assessor (now U.S. Representative) Andrew Hinshaw has observed that the amount of information available only through the assessor's office has not been generally recognized, and much of it is potentially quite valuable to the business community.[20] Hinshaw suggested that this information be compiled by the state assessment supervisory agency for dissemination and that once the state, and even the federal government, recognized the value of the information there would be a greater emphasis to upgrade the quality of the data, thereby upgrading the quality of the assessor's function. Thus far, there is little evidence of the demand for such information apart from the sale of cadastral maps. Hawaii, Maryland, and Tennessee offer prints of maps for sale at nominal prices and annual sales in those states have ranged between $10,000 and $60,000.[21]

To summarize, if the product of the assessment process can be regarded as something more than the basis for the determination of property tax liabilities, then it seems plausible that a strategy for assessment reform can be evolved that is more palatable and powerful than the traditional tax equity arguments. If the assessment process were to be upgraded so that it could consistently produce accurate market value appraisals, rational policies could be evolved to alter property tax burdens so that they are consistent with economic policy objectives, and at the same time the valuation information generated by the process could be utilized in other areas, thereby reducing the net cost of the assessment process.

THE ASSESSMENT PROCESS REFORMED

What would such an assessment process consist of? Regrettably, the most persistently ignored area of property tax administration has been the assessment process itself, and there are no specific models that can be recommended. Nonetheless, our knowledge of what appears to be the best of existing practices suggests the general direction:

Cadastral Maps

Accurate tax maps with land parcels drawn to scale are generally

20. *"Assessment Officials Discuss Current Topics at Chicago Forum,"* IAAO Newsletter Supplement, June 1971, p. 4.

21. *International Association of Assessing Officers, Research and Technical Services Department, "Assessment Mapping and Parcel Identification Systems" (resource paper prepared for the Texas Legislative Property Tax Committee, February 15, 1973), pp. 38-39.*

recognized as a first requirement of a good assessment system.[22] Despite their critical importance to assessment work and their numerous applications in nonassessment work, it is generally believed that large areas of the nation are either unmapped or represented by existing maps that are inadequate because they were drawn inaccurately or have not been maintained. With the continuing refinement of photogrammetric techniques, maps of acceptable quality should be within the reach of all state and local governments, with costs falling in the general range of $5 to $25 per parcel.

Parcel Identification Systems

Parcel identification systems are normally developed concurrently with mapping operations and are the procedures whereby legal descriptions are reduced to a uniform and manageable numerical expression. These codes have been used chiefly in the assessment process to facilitate records management and, to a lesser degree, to organize field operations. Within the assessment field, however, there is a growing awareness of the potentialities of geocode identifiers in the valuation process, and geocode identifiers are recognized as having significant advantages in planning and other nonassessment information systems.[23] Geocode identifiers can be assigned to parcels quite economically if maps are referenced to, or can be referenced to, a coordinate system such as State Plane Coordinate (SPC) or Universal Transverse Mercator (UTM).

Parcel Information Files

Parcel information has traditionally been recorded on "parcel record cards." Although it may be useful to retain such "hard copy," increasingly greater portions of parcel files will be computerized. Implicit in the use of computers is greater regimentation—accordingly, uniform or compatible coding procedures will have to be devised, procedural manuals developed, personnel trained, and edit procedures devised. Field survey procedures will be more rigorous also, and personnel will not be able to exercise as much independent thinking.

Data Processing

Widespread use of automated data processing will be a characteristic of the modern assessment procedures discussed here. This anticipated usage has implications for assessment organization. In

22. A somewhat more detailed discussion of mapping standards can be found in "Assessment Mapping and Parcel Identification Systems," pp. 10-13.

23. See D. David Moyer and Kenneth P. Fisher, Land Parcel Identifiers for Information Systems, Chicago, American Bar Foundation, 1973.

some areas there will be an increased trend towards the consolidation of assessment districts and joint service contracts. More states will also provide central or regional computation centers with terminals in local assessment jurisdictions.

Building Permit Reporting Systems

The use of building permit data is recognized as very important in alerting assessment administrators to potential construction and demolition activities. Receipt of copies of building permits is essential to the efficient maintenance of parcel files.

Real Property Transfer Taxes

Inasmuch as market value is likely to remain the valuation standard, it is essential that assessors have access to accurate information on property transfers. Each state should enact a real property transfer tax act which includes a provision for the automatic transmittal to the assessor of a copy of each property transfer instrument on which the full amount of the consideration is recorded or an affidavit containing the same information.

Refined Valuation Procedures

Mass appraisal procedures should make maximum use of the available market data and be flexible and responsive to rapid changes in market value. In general this will require a greater usage of such statistical techniques as multiple regression analysis. Greater attention should also be paid to the appraisal of unique industrial and commercial properties.

Audit, Evaluation, and Control Procedures

At the present time the techniques for gauging assessment performance leave much to be desired, and research will have to be undertaken before specific standards can be set forth. Nevertheless, workable techniques for objectively assessing the assessment process are essential. Similarly, assessors need control procedures to insure that assessment policies are being adhered to by the assessment staff.

Clearly, an additional investment in the assessment process will be required to bring about the programs discussed here. Moreover, serious attention should be given to the education and training of assessment administrators. Although graduation from college is a requirement for many assessment positions, most assessment administrators receive their formal training in the field from schools conducted by appraisal organizations and state property tax supervisory agencies. This instruction has been quite uneven and, insofar as appraisal techniques are concerned, oriented towards individual rather than mass appraisal practices. It is only within the last two or three years that the International Association of Assessing Officers has been able to develop courses relevant to the assessment process. Assessment administrators have had to develop their assessing skills in a heuristic manner. At the present time college-level education in real estate appraisal is relegated to the real estate departments of business schools and a few junior colleges, and as long as this situation persists it is unlikely that courses will be developed to produce professional assessment administrators. Hopefully, schools of public administration will take up the challenge.

The role of mass appraisal contractors in the assessment process may also change. In a number of states, notably Ohio, these firms have been relied on extensively to perform the assessment function, and in other states they have had a key role in "one-shot" statewide revaluation programs. Although some students of the property tax, and particularly Frederick Stocker of Ohio State University, have wondered aloud whether the performance of the assessment function is necessarily a function that should be performed by government assessment administrators, the prevailing belief appears to be that mass appraisal firms should have a relatively limited role in property tax administration. From a public relations point of view, the industry is currently in a low period as many criticisms are being made of it,[24] including the possibility of conflict of interest for firms which simultaneously represent private industrial clients in a city, and carry out assessments of these firms' properties on behalf of the city. Despite the ballyhoo of computerized appraisal systems, the appraisal industry seems to have been extremely cautious in adopting statistically oriented appraisal techniques and is often careless in the collection of appraisal data. It is in this latter area where there is the greatest cause for concern as data collection would appear to be a suitable activity to be performed by a private service industry.

FEDERAL INVOLVEMENT IN ASSESSMENT REFORM

The Property Tax Relief and Reform Act of 1973, known as S. 1255, was introduced in the United States Senate by Senators Percy and Muskie. In its initial form this bill would authorize approximately $1.2 billion per year in federal property tax relief for low-income individuals to states with a qualifying property tax relief pro-

24. For a sampling of such criticism and the industry's reply to it, see the testimony given by Albert Gore, Jr., Clifford Allen, and William L. Gunlock before the Senate Subcommittee on Intergovernmental Relations of the U.S. Senate Committee on Government Operations, May 3, 1973.

gram and an average of $20 million per year for three years in grants for property tax appeal reforms. In addition, interest-free loans would be available to accomplish more general assessment reforms. After three years, the property tax relief grants would be contingent upon the states' undertaking programs to accomplish assessment reforms.

The assessment field is clearly ambivalent about the proposed legislation.[25] The major issues appear to be: 1) Is there a legitimate federal role in what is generally regarded as a state-local matter? 2) Should assessment reform measures be tied to property tax relief? 3) And are the technical features of the proposed legislation relating to assessment ratio studies and assessment appeals feasible? The attitudes of assessment administrators are also interesting. State-level assessment administrators appear to be largely unconcerned about the federal involvement issue and would welcome the federal financial assistance. Local assessment administrators, on the other hand, are quite divided on the federal involvement issue, and a significant number appear to be philosophically opposed to more "relief." Interestingly, Wisconsin assessment officers as an organization have endorsed the concept of the bill.

With respect to the technical provisions of the proposed legislation, most experts in assessment administration would agree that the importance accorded the publication of assessment-sales ratios in S. 1255 is deserved, and that the taxpaying public must be furnished accurate information about the level and degree of uniformity of assessments if public confidence in property tax administration is to be achieved. Nonetheless, there is considerable concern that the language of the bill dangerously oversimplifies a very complex topic, and that considerable mischief could result. Specifically:

The term "assessment-sales ratio" refers to only one technique for gauging the quality of the assessment product. The more generic term "assessment ratio" would be preferable, and the definition of that term would depend upon the context in which it is used.

The requirements of the section requiring the publication of assessment ratio studies are unrealistic if applied to "taxing" jurisdictions. Many of the 70,000-odd taxing jurisdictions are quite small with, say, less than 1,000 properties, and apart from single-family residences few, if any, sales will take place in them within a year for most of the land use categories described. Even a large, industrial taxing jurisdiction like Detroit, with approximately 16,000 industrial and 25,000 commercial properties, will experience fewer than 300 commercial and industrial sales annually, an inadequate number on which to base

25. This aspect of S. 1255 was a topic of discussion at an "Assessors Forum" conducted by the International Association of Assessing Officers, May 10-11, 1973.

conclusions about a common level of assessment or the average dispersion from the common level. Certainly assessment ratio studies should be conducted for each assessment jurisdiction, but even this standard will be difficult to achieve in those states with large numbers of small assessment jurisdictions.

Some comment should also be directed towards the section concerning assessment ratio study methodology:

1. At present there is no "best existing practice" for conducting assessment ratio studies. Indeed, the very statistical foundation of general assessment ratio methodology as an indicator of "common level" has been challenged in the literature, and the validity of this challenge has not been fully assessed.[26]

2. There are three common ways of computing assessment ratios —arithmetic mean, weighted mean, and median—and other indicators of common level such as the mode have been suggested.

3. There are at present three major uses of assessment ratio study findings: a) in the original assessment process to identify priorities for reappraisal, to test the efficacy of new mass appraisal techniques, to evaluate the uniformity of proposed assessment policies, and to abstract land values and depreciation estimates from improved property sales; b) by assessment supervisory and equalization agencies to monitor local assessment performance and to adjust the aggregate assessments of local assessment and taxing jurisdictions to a common level so that intergovernmental revenue transfers may be made on an equitable basis; and c) in assessment appeals.

4. There is also considerable expert discussion and disagreement on such issues as whether independent appraisals should be substituted for sales data, how instruments or deeds are screened to insure that only "arms-length" transactions are used in the study, whether sales prices should be adjusted to account for differences in financing arrangements, and how to insure that the sample of properties studied in an assessment ratio study was representative of all the properties in the jurisdiction.

The section of the bill dealing with appeal procedures is closely linked to the section dealing with assessment ratio studies and accordingly suffers from the same misunderstanding of assessment ratio analysis. Briefly, there is a lack of distinction between the dispersion in assessment ratios caused by market behavior and the dispersion that can be attributed to the assessment process itself. As drafted, the bill would require upon appeal an automatic reassessment of any property whose individual assessment-sales ratio deviated by more

---

26. Pao Lun Cheng, "The Common Level of Assessment in Property Taxation," National Tax Journal, Vol. 23, March 1970, pp. 50-65.

than ten percentage points from the average assessment ratio. Unaltered, such a provision would smack of self-assessment and would result in a deterioration of the common level of assessment.

No matter what the outcome of S. 1255 may be, the bill represents a fairly sophisticated attempt to induce state legislators to enact property tax reform measures, by linking reform to a politically acceptable program. Some consideration might be given to whether an additional inducement for assessment reform at either the local, state, or national level would be a refinement of the assessment process so that the land data contained within an assessment system would be available to all who could benefit from it.